About the Author

Consumer advocate and organizational psychologist Joseph Éamon Cummins is an ex-affiliate of American Psychological Association and recipient of multiple Best Professor citations. He leads workshops in areas of achievement and resilience, and coaches teams and private clients internationally.

Not One Dollar More!, hailed by critics and consumer advocates as '*a classic*', has been trusted by homebuyers since its first edition in 1995 and has sold over 100,000 copies.

Declared '*Consumer Book of the Decade*' by an American homeowner advisory board, the book has been praised by Money Magazine, Kiplinger's, CNBC, CNN, Business Week, Home, Arizona Daily Star, Chicago Tribune, Philadelphia Inquirer, Denver Post and many others.

The author has also worked as a journalist, negotiator and licensed real estate agent. His recent bestselling novel *On the Edge of the Loch* reached #1 in five Amazon categories.

Tom Wemett, founding member and former President of National Association of Exclusive Buyer Agents, has been an Exclusive Buyer Agent for 25 years. He has offices in Massachusetts and Florida (see Chapter 12 for details).

Praise for Not One Dollar More!

Excerpts here and at the back of this book are from hundreds of comments and letters from homebuyers, media, critics and consumer advocates in praise of the first and second editions of *Not One Dollar More!* Readers' full names are withheld for privacy but are on file with the respective publishers.

What the Critics and Consumer Advocates Said

'Worth its weight in gold. *Every* house in the nation should have this book NOW!'
American Consumers Association

'This outstanding book rates a solid 10/10! — filled with valuable ammunition homebuyers need.'
Robert Bruss, National Syndicated Columnist

'This book is *extraordinary!*'
Tony Robbins, Author of Money: Master the Game and Unshakeable

'No contest — *the* best! A consumer milestone. On-target, easy to understand. Puts power in the hands of the consumer.'
Jordan Clark, Consumer Advocate

'Worth its weight in gold. One of the *great* books on personal finance. Shows how to get a great deal and reads like a novel. A gift to consumers - 5 stars!'
James Scott Tiernan, Jr, Consumer Advocate

'Few book writers can put money into your pocket. Here's one who can! Cummins is surely the new master of negotiation, and a gifted writer. Certainly *the best* and most enjoyable book on home buying. Inspiring!'
Bruce Hahn, President, American Homeowners Foundation

'Not a born haggler? *Not One Dollar More!* helps you cash in on savings!'
Kiplinger's (Worth Getting column)

'This book hands you the advantage — grasp it!'
Barry M. Miller, Consumer Advocate

'Helps the reader from the start. Shows how to hold on to your money, with GREAT anecdotes.'
Andrew Tobias, Author of The Only Investment Guide You'll Ever Need

'THE BIBLE! The classic handbook for buyers, an invaluable resource.'
Homefront (editorial)

'Intelligent, well-written. Offers really good advice. Homebuyers, put this on your buy list.'

Marc Eisenson, Author of The Banker's Secret

'An outrageously good book! Read well what Cummins writes, it could make all the difference.'

Kathleen Smith, Author of Prosperity Reigns

'DON'T loan this book. You won't get it back!'

Sam Alexander, Consumer Advocate

'A wealth of detail as it takes you right up to the settlement table.'

Philadelphia Daily News

'*Not One Dollar More!* — a book with great promise for homebuyers.'

Dr Wayne Dyer, Author of Your Erroneous Zones

'A blueprint for saving money. None of the complexity or tedious language of other money books. The reader is helped with examples and entertaining anecdotes that communicate important know-how.'

TV Review

'Real estate agents and sellers should also study this book'

San Jose Mercury News

'*Not One Dollar More!* Sound Advice!'

Denver Post

'Terrific! An excellent book.'

Business Radio Network

'A wonderful money guide for homebuyers and those who long to be.'

Cable News Television

'Shows clearly how to buy a home without paying too much for it.'

Philadelphia Inquirer

'An indispensable book!'

Bob Pisani, CNBC TV, Host of 'Money Talk'

'This *really is* a GREAT book!'

George Chamberlin, KCEO Radio, San Diego, CA

'Outstanding! Secrets of *invisible negotiation* and getting the best deal.'

HomeBase

What Readers Said

'We are grateful to you and your book for saving us $24,000. We will recommend *Not One Dollar More!* to other homebuyers. Many thanks!!!!'

Peter and Diane, Pittsburgh, PA

'So much better than anything else written on the subject.'

D.L.T., Attorney-at-Law, NC

'With the help of Bill Wendel's Real Estate Cafe (Cambridge, MA) and *Not One Dollar More!* we got $33,000 off the asking price of $275,000. The book is such an incredible resource for first-time homebuyers like ourselves.'

Caitlin and Doug, MA

'Joseph Eamon Cummins is sharp and so good to read, a wonderfully interesting writer. He should be writing in the *Los Angeles Times* or some big daily newspaper like that.'

R.T.H. Jr, San Diego, CA

'Your *Not One Dollar More!* is just extraordinary as a resource for buyers. I'm an attorney-broker providing negotiation and consulting services to homebuyers. Your book has elevated the profession. BRAVO!'

M.R. LeB., Attorney-at-Law, St Paul, MN

'*Not One Dollar More!* gave me confidence, reminded me that I'm in charge, not the real estate agent, not the seller, but me and my cash.'

Ron A. C., Rochester, PA

'Fantastic book! Details I never saw or heard before. Everybody should read this book, buyers and sellers. Have recommended it to everyone.'

B.Y., Woburn, MA

'Your book has been truly a revelation to me. I cannot thank you enough for the skill with which you make the know-how accessible. Unfortunately, I made a bad mistake before reading your fantastic book!'

Matt B, (by email)

'I wish I had this information 25 or 30 years ago. It would have made a big difference to my finances. One thing is for certain, I'll make sure my son reads it.'

Guy D., Wedowee, AL

'Creating wealth is hard. I've read all kinds of books searching for good answers. This book fills a definite need, the know-how of creating personal wealth. It's reliable, down to earth, and best of all, has great concrete examples (and) anecdotes.'

J.I., Philadelphia, PA

'Upon arriving in Indiana, we had two weeks to find a home before I started work. We followed the book's suggestions, looked at 34 homes. We offered $92,000 on a house listed at $110,000. We bought it at $97,000, a single-story rancher two miles outside town. You saved us $13,000!'

G. and D. R., Ft Wayne, IN

'Thank you for a fascinating book!'

Evelyn and Gil B., York, ME

'EXCELLENT!! Inspirational, easy to read, a great confidence builder, advice only your best friend would give you, if only they knew it. BRAVO!'

Chris M., Mays Landing, NJ (from Amazon.com)

'Don't be another real estate victim! This book provides the tools with which to fight back. Mr Cummins weaves concepts and real-life illustrations together to create an informative, inspiring book.'

E.L., Los Angeles, CA (from Amazon.com)

'An excellent book. Reading it every day looking for a home. Using your suggestions we've already been able to get reductions in asking prices.'

Sue T., New York, NY

'Absolutely the best! A unique perspective on home buying. Empowers you to select, negotiate and buy — or reject! — a home on YOUR terms.'

A reader from New York City, (from Amazon.com)

'Everybody should read this book — buyers and sellers.'

Bob Y. Woburn, MA

'I'm in commercial real estate. I found the book fascinating. Excellent negotiation tips and a wealth of great information. I could not have asked for a better book.'

Bob R, Arlington Heights, IL

**See back of book for
Readers' Success Letters and Amazon Reviews**

NOT ONE DOLLAR MORE!
HOW TO SAVE $3,000 TO $30,000 BUYING YOUR NEXT HOME

A Plain-English Guide

THIRD EDITION

Joseph Éamon Cummins

WITH TOM WEMETT

MOON ABBEY MEDIA

NOT ONE DOLLAR MORE!
How to Save $3,000 to $30,000 Buying Your Next Home
by Joseph Éamon Cummins

First published 1995, second edition 1999. This fully revised third edition 2017
by Moon Abbey Media, an imprint of MindWave Ltd (Irl).
Trade enquiries: NotOneDollarMore@gmail.com

PB 1: 0: 0:

A CIP catalogue record for this title is available from the British Library.
This Trade Paperback ISBN 978-0-9935452-9-0
eBook ISBN 978-0-9935452-8-3
ASIN:
Audio book for release in 2018

Book design by Maureen Cutajar.

Codes 1-5: P2234 P3345 P4456 P5567 P6678

** Website & Contacts **
For interviews, articles, media info and Q&A visit book website:
www.NotOneDollarMore.com.

For bulk purchases, education discounts, sales promotions, etc,
contact Moon Abbey Media at NotOneDollarMore@gmail.com.

** Training, Coaching, Speaking **
To book author for workshops, conferences, speaking engagements,
interviews, or for group or private coaching: NotOneDollarMore@gmail.com.

** Reader Review Request **
The author would be very appreciative if you'd write a short review of this book,
on Amazon preferably, or if you prefer on GoodReads, Barnes & Noble,
or other book reader website. It really makes a difference.

Many thanks!

DEDICATION

for Desi,
comrade of many odysseys,
for his fortitude and friendship.

Table of Contents

Dear Homebuyer . . .

This is more a workshop than a book!

The 'Smart Buyer' know-how you need
is laid out in stories, lessons, examples and
real-life case studies so that it embeds
automatically in your brain — unlike books
that leave you remembering nothing.

You can read any chapter as a stand-alone guide.

You'll learn how to get the best deal possible
on your next home purchase, how to get the
best mortgage — and how to protect
your present and future wealth.

My aim is not just to teach you,
but to inspire you.

Joseph Éamon Cummins

Introduction

The real purpose of books is to trap the mind
into doing its own thinking.
— Christopher Morley

Congratulations, you belong now to an elite group made up of what I call 'Smart Buyers'. You're in a small minority.

It would have been easier not to write this book! To turn a blind eye. But my concern, like that of many consumer advocates, has always been about the ethics of the system, the fact that homebuyers are unknowingly vulnerable, not adequately informed or protected by an industry that purports to serve them. That's why I wrote the book. I have no financial interest of any kind in the real estate or banking industries, nor am I part of either.

Not One Dollar More! has been helping homebuyers for twenty-two years. And each year millions more, from first-timers to retirees, make one of the biggest high-risk decisions of their lives, to buy a home. Most do this with far too much risk and far too little know-how — and without *even one* professional confidant or mentor! There is no *un*-selfish justification for such a system. Yet it continues.

You will find here ideas *not* found elsewhere. I can say with certainty that the book you are holding can put money *into your pocket,* and just as surely it can stop others taking money *out of your pocket!*

Here's why:

In the US alone over five million homes will be sold this year. That's around nine million buyers signing on the dotted line (80% are couples). The vast majority will *not* prepare well enough to avoid over-paying and other serious risks. Only a small number, among whom you now stand, will do what's necessary to protect their interests.

Whether you're a first-timer or an old hand at real estate matters not. The information here can bring you peace of mind and significant savings. *Not One Dollar More!* can do this because it takes a stand — without apology.

It is *100% pro-homebuyer.*

It stands against deception and unfairness, against the all-too-common shifty and misleading practices that can steal your money and turn you into a victim *without you ever realizing it.* And I mean *ever.*

It's also a practical book with no silly overloading, a book that has served generations of homebuyers before you. You'll find it easy to understand. And you can trust it. The lessons come from hard-won *real-world experience*, real estate and beyond.

With this new edition I am as certain as I was with previous editions that no other book like it exists. Over 100,000 homebuyers have relied on it, so far, and that's *not* counting couples, pass-along readership or online re-sales.

The advice and guarded secrets you'll find here come not only from my personal involvement in buying, selling and negotiating, but also from the thinking of men and women who as a rule do *not* share their expertise. And from extensive research and detailed notes I recorded over a span of decades. It comes too from what I've learned and taught while working in psychology and human behavior fields, particularly in the areas of influence and achievement.

But it's not an encyclopedia! My mission is simpler: To help you win the 'mind game' and the 'money game', both of which you cannot avoid when you buy a home. And in doing this, to make you richer and happier. Since the mid-1990s, top consumer advocates and countless readers' letters say this is precisely what *Not One Dollar More!* delivers (see readers' letters at back of book).

You'll notice right away it's not a mishmash of selling agents' advice. I should think not.

Let's talk straight here before we go further: Traditional selling agents and real estate salespeople pledge to get the best deal for the seller — *only* the seller — not for you, the buyer! Can we ask the fox to guard the farm yard?

I think not. But such dubiously authored 'homebuyer' books are plentiful, along with mountains of literature and online 'advice blogs' written by agents and salespeople who represent sellers' best interests!

Odd, isn't it? And worth remembering. A blatant conflict of interest.

It's no different when you are out there on the street. How can these traditional real estate agents and salespeople be expected to give *you* objective advice; you, the party they *do not* represent? The party to whom they *do not* and *cannot* pledge loyalty or confidentiality or obedience or full disclosure? The party they *do not* and *cannot* work for to get the lowest price or best terms?

They can't! Clearly.

And they should not. Because, by law, in every home sale your local traditional listing agent and selling agent *must* give 'fiduciary responsibility' *only* to the seller — never to you, the buyer. This legal requirement known as fiduciary responsibility obligates these agents to give to the seller, and *only* the seller, the following: undivided loyalty, confidentiality, obedience, honesty, and full disclosure of all information that furthers the *seller's* best interests, along with due care and diligence. This is because in law the seller is the agent's *client*; you, the buyer, are the *customer*. Legally this makes a world of difference.

I said above that this book stands for something. It does. It stands for you! And it stands up for you. Its responsibility is *only to you,* the homebuyer.

Not even in real estate can one serve two masters at the same time, though different types of real estate professionals — dual agents, facilitators, transaction brokers, and salespeople — *appear* to do so. But as we all learned early in life, appearances are often deceptive. You'll read more about this soon.

Do you see why you need to be well informed? Is it becoming clear why you must know how the game is played?

The Power of Invisible Negotiation

This is a book about 'invisible negotiation'. I created this term early in my career, for specific reasons. First, it is not the negotiation you probably think of when you hear that word. It is not bartering or bargaining, as those terms are generally meant. It does not require you to talk tough, look intimidating, argue aggressively, act like an expert, pound the table, make threats, or issue ultimatums. And it certainly isn't haggling or bickering.

Best of all, it doesn't lead to dispute or bad feelings between you and the real estate salesperson, or between you and anyone.

So what is it?

It's a way of getting what you want by using *uncommon* know-how. Without anyone even suspecting you are negotiating. And here's what you might find ironic, these 'invisible' skills are known to few people. Typically, because those who know them fear they'll lose out by sharing them.

Yet, the basic skills of invisible negotiation are easily and quickly learned. No tedious study is needed. In fact, you'll find yourself in tune with the logic of it when you see it here in action. As soon as you grasp these tips and tactics you'll use one or more of them when your money is on the line — which is any time you buy a home. I'll show you how to do this in simple and powerful ways.

This Book and You: Making It Really Pay Off

In the first edition of *Not One Dollar More!*, over two decades ago, I promised to reveal these techniques to readers in *interesting* and *readable* language, to explain in plain English how to avoid the most costly mistakes homebuyers make. You're now holding the fully revised and updated third edition in your hands. It will help you protect your money and other interests when you are potentially most vulnerable.

But only if you use it!

You do *not* need to read every chapter or become familiar with all sections. Any serious approach by you will embed powerful techniques in your brain. These will automatically become part of how you think, talk, and act. Soon you'll start seeing yourself as a confident and quietly capable negotiator.

That message bears repeating: The secret to learning lies in action. From the moment you first put this know-how into practice you'll sense that you are taking control — even when you're only rehearsing (which, by the way, is a good idea). You'll also find yourself using these skills in numerous non-real estate situations.

But can't I just rely on instinct and intuition? you ask.

No! The risks are far too great. Even the most experienced negotiators prepare; they form a basic strategy (simply a 'plan'). To do less is naive, even reckless.

Forming your strategy will be easy when you follow the tips and tactics explained here. This will bring you a double benefit, because the skills you'll learn are also your first line of *defense*. They equip you to spot tricks, tactics, and deceptions being used *against* you, and to counter them.

It will serve you well also to remember that list prices, asking prices, sellers' positions, and what salespeople suggest is an 'appropriate' offer — are never to be taken as rigid. Virtually every buy/sell transaction has negotiation room. Sure, sellers might huff and puff and balk at an offer, insisting that you pay more than they are in fact willing to accept (or will later agree to accept). A negotiation is a dynamic, moving thing, a constantly shifting exchange.

Therefore, note this critical point:

> *The seller's and salesperson's thinking, flexibility, and price expectations are influenced and changed by you, to your advantage, as you apply the skills of smart buying!*

Never overlook the fact that you, the homebuyer, are the one who is *least* protected and most likely to lose out. By being a smart buyer you simply level the playing field. When the agreement is sealed (the one your negotiation know-how shaped) the salesperson and seller *both succeed* in their individual goals. Don't ever doubt this, despite what any other party claims.

Even when you are using an Exclusive Buyer Agent (which, by the way, is the single best advantage a homebuyer has — much more on this later) you must take 100% responsibility for your own success. Your success is *not* the responsibility of the seller, and *not* the responsibility of the amiable agent or obliging salesperson. You have no one's loyalty, confidentiality or best efforts protecting you — these safeguards are pledged by the traditional salesperson and agent to the seller. That's the law, as noted earlier.

Later, in the ToolBox section, you'll find advice and information on other professional services that stand ready to assist you.

Whether you are experienced or not, big budget or small, just married, millennial, baby boomer, mid-career, retiree, country folk or city dweller, you'll be able to recognize problems and save significant time and money by staying aware of what is revealed in *Not One Dollar More!*

A Pawn in Somebody Else's Game?

Let's face it, the two biggest risks you face when buying a home are to:

1) Your money
2) Your peace of mind.

In other words, hard-earned cash and happiness! Much too important to surrender control to others. And you don't have to.

As a smart buyer you'll feel the power that comes from controlling the process rather than being a pawn in somebody else's game. But first comes learning how to forge a good deal.

The fact that you are reading this book suggests you recognize the need to protect yourself against loss. But if you are not going to lose, who is?

Negotiating successfully does *not* mean taking advantage of anyone. On the contrary, it brings equality and fairness into the transaction. That's because the seller always retains the right to refuse any offer you make, say no to any condition you request, or break off the negotiation. By negotiating smartly in your own interest you are simply doing for *you* what the seller and the salesperson are doing for both *their* benefits.

When you make an offer, the seller can accept, reject, or send a counter offer back to you (a counter offer says: 'No, but let's keep talking'). Nothing you do will take any of these options from the seller. And when you reach a well-negotiated agreement, both sides gain, and so too does the salesperson, a point we'll look at in more detail.

Read Any Chapter In any Order: A Structure for Learning

I've seen credible national surveys that say that a large percentage of readers don't read past half way in the books they buy. With how-to books it's often because of complexity and heavy language. In *Not One Dollar More!* you'll encounter nothing of that sort — just straight talk.

However, more than straight talk is needed when writing about the often confusing fields of home buying and mortgages. For that reason, I've built in learning aids that make it easier to grasp and retain information that is critical to your wealth and contentment. The early chapters might seem basic; they have two purposes: 1) To show you *why* you need to know what comes later, and 2) To provide a *solid foundation* that will help you learn better how to achieve your goal.

As a long-time teacher and trainer I know that repetition is a rich learning tool. The more you encounter an important idea the better it takes root in your thinking. I would do you a *disservice* if I did not intentionally repeat critical points. As a result, you are likely to learn more than you've learned from any other book. This also allows you to skip ahead or read chapters in almost any order. As I said, it's as much a modular workshop as a book.

No doubt you'll notice too that *Not One Dollar More!* offers detailed guidance on your *behavior* and how this can work for or against you in negotiation (no other comparable book does this). That's because your behavior reveals, persuades and communicates more strongly than anything you *say*. It can win you success — or give you away. In fact, how you behave determines your personal power. And personal power is the single most important ingredient in producing positive results in any challenge you take on in life.

As you'd expect, I won't tell you what to buy or where to buy. Just how to acquire the home that's right for you, at the lowest price and best terms possible. And how to protect yourself from wealth-stealing pitfalls, bluffs, tricks, deceptions and pressure, whether your goal is a rancher, condo, townhouse, farm or something else.

The Key Ingredient — Action!

To get a deal you can have faith in and feel happy about you'll need to know what happens behind the scenes in real estate. After that, common sense and just a few easily learned skills will get you your goal.

Later chapters will help you build and maintain your confidence as you move into action. You'll help yourself by remembering that knowledge by itself is *not* power. Until it is used productively it has no actual power.

And when the time comes to step up to the plate, bear this fact in mind: Whatever a listing agent, salesperson or selling agent might ask you to believe, accept, or agree to, they are not committed to protecting *your* best interests or *your* money. Their objective is to sell you the home you want (or possibly one you'd do better to let go) at the highest price they can convince you to pay. They pledged to the seller they would do this, and so they will.

So, answer for yourself this key question:

Is it sensible to accept unquestioningly the arguments, logic, opinions, or reasoning of a person who is pledged to get the most dollars possible *out of you?*

I wrote *Not One Dollar More!* with one simple objective in mind: to show you how to protect yourself. When that protection is in place, the benefits to you are many, including:

- You get the home that's right for you
- You save a lot more than loose change
- You gain security and peace of mind
- You *never* need to question your decision.

The hard reality of home buying is this: Hanging in the balance in every purchase is thousands of dollars, frequently tens of thousands, and even more in some cases. All up for grabs! This is *your* money. Every penny of it! *Because you are the only party putting cash on the table.*

If you are beginning to feel worried, good. Let this awareness sink in. And let it sink in that no seller or selling agent or traditional real estate salesperson is your confidant; none of them are looking out for your best interest. They are not in your corner.

Not One Dollar More! is!

Let's get to work.

PART ONE

HOW NOT TO LOSE:
THE FIRST STEPS

CHAPTER 1

Come Into My Parlor . . .

Be wiser than other people if you can,
but do not tell them so.
— G. K. Chesterton

Buying and selling real estate is a game, pure and simple!

A game in which professionals and amateurs compete side by side. What's wrong with that, you might ask.

Answer: Something potentially very costly to you!

Because typically only one party is adequately protected and professionally represented throughout the entire purchase/sale transaction.

And it's not you!

You, the homebuyer, stand on the other side with your best interests entirely unrepresented or inadequately represented, ineffectively prepared (typically), and uninformed about the game rules, and the traps and tricks and mistakes that can separate you unfairly and unethically from your hard-earned money.

And we're talking here about big chunks of money, as you will see.

So, bright as you are, you nonetheless run a high risk of being out-maneuvered, outwitted, and outgunned.

And here's the kick in the pants — *without you ever knowing it!*

This is why the majority of homebuyers hand over thousands of dollars more than is necessary, accept inferior terms, agree to deals that so easily could have been better, and sometimes end up with 'the house from hell'.

Based on what I've seen in real estate, privately and professionally, I believe that homebuyers' lack of know-how and basic negotiation skills cause them to pay more than they need to and accept terms far from the best attainable, in 95% of purchases. It's the same when buying from private sellers.

With a little extra awareness and a handful of self-defense tactics you can avoid the biggest wealth-stealing and peace-of-mind-stealing threats. As you read on you'll learn and remember what you need to know.

Knowing What You Are Up Against

Ironically, once in a while a nervous buyer lands an unpredictably good deal through a combination of his own hesitation and the seller's resulting frustration. This fact reinforces one core principle: specific human behaviors (indecision and procrastination in this case), when used *intentionally* and *strategically*, can be profitable tools. And there are others, which you'll discover here.

In practice, the average homebuyer lacks critical know-how, uses few if any tactics, and rarely gets within a couple of thousand dollars of the seller's lowest acceptable price or best terms. Far too many miss the boat altogether and grossly over-pay, or end up with a house or an environment full of nasty surprises.

In a later chapter I'll describe in detail how I witnessed an unprepared and poorly informed buyer pay *one hundred thousand dollars* more than the seller was willing to accept on that same day. This enormously expensive mistake didn't happen on a $2m property. The unfortunate buyer paid $280,000 when he could certainly have bought the property there and then at or close to $180,000.

Yes, this is an exceptional case. And it illustrates how wrong things can go when a buyer lacks the astuteness to protect his own financial wellbeing, or when he lacks the ability or willingness to use simple tactics.

I'll assume, for the most part, that you plan to buy through a real estate agency. But almost everything you'll learn here applies in *any* transaction in which you will be asked to hand over money or make a commitment to purchase. You'll learn through stories, examples and actual case studies, and you'll read precisely what you can do and say in different situations.

Whatever your plan or budget, I can offer you no better advice than this: Learn and apply at least some of the techniques you'll find here. They are not difficult to grasp or use. And they are not *anti* the real estate profession. Once you know what you are doing, a good real estate salesperson can be an excellent source of necessary information and assistance.

However, an Exclusive Buyer Agent is the *only true ally* of the homebuyer, something we'll say a lot more about.

When I refer to any professional whose job it is to list or sell property, I will generally use the term 'salesperson'. I do not use 'Realtor' because this refers only to members of a trade organization, the National Association of Realtors (not a state or federal licensing body); many real estate salespeople are not members.

This book stands against deception, misrepresentation, lack of representation and questionable practices, all of which are tolerated and common in buying and selling property. In contrast, everything I have written here is unapologetically in the homebuyer's best interest.

Few books dare make that claim!

Because most 'homebuyer' guides in your local bookstore or real estate office are written by traditional real estate agents, all of whom are hungry for homebuyers *as customers*. You, the buyer, as we saw earlier, are *not* their *client*. So, looking out for *your* best interest is out of the question; they give this pledge *exclusively* to the seller. That's what sellers pay for and expect. Consequently, you need to question the source of all 'homebuyer advice'. Is it coming from somebody who serves the seller's best interests? Or yours? Or neither?

Whether on paper, online, or on the street, when your best interests are not being served exclusively, you are without a *confidant,* without an *advocate,* without *undivided loyalty,* without *full disclosure,* without *unbiased advice* and *direction.*

In essence, you are entirely *un*-represented — and vulnerable.

Not One Dollar More! addresses this imbalance. By grasping what's in these pages you can put significant 'saved' cash in your pocket, and look forward to a purchase you won't have to wonder about, worry over, question or regret.

But no book eliminates your need for expert legal advice; seek this before you begin your home search, and do the same with financial and mortgage advice.

You'll find here also a comprehensive home-financing section that makes mortgages simple and understandable. I'll tell you things you've *never* been told before, and I'll show you cost-free 'mortgage tricks' that can save you a small fortune with *zero risk to you.*

Along with that, I'll help steer you around the most common mistakes and dangers inherent in buying and financing your home.

Starting now, this is your challenge: Become a *Smart Buyer.*

Decide you are going to achieve the lowest price and best terms attainable, and obtain guaranteed approval on the best home loan for your circumstances. This book will help you achieve both.

You are already on your way.

However, before moving into the book I felt you'd benefit most from being clear about the different ways agents can 'represent' you when you go looking for a home. Some forms of representation, I believe, are downright dangerous to your wellbeing. The big mistake — made by the vast majority of buyers — is thinking your best interests are being served, when in fact they are not.

It's a costly mistake.

However, there is one form of representation that all homebuyers should insist on. By understanding this now, you'll find the rest of the book even more helpful.

It can seem confusing, but I've put it into plain-English in the next chapter.

CHAPTER 2

When 'Your' Agent is Not Your Agent at All.

Who is Really Looking Out for You?

*Oh! what a tangled web we weave when
first we practice to deceive.*
— Walter Scott

First, the whole area of homebuyer representation is a mess. It is hugely confusing to buyers, and even to real estate salespeople. Adding to the problem is the fact that real estate laws and regulations vary from state to state.

The net outcome is this: Few home buyers ever realize that the real estate salesperson showing them homes may have no legal obligation to advise them, honor their most confidential details, or look after their best interests — despite appearances suggesting just the opposite.

Yet in every purchase, the homebuyer's biggest need is for full and exclusive representation and undivided loyalty from an agent. Nothing less is safe or sufficient.

Brokers are free in most states to provide different forms of 'representation' to buyers, including acting as 'transaction brokers', 'facilitators' and 'dual agents'. All three of these mean you get no fiduciary obligation: no pledge of undivided loyalty or obedience or full disclosure. So in all three cases neither you *nor* the seller is fully represented. This makes no sense, certainly not to consumer advocates who have lobbied for decades for full and exclusive representation for buyers, and even less sense when you are making the biggest financial decision of your life.

You might well wonder what's behind all this.

By serving buyer and seller at the same time, transaction brokers, facilitators and dual agents earn double commissions (known as 'double dipping'). The entire commission stays in-house, because there is no out-of-house agent or Exclusive Buyer Agent (EBA) to have to share it with.

Recently things got even muddier. Many states have adopted another type of representation called 'designated agency', in which two agents from the same agency can separately represent buyer and seller, which you'll read more about below.

If you're confused, that's a perfectly reasonable reaction. But there is a safe solution.

You don't need to wrangle with all this complexity if you keep one simple point in mind: As a homebuyer you need an agent who'll represent *exclusively* your best interests. You deserve no less in any major financial transaction. Never assume you have full exclusive representation and undivided loyalty until it is confirmed verbally by the agent and spelled out in a written disclosure stating clearly that this is what the agent *and* the agency is providing.

Simplifying Agency Relationships: What You Need to Know

An agent's fiduciary (legal) obligation to you is established only when the agent or salesperson agrees to act fully and *only* in your best interest in helping you find and buy a home. Transaction brokers, facilitators and dual agents are not in fact 'agents' in the above sense; they do not pledge fiduciary obligation or undivided loyalty to you. A true agent, on the other hand, is required to place your interests ahead of the seller's interests, and ahead of their own.

In practice, home buyers rarely receive exclusive representation.

The laws governing agency are part of common law and are similar everywhere. Nevertheless, because state regulations differ, real estate agencies can provide different forms of 'representation' to homebuyers. Let's see if we can simplify all that and understand what can hurt you and what can help you. Here are the common forms of representation (agency) offered to homebuyers:

Exclusive Buyer Agency: An Exclusive Buyer Agent represents the best interests of the homebuyer *exclusively*, from start to finish, which means you and *only you* are being represented. An Exclusive Buyer Agent *never* lists or sells homes, nor does the company he or she works for. This is the gold standard and should be your first choice.

Another big advantage is that typically an EBA will show you more homes, including for-sale-by-owner homes. Ten, fifteen, even twenty or more is common. You will never be expected to buy from an edited list of 'selected' homes that are most rewarding for the salesperson. Rather, you'll get to consider all homes on the market that meet your requirements.

To find an EBA near you see www.NAEBA.com.

If no EBA is available in your area, see if you can find a 'true' or 'single' agent. Unlike an EBA, a true or single agent, and his or her company, represents buyers *and* sellers but pledges never to represent both in the same transaction. Therefore, this agent can offer you exclusive representation and is an excellent alternative to hiring an EBA. True or single agents, like EBAs, never practice dual agency, designated agency or transaction brokerage. With an EBA or a true or single agent working for you, you never need doubt who is being represented; because both *always* and *only* represent your best interests. So, when you are screening agents (often best done by phone), ask this question:

Can you represent my best interests exclusively all the way through my home search and including closing?

If you cannot locate an EBA or a true or single agent, consider a third option: hiring a traditional agent from a small office with few listings to represent you exclusively. However, if it happens that you become interested in one of this traditional agent's own listings, he or she would need to be willing to allow you to be represented by another agent from a different rest estate company in negotiating for the home (naturally, to avoid conflict of interest).

Every consumer advocate I've worked with or interviewed, and everyone in the EBA community, believe exclusive representation is the safest, most ethical and best form of representation, and all advise homebuyers to accept nothing less. I strongly agree. Be certain this is what you get.

Designated Agency: One real estate company (brokerage) designates (appoints) two of its own agents: one to represent the buyer exclusively, the other to represent the seller exclusively. To the unaware this looks reasonable. It isn't! It is filled with risk and conflict of interest. It requires the salesperson working for you, the buyer, to hide all your details from the salesperson working for the seller, even though they are colleagues working side by side, usually in the same office, habitually sharing buyer information over lunch or coffee and in sales meetings, with commissions at stake for both agents.

Designated agency also means the agent would need to lock away all notes, files and information relating to you, and require their fellow salespeople and employees, and all others associated with the agency, not to openly discuss or disclose any of your details — in an industry in which deals and commissions hinge on exchanging buyer information. Is it even possible?

Designated agency is an 'in-house deal'; one hundred percent of the commission goes to just one broker (because both designated agents work for the same agency). Consumer advocates have described it as a farce, subterfuge, a fiction, and misleading to home buyers. They also point out that designated agency is not legal in any other profession, where 'agents' in the same company must negotiate *against* each other — the conflict of interest is blatant and absurd. I advise buyers against this form of service, when it is avoidable. When it is not avoidable, the tips and techniques in this book are your safeguard.

Disclosed Dual Agency: The 'disclosed' part of dual agency means that to be legal this form of 'service' must be disclosed to and agreed to by buyer and seller from the beginning. In dual agency, one or more agents or salespeople provide services to both the buyer and the seller but *cannot* represent the best interests of either, and *cannot* advise, advocate for or negotiate for either. This means buyer and seller must both do without undivided loyalty and without their best interests being represented in one of life's highest-risk financial transactions. Dual agency also causes a lot of stress among agents; it is full of risk to all parties and should not even be considered by home buyers.

Transaction Brokerage: One agent or two agents at the same real estate agency may provide services to the buyer, the seller, or both, with *no* agency relationship with either party. This means no fiduciary duties of undivided loyalty or full disclosure is given to buyer or seller. Agents acting in this way are sometimes referred to as 'facilitators'; they work to bring a deal together but provide home buyers with none of the *critical* services of an Exclusive Buyer Agent. As a buyer you are entirely without an advocate here. Certainly not what you need.

'Buyers' Agents': Most traditional listing and selling agents can in certain circumstances call themselves a 'buyer's agent'. Many do it to attract smart buyers, the buyers who demand confidentiality, full disclosure and undivided loyalty from an agent.

This agent may be able to represent you as a single or true agent, which means your interests are being exclusively looked after. That is, until you want to buy a home listed for sale by the agent's company. Then something has to give, because this 'buyer's agent' is *not* an *Exclusive* Buyer Agent (EBA); they also sell homes and represent sellers' best interests. This means they are similar to designated agents in how they operate, but the term 'designated agent' is not used in every state. Instead, 'buyer's agent' or some variation of this term is used.

Consequently, when you'd like to buy one of their listings there's the problem. Who will the agent or the agency then be representing, you or their seller? Keep in mind, this agent already knows lots of confidential details about you, things you would never want any seller to know. At this point, the agent will probably ask if you'll go along with him or her switching to acting as a dual agent or designated agent or transaction broker, none of which is what you require.

For you, at that point, no good solution may be possible; you're in a fix. You wanted to be fully and exclusively represented but now you are being asked to settle for much less. It's an easy fix to get caught in — a problem that cannot ever happen when you work with an Exclusive Buyer Agent. EBAs *never* list or sell homes, which means you'll never get caught in a conflict of interest. EBAs also never practice dual agency, transaction brokerage or designated agency. Naturally, this is the *only* form of agency I recommend. And what all home buyers should demand.

To learn more about engaging an Exclusive Buyer Agent, see Chapter 11, *How to Find and Work With an EBA — and Why You Should*. And to learn why EBAs choose to represent only buyers, you can read what some of the nation's top EBAs have to say; I interviewed twenty-four for Chapter 12, *Why Be an Exclusive Buyer Agent? Top Professionals Respond in Their Own Words.*

When you set out to buy your next home you owe it to yourself to demand undivided loyalty, confidentiality, full disclosure and exclusive representation. Unfortunately, however, EBAs are not yet available in all areas across the country — which is another reason I wrote this book. And even when you find an EBA to work with, it still pays to be a smart buyer — well-informed, streetwise, and able to partner productively with the EBA.

Right now, the next short chapter looks at 'money' from different perspectives, and how this can help you stay ahead of the game.

CHAPTER 3

It's Your Money — But do You Know What it's Really Worth?

The obscure we see eventually,
the completely apparent takes longer.

— Edward R. Murrow

You might think this is an odd chapter title. But *do you know* what your money — specifically the amount you hand over and the price reduction you negotiate — is really worth?

Whether you answer Yes or No, it will pay you to read this chapter.

As before, when I use *mortgage* I also mean loan or trust deed; no distinction is needed here. And with home loan interest rates I'll standardize on 5% in examples (no heavy math, and all figures are rounded to nearest dollar). Keep in mind too that the tax advantages in owning property are outside the scope of this book; your tax advisor may be able to help you save even more than is apparent here.

To start, a few facts might surprise you and help you appreciate further where savings are possible. Let's assume you have pre-approval for a 30-year mortgage at 5%, and the seller has just accepted your offer. You've negotiated a modest $3,000 saving off the list price of the home. What's your next move?

You have *two* options.

When a Dollar Is Not Really a Dollar

Option 1: Take a smaller loan. Tell your lender you got a better deal than you anticipated and will therefore need a smaller mortgage.

Straightforward enough? You saved $3,000, so you pat yourself on the back and tell everyone willing to listen that $3,000 is not small change (and it certainly isn't). But, not so fast. If you look deeper you'll discover you did better than that.

Realistic examples (which you'll find throughout this book) bring these points to life and make them easier to grasp and remember, so let's add a few details.

Example A:

You planned to borrow $100,000. But now you'll need $3,000 less. So you take a $97,000, 30-year mortgage at 5%. If you don't pay off this loan early, you'll pay back $187,500 in Principal plus Interest.

Had you failed to negotiate that $3,000 price cut, your P+I payback on the $100,000 loan would be $193,250. Surprise, surprise! What looked like a saving of $3,000 is in fact $5,750 over the life of the loan.

Let's see how:
- Mortgage 1: $100,000 for 30 years at 5%. You pay back $193,250
- Mortgage 2: $97,000 for 30 years at 5%. You pay back $187,500
  Savings: **$5,750**

You saved not $3,000 but $5,750! Big difference. Now, what if you managed to negotiate a bigger price reduction?

Example B:

Let's assume you got the seller to accept $10,000 less than the advertised price. Now you'll need to borrow only $90,000.

Over the 30-year life of this loan, you'll pay back $19,320 less than if you had borrowed the $100,000 you otherwise might have done.

Here's how:
- Mortgage 1: $100,000 loan for 30 years at 5%. You pay back $193,250
- Mortgage 2: $90,000 loan for 30 years at 5%. You pay back $173,930
  Savings: **$19,320**

In both examples your negotiation success was worth significantly more than it seemed. Logically, the bigger the price reduction the better it gets. You can confirm these figures and play around with other scenarios on any online mortgage calculator.

Let's take this further.

If you get the seller to agree a $30,000 price reduction you cut your payback figure by $57,970. That's the difference between paying back a $70,000 loan and a $100,000 over 30 years at 5%.

Here's an important point to remember: Reducing a loan of *any* size by a specific amount ($10,000 for example) will bring you the same total savings.

Let's illustrate that point using our 5% loan:

If you borrow $90,000 instead of $100,000, as we saw in Example B, your payback figure went down by $19,320. Had you borrowed $50,000 rather than $60,000, you'd still save the same $19,320. Or if you borrowed $190,000 instead of $200,000, it's the same again, a saving of $19,320. You can see it has nothing to do with the loan size, just with the reduction in loan amount. That's it with the math, for now.

Recap: When you negotiate a reduction in the purchase price, this allows you to reduce your loan by the same amount. Reward, you save money on the day of purchase and go on saving *additional* money over the life of the loan, whether you hold it for 30 years or not. Because a smaller loan means smaller monthly repayments *and* a smaller loan balance to pay off when you sell. And, of course, you own more of the home from day-1 (your equity is bigger) and the lender owns less, which is always something to cheer about.

I said you had two options when you negotiate a price reduction; here's the second:

Option 2: Instead of taking a smaller loan, as we just saw, take your savings in cash. Stay with the original loan amount but reduce your down payment by the price cut you negotiated.

Let's see how. Buyers might commonly put down 5-10% in cash. However, if you are trading up or down you could plan a down payment of 30% or more, which is ideal for this option to work well. It won't cut the size of your repayments but it's an attractive alternative.

We'll assume the salesperson has been adamant; the seller won't accept less than $250,000. So far, you've been negotiating without success. But you want the home and are almost ready to go forward. You'll put down $50,000 and take a pre-approved loan of $200,000, if you have to. That's your plan.

But at the eleventh hour (when most concessions happen) your last offer of $240,000 is accepted. So now you decide to put down just $40,000 (not $50,000) and stay with your $200,000 loan. Since you had $50,000 earmarked for the down payment, you now have $10,000 in your pocket that you were willing to hand over.

How you spend it is your own business.

Obviously, this option depends on the size of your down payment. If you only have enough cash to meet the minimum required down payment you won't have room to reduce it (in the example above we were free to reduce the down payment from $50,000 to $40,000). Nevertheless, you *can* still go with Option 1, taking a smaller loan, with all its benefits.

What's in It for You?
Hard Cash and Peace of Mind!

When I speak on how to negotiate I'm frequently asked: 'As a non-professional negotiator, what kind of success can I expect?'

Coming from homebuyers this looks like a single question but there are, in fact, two questions being asked here, and both need to be addressed:

1. As a layperson *homebuyer* can I expect to negotiate successfully?
2. How much can I save?

The answer to Question 1 is: Yes! The answer to Question 2 is: It depends. You'll read case studies and see realistic examples in the following chapters. But let's explore a little further here.

The Advantages of Being a Non-Professional

Being a non-professional is a big advantage. As you read on you'll realize the truth of this. Don't for a moment think otherwise.

Here's a lesson worth learning from expert negotiators: They *don't* broadcast their skills and they typically favor a low-profile, with good reason. Because one of the best-kept secrets of negotiation is this: Success comes from acting and sounding genuine, ordinary, reasonable, non-expert, detached, non-threatening and even somewhat indifferent. The slick, aggressive, high-power, ego-driven negotiator is a myth, the stuff of Hollywood and dramatic novels.

In the real world, negotiators rely on being subtle, empathic, respectful — and firm when they have to be, even stubborn. They prepare well, gather relevant information, and employ tactics and persuasive communication. None of this is outside the capability of the ordinary person.

In the business world, when it is known that a *professional* negotiator is acting for one side, the other side raises its alertness level and puts counter strategies in place. The attitude is: 'You might be a hot-shot negotiator but you will not get the better of us.'

As an *amateur* you won't provoke such defensiveness. Nonetheless, success will rest ultimately on how you handle yourself, which is what you're learning here.

To start, keep in mind that list prices and selling prices *are not* carved in stone. The smart buyer's best approach is to consider *everything* negotiable, despite how convincingly you are told otherwise. Sellers and their sales agents will *never stop* trying to get you to pay more money than you want to. That's their right. In fact, it's the listing agent's, salesperson's, and selling agent's duty. And it's why you need to play your cards well.

Unlike most homebuyers, you won't rush in. You'll ready yourself for negotiation. You'll learn first about how people behave in particular situations, then how to influence their reactions. These are two of the main goals of this book. All the common tricks and tactics are covered. But, for you, the penny will drop in earnest the moment you recognize the specific tactics sellers and salespeople are using to pressure you to say yes. It's something of a real-world shock, being able to see through how others are attempting to control your thinking. You'll need to stay alert, and motivated!

You stay motivated by keeping a picture in mind of the money you'll stand to save, the safety of the deal you'll sign, and the long-term peace of mind you'll gain. And by remembering that concessions usually appear when everything seems to say they won't.

Who Will Take the Role of Negotiator?

House hunting couples should decide early which of them will take the role of negotiator. It works best if the other partner adopts a quieter profile, remains more detached in face-to-face discussions. This works to reduce the effectiveness of the other side. And it's for no one to know but you. The less they can read you, the better.

Your success will depend also on how well you do what all homebuyers *should* do — gather relevant information before heading out to view properties or engage with salespeople. You don't need to do a lot of work. Just gather details of asking and selling prices of homes already sold, information on homes currently for sale, neighborhood characteristics and trends, the condition and direction of the local housing market, and so on, and get guaranteed loan approval from your lender (but make sure first that you read the chapters here on saving money on your mortgage).

With this data in hand, and with the ability to use simple negotiation techniques (and neutralize those used against you) you'll possess more power and potential than 95% of homebuyers.

The benefits — hard cash and peace of mind — come from putting this power into action. And always remembering that it's *your* wealth and *your* money that's at stake. And *it is* at stake, as you'll discover in coming chapters.

What Can You Expect to Save?

This is a question everyone wonders about and, as I said above, there's only one answer: It will vary.

A lot depends on the price range you are buying in, and of course market conditions and the seller's circumstances. But this is how it's always been; you negotiate regardless. You might be happy to save $3-8,000 off a home listed at $150,000. On a $250,000 home you might hope for $7-16,000. These are deliberately conservative figures; I would personally aim to save more in both examples. Saving $12,000-20,000 off an asking price of $250,000 is not out of reach. Readers have written unsolicited letters and posted accounts online of having achieved these and bigger reductions.

Let me be clear here about one other point. By 'saving' I don't mean the 'extra bit' some sellers add on to what they believe the house is worth. 'Room to negotiate' or 'room to come down' is how salespeople refer to this padding. When you negotiate you'll have a good chance to save more than this padding. In later chapters you'll see examples and case studies that illustrate how this can be accomplished.

Factors That Influence Your Success

There is no perfect negotiation climate, never was. Any time you buy property, both negative and positive factors will be at play, and often the unexpected will crop up to influence the outcome. It's important, therefore, to allow nothing in your situation to deter you from negotiating. Because it's *only* through negotiating that you *discover* what's there to be won.

Here are common factors that can affect outcomes:

1. The economy locally and nationally; and more specifically, how well or badly real estate is selling in your search area.
2. How anxious or motivated the owner is to sell. The seller and salesperson are unlikely to volunteer this information; you'll learn here how to discover it.
3. The owner's *real* reason for selling. This can be critical not only in relation to price negotiation but also regarding the health of the home and the suitability of the neighborhood.

Obviously, you have no control over the economy or the owner's reason for selling. But there are always factors within your control. Your task is to notice these and use them to your best advantage.

As any experienced negotiator will tell you, bargains don't drop out of the sky, despite the fact that most of the homes you show interest in will be described by the salesperson as 'a bargain' or 'a rare opportunity'. But 'bargains' (read, genuinely good deals) don't happen like that. They are rarely 'found'. Genuinely good deals are created through negotiation — by smart buyers. And patience and determination are requirements.

Working in the human achievement field I see repeatedly that no matter how strong a person's determination, if they have more than one good reason for taking action they are more likely to follow through and reap the benefits. Let me try give you that advantage now — and relate it to money and *value*.

Not Just Dollar Bills:
The Alternative Values of Your Money

The real price of anything is the amount of freedom or time or money or worry or effort or opportunity you exchange for it.

Every dollar in your wallet has a *price tag* stuck to it. To put it there you've had to sacrifice, endure or spend something.

This has special significance for homebuyers and can be better understood — even proved — if we look at a few yardsticks by which we can measure the *real* value of money.

The following examples describe how to recognize the *actual* benefits you achieve when the seller accepts your lower offer. These 'alternative values of money' should fuel your motivation.

Money has Sweat Value

Like most people, you probably put in 40 hours at the office or factory every week. And let's say you take home a net wage of $400 each Friday. Consequently, your money has sweat value.

Our hypothetical saving of $3,000 from earlier can now be viewed in that context.

- A $3,000 saving represents 7.5 weeks of your working life ($400 x 7.5 wks = $3,000). Or, said another way, you worked 300 hours to earn that $3,000 savings (7.5 wks x 40 hrs = 300 hrs).
- At the same take home salary of $400 per week, a $10,000 saving represents 25 weeks of toil ($400 x 25 wks = $10,000); and it took you 1,000 hours to earn it (25 wks x 40 hrs = 1,000 hrs).

But maybe you earn above the average and take home $667 weekly.

- That $3,000 you negotiate off the asking price is then equal to 4.5 weeks of your life at work ($667 x 4.5 wks = $3,000); and it took you 180 hours to earn it (4.5 wks x 40 hrs = 180 hrs).
- On the same $667 weekly salary, a negotiated saving of $10,000 means you had to put in 15 weeks of work ($667 x 15 wks = $10,000); and it took you 600 hours to earn it (15 wks x 40 hrs = 600 hrs).

Sweat value (your labor, time and thinking) is one 'other' important way to view the value of the price cut you negotiate.

Here are more:

Money has Savings Capability Value

How much on average are you able to save each month? If you don't know the answer it's worth figuring out.

Let's assume that by cutting back on luxuries you manage to stash away $3,000 over a 12-month period. At that rate, the $3,000 price cut you negotiate is equal to *one year of personal saving* — without you having to sacrifice time or expend the effort to stash away the $3,000 from your salary.

If you can save $3,000 annually, a price cut of $10,000 would take you 3.3 years to accumulate. So, a $10,000 price concession, means you are putting 3.3 years of personal savings into your pocket *in one go*, again without any of the sacrifices required in saving it from salary.

And if you can save only $2,000 per year from your pay check all of these negotiated price reductions are worth correspondingly more in savings value. For example, a $10,000 price concession on a home purchase would take you five years to save from your pay check. And so on. You need to see money this way.

Money has Purchasing Value

A sum of $3,000 invested early for your child's education could make a big difference. Putting away $10,000 might guarantee you a more comfortable retirement. Either sum might buy you a whole new wardrobe or take you on a European vacation. The wardrobe and vacation have no investment value but either might be precisely what's best for you at a particular time.

Here's the point: The money you save on your next home purchase is yours to do with whatever you choose. It's yours, not someone else's. Whether you spend it today or invest it, it has real purchasing value.

I am giving you these examples to illustrate that money, when you earn it, save it, or spend it, has value beyond countable green dollar bills. Cash in your hand is a means of making life more fulfilling. That's exactly what you stand to gain by being a smart buyer — choices. Big or small, any price concession you negotiate can be used to improve your life. Negotiation is *never* just a numbers game.

Money has Peace of Mind Value

You already know this feeling. The particular euphoria you experience when you negotiate a good deal or make a particularly rewarding decision. It doesn't apply just to home buying. Any time your actions safeguard your personal interests or wealth you feel it deep inside. More so when you've been smart enough to prevent another party taking advantage of you. Then you sit back and reflect, and you know that you'll go on enjoying your success for a while to come. This is peace of mind value.

All that may be so, I hear you say, but what if you are one of the lucky few who are independently wealthy? Does any of this really make a difference then?

It might surprise you to learn that readers of *Not One Dollar More!* fall into every wealth category, including millionaire and beyond. I discovered this from communications with readers all over the globe. Also, my professional work has reminded me constantly that it's almost impossible *for anyone* to acquire and hold on to wealth without understanding the real value of money. To people in all tax brackets, one dollar *saved* is almost always worth more than two dollars earned, which underscores the fact that $10,000 saved is worth at least $20,000 earned. So, to answer the question above: Yes, saving money does make a difference to people at all wealth levels.

Note: As you absorb the skills of negotiation you'll probably feel that some of what you read here doesn't gel with what you've heard. The misconceptions about negotiation are many, and there are few reliable sources to learn from. As I mentioned earlier, expert negotiators, like top magicians, rarely reveal their secrets.

But, you can be certain the techniques explained in *Not One Dollar More!* do work. Used well they can add significantly to your wealth, regardless of what you are negotiating for. I've been applying these methods profitably for decades. I've taught them around the world to diplomats, lawyers, sports coaches, salespeople, consultants, mediators, psychologists, and others.

You never need to follow my advice slavishly, or speak the exact words I give you for dealing with salespeople and private sellers. But you do need to recognize the logic in these lessons, then apply what you learn and add common sense. Negotiation allows few opportunities to correct errors made through acting impulsively, and even less room to backtrack or delete what you have already communicated.

Good negotiation is power, the power to protect your best interests and enhance your quality of life. I am certain you'll recover the cost of this book hundreds, or maybe thousands, of times. *Not One Dollar More!* might in fact prove to be your *biggest-ever* return on investment.

I sincerely hope so.

For that to happen, you must believe in your ability to negotiate. I mean genuinely believe. I've already begun helping you do that, though you probably haven't noticed; your brain has been quietly primed for what's ahead, going into action — next chapter.

PART TWO

PREPARING TO WIN

CHAPTER 4

Going Into Action

*Always be on your guard because you are one
of all the people who can be fooled some of the time.*

— Anonymous

Your decision is made. You're going to search out and buy the kind of house you've been longing for. Maybe you'll call it home, rent it out, or renovate and re-sell. None of that matters.

What matters is what you do next.

You *should* start by finding an Exclusive Buyer Agent and be guided forward from there. This is by far the safest and potentially more rewarding decision you can make. However, that does not mean you can afford to be a passive, uninformed consumer. So, from this point on I'll assume, for learning purposes, that you must look out for your own wellbeing, that you have no EBA on your side. But everything you learn here will stand good to you whichever route you take.

Most buyers start by scanning property websites and checking local newspapers and property magazines. Before long this gets tedious. They then decide it's easier to meet with a real estate salesperson and discuss homes they've read about and others they have yet to discover. They pore over the agency's listings and narrow down to a handful that look interesting, then ask all the relevant questions about each one, things like:

- Age, condition, size
- Local amenities, local authority plans for the area
- Property taxes, schools, transportation, neighborhood crime rating
- Why the home is being sold, length of time on market
- What's the lowest price the seller might accept
- Does the price of the home represent good value, and so on.

And if it's you, while all this is going on you answer questions about yourself, your needs, your money, your motivation, your life, your partner, your family, your profession, your salary, your job commute, your limits, your loan, your time frame, your deadlines, and other vital, personal and confidential matters.

Later that day you call the salesperson for additional information on two of the homes she managed to show you and one or two others you might want to look at. The salesperson invites you to re-inspect both properties and mentions that she has identified another especially attractive home you should view, which she believes suits your needs perfectly and is priced very competitively. So you set an appointment and in the meantime begin imagining that it won't be long before you get what you're looking for and all the hard work is over.

It's that easy! That's how it should be done, right?

All wrong!

Wrong if you are to have any chance of negotiating successfully. Or any chance of buying at the seller's lowest acceptable price or on the best terms. Certainly not the way to protect your money, or guarantee you'll get the best deal available, or even a good deal. Not the way of the smart buyer.

But it's exactly the way to open yourself to being disadvantaged and vulnerable and to overpay for what you buy.

Hold on, you say, isn't this how everyone buys a home? Not the top five percent that I call smart buyers — and now hopefully not you.

It never ceases to amaze me that so many people search for and buy homes in this manner. Unwitting, over-trusting, inadequately prepared buyers virtually always pay more than they need to, accept inferior terms, and buy homes with problems they don't discover until it's too late. In fact, the average consumer employs more checks and safeguards when buying a car, or even a washing machine, than when buying a home. They walk naively into a high-risk, professionally controlled, commercial environment that is working against them from the start, taking few if any steps to protect their money, peace of mind, or confidential details.

And they rarely end up with the outcome they deserve!

If the above house hunting process sounds familiar, let yourself relax. These are not just the mistakes of amateurs. Professionals, with millions of dollars to spend, make the same mistakes.

Here's some evidence:

While writing the first edition of *Not One Dollar More!* I happened to be giving a series of short talks on negotiation for 110 non-real estate executives. I decided to poll them on how they went about buying a home. And was I surprised! Of these 110 senior executives, who each day made big decisions involving people, resources and money, only six said they had used a prepared strategy to ensure they got the best deal possible.

So what, you might think, every buyer has common sense and tries to avoid paying more for a home than they have to. This is true, of course. And if common sense and intention were enough, there'd be no over-paying, no mistakes, and no vulnerable buyers. But that's not the real world. Negotiation success requires insight, know-how, and a basic strategy. Good results come from *deliberate, informed* actions. Home buying can never be a naive undertaking.

I'd be willing to bet that virtually all of those 104 executives who went in without preparation and a strategy gave money away, and here's the real sting — without *ever* realizing it — except perhaps now on reading this! Their responses highlighted their mistakes; it was as if they had been *conditioned* to believe there was only one way to go about buying a home.

Nonsense.

Let me be blunt: Smart as these professionals were, all but six failed to safeguard their interests or their wellbeing when their money and peace of mind were at risk.

Their big mistake was that they talked with the real estate salesperson much too early and much too openly for their own good.

Before we look at a better way, here's some advice on using online services. The question I hear asked a lot is this: *Should I or shouldn't I use websites like Zillow, Trulia, Realtor.com and similar?*

Property websites like these can be useful for getting an overview of homes, prices and neighborhoods. But most of them make money by selling your personal information to agents. Generally, if you register or input information expect sales calls and attempts to get you to use a particular agent. In my view, none of these sites provide sufficient (if any) consumer protection alerts or know-how to buyers. For example, registering online as a homebuyer can lead to you being seen as 'belonging' to the agent who paid the most for your details, even though you might not intend or desire this. The first agent you talk with about properties — online or not — can demand a commission even when you don't buy the property through him or her. This doesn't always happen, of course, but it can, and it has done. It can be quite messy, even making it difficult for an EBA to work with you (because the EBA's commission can be claimed by the first agent you spoke with). So, stay aware of the potential consequences of giving your personal details to anyone, online or not. And when you are working with an EBA, always make this known when speaking with other agents.

At Open Houses it's the same. The agent wants your name, contact number and other personal details about you and your situation. Tread carefully; your name is enough to hand over, at least for now. If you are working with an EBA, say so, and that you'll be in touch if you're interested. If you are going it alone, everything in this book applies.

Caveat: Never disclose information you expect to be kept confidential, except to the agent who will be representing you exclusively — ideally an EBA.

The First Commandment: Don't Rush In!

Note: No challenge should begin with face-to-face contact with an individual who is not on your side.

Does this mean you must view the seller and salesperson as your competitors? Yes! Though not in the combative sense. The inescapable fact is this: The seller and you are in opposition; you each want the best financial deal and best terms — you have *opposite* objectives, you want *opposite* outcomes.

As we saw earlier, the listing agent, selling agent, and salesperson who show buyers around, all work for the seller; all are trying to get you to pay, and agree to, what *the seller* wants. The law, and the contracts they make with the seller, obligate these agents and salespeople to act in this way.

Homebuyers rarely realize or understand the implications of this.

As an unrepresented buyer, the odds are stacked against you. Not because that's the way it *should* be; it certainly isn't the way it should be. But because that's how the system works — unless you employ your own Exclusive Buyer Agent, which is the smartest move you can make (see Chapters 11 and 12 on EBAs).

OK, if that typical approach is wrong, what else is worth knowing, apart from the idea of using an Exclusive Buyer Agent?

Let's answer that by considering a few common situations in which you hand over money in exchange for products or services. Note what happens as your spending increases (bear with me on this, I am embedding a principle in your unconscious).

Typically, you won't think too hard or long about spending $20 for an item of clothing, especially if it's something you feel you need; your decision to buy is almost automatic, you hand over your $20 without fuss. Deal done.

When it's a $230 pair of shoes your decision isn't so quick or simple; you'll think harder and longer. But your hesitation won't go on forever; you deserve to treat yourself, you rationalize, and Italian slip-ons will look perfect with your new designer suit. You hadn't planned the expense but after mulling it over you decide to go ahead. However, you're aware that with this purchase you expect more: attractiveness, craftsmanship, comfort, and a higher level of service and satisfaction. Or you won't part with your $230.

Later, when you get home, you discover that your just-out-of-warranty TV is kaput. Not worth fixing, is what your dial-up repairman says. You're low on cash but you need a TV. So you search the online stores and newspaper ads, comparing brands, features, styling, size and price, and you short-list two models. You then call the best store and ask if a sale is imminent or if any discounts are available on your preferred model. The salesman says no to both. You tell him you're disappointed and remind him that you're a long-standing customer, and that his competitor has a store-wide sale starting this Saturday. His own store, the salesman responds, carries the lowest prices in town, but, for you, as a once-off gesture, he'll allow you a five percent discount, throw in a free remote, and give you a six-month free subscription to your favorite movie channel — provided you buy either of your two selected models before 5pm tomorrow. So you drive to the store, request a full demonstration, check all the controls and the picture and sound quality, make sure everything is just as you desire, seek assurance on the store's full-refund-if-not-satisfied policy and the manufacturer's two-year warranty. And only then, finally, you hand over your $750, roll out your new TV and head home.

What on earth, you ask, has all that got to do with real estate? Well, everything. Let's see.

With all three purchases you behaved differently. As the price went up you took more time preparing, communicating, inspecting, strategizing, and deciding. You also looked for progressively more assurances and guarantees. With the most expensive item you even pressed hard for a discount, stating that you had *choices*, and that you might spend your money elsewhere if you didn't get your way.

And your TV-purchase strategy worked, due to a fundamental principle of negotiation: Because you recognized you had *power*!

No, you didn't consciously strategize everything. But you intuitively understood that the seller needed what you could provide — money, a guaranteed sale, cash on the table, business done, commission in the salesman's next pay check. The salesman's behavior (his discount offer and extras) told you loud and clear that he desired your cash more than you needed to buy *his* TV.

Question: What else of significance did you do, consciously or unconsciously? You recognized and made clear to the salesman that you could take your business elsewhere, get a sweeter deal, buy a different model, get better value for your money, a bigger discount, and maybe more extras. What *your* behavior said to *him* was that you knew you were in the stronger position.

But were you?

Maybe not. Could be you would have bought his TV even without a discount. Could be his competitor had sold out of your preferred model or had it at a higher price. But who knew any of that? Not the salesman. And that's the point. What he 'knew' was that the sale could be lost, a willing, motivated, cash-ready customer could walk unless he got concessions.

Well, well, it seems like you had a strategy after all.

Who was it that made the salesman think that way? Clearly, it was you. *You* put those thoughts in his head, *you* pulled the strings, *you* controlled the tone and progress of the negotiation, and eventually *you* set the final price and terms.

You had power.

We saw earlier that, in negotiation, having options and alternatives, or the other side believing you do (like the TV salesman), puts power in your hands. Your power comes from the story you place in the other person's head — whether you are holding any 'real' advantage or not.

Simply, what it comes down to is this:

When the other side believes you have power — the power of choice — you do! That's the message you should be sending from your first contact with anyone you'll later negotiate with, in home buying or otherwise. Make a mental note now of the significance of power in negotiation — actual power and perceived power. This is critical to getting the outcome you desire. By 'outcome' I mean the lowest price and best terms possible, with no nasty after-purchase surprises or hidden problems of any kind.

Let's investigate closer this phenomenon of power.

Power and Predictability

Over the years I've made a point to open my negotiation workshops with this basic caution:

If you forget everything else you learn over the next few days, be certain to remember one thing: Never give away your power!

The thinking you'd put into buying a $750 TV will serve you equally well when buying a home of any price. One core reason is this: In every legitimate negotiation, the seller wants and frequently *needs* your agreement, be it to hand over cash or do something else.

The person-to-person exchange is at the heart of negotiation and has been extensively studied by psychologists and others. We've learned that human behavior is surprisingly predictable in particular circumstances (you'll experience some interesting examples as we proceed). Whether the people involved are property sellers, agents, store clerks, army generals, business executives or politicians, all behave reasonably predictably in specific situations.

So, here's the question: How can you use this knowledge to your advantage?

First step, gather the information you need. The more you learn about sellers' wants and needs, the more predictable they become. You'll see this more clearly if you pull back a little from the anxiousness of the action. What you know about a seller's circumstances and the property under consideration gives you a distinct advantage, which means an opportunity to influence. By influencing the seller's thinking you affect the outcome. Much of the time you do this via the salesperson or listing agent who presents your position, your questions, or your offer, to the seller. In for-sale-by-owners you're likely to be doing it face to face with the seller.

The better your information, the greater your potential power. And the clearer you communicate your message — to the salesperson or seller — the stronger your effect.

Naturally, power and predictability relate to information and how you execute your strategy. But caution is called for because information is a two-edged sword. It works for you when you possess it and use it. And just as surely, information about you in someone else's hands can work against you. This is one big reason the real estate salesperson wants to know so much about your personal circumstances.

Let's see what this means:

The more the salesperson or seller knows about you the weaker your power becomes. Here's what you *don't* want them to know:

- the *intensity* of your desire for a particular home
- the *depth* of your needs
- the *strength* of your attachment to a home
- the *urgency* of your situation
- the *level* of your enthusiasm
- the *pressure* of your spouse
- the *preference* of your spouse
- the *excitement* of your kids for a particular home
- the *extent* of your wealth
- the *size* of your salary
- the *ease or difficulty* of your commute
- the *amount* of your savings
- the *limit* of your budget
- the *demands* of your job
- the *due date* of your pension payout or inheritance
- the *cash-in-hand* you'll get from your current home sale
- the *fullness* of your satisfaction with a seller's counter offer
- the *firmness* of your preference
- the *give-up-ability* of your conditions
- the *flexibility* in your offer price or your position
- the *nature* of your strategy
- the *secrets* you learned from this book
- . . . and so on.

You must become a sponge, eliciting and absorbing details and insights (without being unethical, of course). At the same time, you disclose nothing about you or your situation that can be used against your best interests, nothing that will weaken the *power* you've been building since you first set out to buy a home.

Instead, you reveal only those details you have deliberately orchestrated, thereby reducing your vulnerability and bringing advantage on your side. We'll go through shortly what and how much to reveal. Before that we'll explore some thinking closer to home, another important part of your preparation.

Knowing What You Need and Knowing What You Want

Why do you want to buy a home?

Only you can answer that, but answer it you must. Being clear about your dominant motive, your most compelling purpose, will inform and support your decision making later, when the pressure mounts, as it will.

The question might seem unnecessary, something you'll know intuitively, but once again be guided here: Negotiators will always contemplate and clarify the 'why' that will drive their actions before setting out.

Perhaps this will be your first house and you're totally excited about the reality of being a home owner. Or it could be that your current home is too small, too big, too noisy, in a declining suburb, or that you need to escape neighbors from hell. Or possibly because you see property as a good long-term investment, a way to shelter your money from taxes. Or because you want to start a vegetable garden, or get a dog, or have more open space outdoors. Only you can say.

The reason I'm pushing this point is important. When you're clear, really clear, about your dominant buying motive, you'll be clearer about exactly what it is you *need* and *want* in the home you are seeking.

Buy a Notebook — Now!

I'm a strong believer in writing things down, and you should be too. Before you make contact with any salesperson, call any realty service, register on any website, or inspect any home, buy a good notebook with lots of pages. It will prove a godsend many times during your search, because almost *everything* goes in it.

Start by making a list of your *must-haves,* those things you consider indispensable. For now, only must-haves. Do you require three bedrooms? A family room or study? Need to be close to public transportation? Or within walking distance of a convenience store? You get the idea. These are not emotional items you'd *like* to have; they're necessities. Write them down.

And here's the reason this exercise is so important. The time pressure and emotional tribulations that are part of researching and inspecting properties, on top of your daily work-life challenges, can cause you to compromise on what you actually need.

Your list of must-haves will keep you focused and on track. Of course, you are free to change your thinking and modify your list, but do so only with good reason, only changes that serve your needs and spring naturally from your circumstances. Never changes that serve the salesperson's or seller's interest alone, or changes induced by your own weariness or frustration. In other words, changes you can live with and feel happy about, because in the end nothing less will satisfy you.

When you are prompted to alter or delete from your must-have list, bear in mind that this suggests the item was *not* a must-have in the first place. You need to examine now why you put it there, before you alter or delete it. If your must-have list is solid it is unlikely you'll make changes, unless you radically re-think your needs. So, construct your must-have list thoughtfully, and if you are tempted to change it be certain the change is merited.

The danger in not having a must-have list is that pressure, anxiety, tiredness, excitement, or someone else's self-serving opinion can affect your judgment and cause you to make a decision you'll later find hard to live with.

Two examples: road traffic and traffic noise. If you hate the sight or noise of traffic outside your door, there's probably zero chance it will ever stop bothering you, regardless of the attractiveness of the home or the salesperson's suggestion that you'll soon tune it out. You won't. It's this salesperson's suggestion you should tune out.

For all the above reasons you'll need also an *elimination* list, all the factors that will eliminate an otherwise ideal home from your consideration. Like your must-have list, in the heat of the moment your elimination list will prevent you from convincing yourself, or being convinced by others, that you can overlook one or more elimination factors. Because it's written down, your resistance will be stronger, and your chance of getting exactly what you need will be enhanced.

Together, your must-have list and elimination list will save you many hours discussing and inspecting unsuitable homes that waste of your time and delay your search.

Finally, all your *would-likes* can form another list, if you feel this will help you. Your would-likes are familiar to you and can be sacrificed, if necessary, for an otherwise ideal home. Whether you list would-likes or not, keep a picture of your ideal home in mind at all stages in your search.

Now, let's turn our attention to your budget and how to manage it.

Three Money Limits: How to Set Them and What to Reveal

Before your search begins you will need to know your *borrowing limit*. The time to do this is *before* you start looking at homes, not when you have found an ideal property.

Instead of pinning your hopes on one lender, investigate two or more options for the mortgage you require. Talk to mortgage reps, loan officers, knowledgeable agents, buyer brokers, and so on. Compare costs and fees on the kind of loan you will look for. Who will give you the lowest interest rate and, when all costs have been counted, the best annual percentage rate? There's an extensive how-to section later of mortgages and financing.

When you find out the loan amount you qualify for, see this as the maximum figure available to you, but not necessarily the amount you will spend. By knowing your borrowing limit you avoid indecision and can act confidently if an unexpected opportunity arises.

Here's an example:

Assume you requested to be pre-approved for $180,000 and you got the OK on that figure. A few days later your dream home shows up. You hesitate because the price is higher than you wanted to spend. You'll negotiate, of course, but it's clear you'll need a bigger loan. Doubt and anxiety set in. You're not sure the home is within reach, which injects uncertainty into your negotiating; that vital energy and conviction is absent. You're now disadvantaged. You lack essential information. Postponing your interest or starting over might not be feasible, or might seriously work against you, even though you might in the end drag some kind of deal together. The whole episode is less than ideal.

You see, you asked your lender for $180,000, but your *borrowing limit* might have been $210,000. That information is no good to you if you don't have it when you need it, or if you cannot get an immediate Yes from the lender.

I'm not recommending you take the biggest loan you can convince your lender to give you. You might never spend anything close to that figure. But it's helpful to know. And even more helpful to have approval for that.

How Much Do You Want to Spend?

Let's get back to a core question: How much are you willing to spend? This will be asked of you every time by realty salespeople. Write the figure in your notebook before you begin your search.

Now, here's my advice — and it will go against everything you'll be told — *never* divulge this figure to a salesperson or private seller. It's for you to know, and only you. As we go on you'll see the logic in this.

Now, in your notebook, write these *two* figures.

The first is your *comfortable spending limit,* the amount you ideally *want* to spend. You arrive at this based on considering how a lump sum down payment and loan repayments will affect your quality of life, including how much you'll have left over for discretionary spending each month. Be sure that your comfortable spending limit enables you to get the features and quality you desire in a home.

The second figure is your *upper spending limit.* The same considerations apply here, how it will affect your quality of life and discretionary spending level. You can afford this amount, and are willing to spend it, but only for a special home that represents exceptional value. When a financially out-of-reach home grabs you, your emotions will shout *I want it!* but your notebook will say *No!*, providing hard evidence you cannot afford to overlook.

I'll illustrate this because it's a trap I've seen too many homebuyers fall into. Let's assume you are *comfortable* putting down $30,000 and borrowing $150,000. And although it's not part of your plan, you could go to your *upper spending limit* for a once-in-a-lifetime home: $30,000 down payment plus a loan of $180,000.

Here's how that might look:

Notebook:
$30k down payment, *comfortable* spending limit: $180,000
$30k down payment, *upper* spending limit: $210,000

Both these 'limit' figures are in your notebook. The third figure, your *borrowing limit,* as I said earlier, is stored in your brain (or, if necessary, in your wallet, for your eyes only) along with a note of how much cash you have available for down payment.

You'll notice there's little emotion in this exercise. Successful 'negotiation does not arise from emotion but plays to emotion'. We'll see much more of how this works further on. For now, note that all your big financial commitments, such as buying a home, need to be guided by rational, pragmatic thinking and solid preparation, never heat-of-the-moment temptations.

As we noted earlier, *instinct* and *intuition,* which many people boast about possessing, are often dangerous substitutes for basic negotiation know-how; they cannot be relied on in place of good planning and preparation. Too much of your hard-earned cash, and a lot else besides, are at stake.

Recap: Understand and be resolute about three figures — your: 1) *borrowing limit, 2) comfortable spending limit,* and *3) upper spending limit.* This will support your decision making in financial situations.

Research: Finding Out What You Need to Know

Information gathering is imperative, even for buyers who, for whatever unwise reason, choose not to plan strategically.

The objective of research is relevant, reliable information, and the product is responsible action.

A recurring challenge I face in teaching negotiation to corporate types is to get them to make use of their research data. Even governments spend millions of dollars gathering statistics (information) on things like the number of people living below the poverty line or the national level of illiteracy. Too often, however, no rectifying action is taken, a case of information existing for its own sake rather than as a catalyst for positive change.

Only when someone *acts* can the status quo change. I recall Bob Geldof saying something like this to world media before the 1985 Live Aid concerts to relieve famine in Africa. He was right. Frequently, what individuals (and corporations) need most is to be shown how to use information to achieve specific goals.

In home buying, good information is vital and relatively easy to acquire, and it will usually determine the quality of deal you end up with.

But where do you start? You already have! You're well on your way at this stage.

Your New Surroundings

Your focus now shifts to location. Which neighborhoods interest you? This goes in your notebook. Which areas fit into your budget on first look? Narrow your focus by eliminating areas you know you can't afford; but stay alert for the occasional lower-priced home in a better neighborhood (often a sound strategy).

The quickest way to get a feel for the affordability of a neighborhood is to check relevant websites and the real estate sections of local papers. But be careful online that you don't *unthinkingly* hand over your personal details or contact information just to gain access to a site, something I'll return to later with a warning.

You're in the preliminary research stage, so it's still too early to talk with sales-people. Friends or associates who live in your selected area may be able to provide details of recent sales, prices generally, property taxes, how the area is developing, age breakdown, crime, schools, and other details important to you.

Continue noting details of asking prices and actual selling prices of homes that are similar to the home you have in mind; this activity goes on for as long as your search runs. Whenever possible, make a note of the difference between initial *asking price* and the *selling* price. An initial list price of $215,000, might later have been reduced to a new asking price of $205,000; however, a smart buyer might have got it at $195,000. This type of information is helpful but sometimes not easy to acquire, though local websites often publish raw details (when you work with an Exclusive Buyer Agent this is no problem).

Of course, local realty offices have all this data. However, if you call them about specific properties or prices, tell them you are just 'keeping an eye on the market' and are not yet ready to buy, adding that you may talk with them later. Agencies are run by business people; so, as a prospective customer you'll probably get the information you need. Stress that you require actual figures, not vague ones. Tell them it's 'too early' to discuss your needs, and say no to the offer of a call-back.

So far, you have avoided face-to-face discussion of your situation with a real estate salesperson. That's how it should be. Everything you have done to this point has been to ensure you are adequately prepared, which is the first key to your success. You can think of it as forging your armor before you enter the arena.

I hope I have convinced you to think hard and come up with answers to critical questions. At this point you should have a mental picture of the home you'll search for and be clear on the mindset and information that will protect you as you move forward. This early work should have taken just a few days at most.

Let's review your notebook contents:
- Your borrowing limit
- Your comfortable spending limit
- Your upper spending limit (in the event you discover an outstanding bargain that's too good to miss)
- List of must-haves
- List of factors that will eliminate any home
- Names of your preferred neighborhoods or locations, ideally in order of preference
- General information on prices, taxes, schools, amenities, planned developments, dominant age groups, crime stats, and so on, in your selected areas
- Examples of list prices and actual selling prices, as recent as possible, and brief descriptions of the properties concerned: age, size, bedrooms, family room, kitchen, dining room, condition, garage, block size, etc.

As you gain confidence in your skills as a negotiator you'll feel tempted to by-pass this early work. Please don't. *Not One Dollar More!* was written with a commitment to give you what you need to protect your best interests and get the best deal possible. That prize will depend to a large degree on how well you prepare *each time* you set out to negotiate.

Next we'll move to face-to-face negotiation. This is where the information you gathered and the thinking that's reflected in your notebook take on real significance. Very soon you'll feel capable of holding your own as the salesperson goes to work to get the highest price and best outcome for the seller — out of you.

You'll also learn to recognize when tactics are being used against you, and how to neutralize them.

Let's see how next.

CHAPTER 5

What You Need to Know to Protect Your Money

When you have to make a choice and don't make it,
that in itself is a choice.

— Mark Twain

It has always surprised me that even the smartest of people, those you'd think of as diligent and organized, are just as likely to approach buying a home in the same casual and naive manner as the majority of buyers.

Perhaps it's because they're less street-wise than they need to be. In this game of real estate, being less than street-wise is a liability that can cost you dearly.

Despite inducements, and your natural inclinations, placing complete trust in any person anxious to sell you property is something you *never* do. Caution is always called for. Trust should be traded in minute quantities only when you are certain it has been earned. Your first impressions — no matter how much you fancy yourself as a judge of character — will *not* provide that certainty.

Here's my best advice: Reveal only information about your circumstances that is necessary, and verify each potentially significant 'fact' told to you by real estate salespeople and private sellers.

That's the first step in developing a protective strategy — intelligent skepticism. Here's an example of where a fortune could have been lost — or saved.

Case Study: Millions at Stake

I was presenting a seminar in Australia on problem solving and personal achievement. At the end of the final day, one of the participants (I'll call her Kathleen) presented me with a challenge I found impossible to turn down. What happened next illustrates a frequent occurrence in real estate.

Kathleen was a business executive who had been negotiating for the purchase of a four-story building on behalf of a corporate client. She asked if I would inspect the property with her and the salesperson. I first looked over the research she had gathered then acquired additional details. Next, I inspected the building and spent one hour with Kathleen and the salesperson.

Our 3-way discussion was cordial. The salesperson was clear and assertive. The property was for sale at a price of ten million dollars, which, he stressed, was below market value (that sounded odd — why would someone sell below market value?).

Weighing up what I heard and observed, along with the research and my own enquiries, I suggested to Kathleen that if her client was serious about buying the property they should hold off, do absolutely nothing. My reading of the situation made me feel the eventual selling price might be closer to $5m. She went along. So I outlined a strategy I felt would give her the best chance of buying at the lowest price possible. Timing and persistence would be critical.

Kathleen followed the strategy, which meant engaging briefly in two further telephone contacts over the following ten days, both initiated by the salesperson.

Five weeks after I first met the salesperson he phoned Kathleen to tell her he had received an offer of $3.5m and the seller had rejected it. And, you guessed it, he asked if she would be interested in submitting an offer.

In the end, Kathleen's client decided against the property, but I'm sure the point is clear. The strategy used here can be just as effective in buying a residential home and is explained in detail as we move through this book.

For now, let's play a guessing game. Based on what you already know, how much do you think Kathleen's client might have bought the property for? Ten million? Eight million? Six million?

Working with more details than I've given you, I believe between $3.5m and $5m might have sealed the deal.

Your reaction — and a logical one too — might be that this is all the building was worth. It was probably grossly overvalued at $10m, you say. Maybe that's correct. But price is not the most important lesson here.

Consider this: What percentage of prospective buyers would have imagined a 50% reduction (or more) in the list price? Few, I'd say. Especially since the salesperson said more than once that another buyer was showing serious interest at $10m. How many 'lost millions' might this have cost an unwary buyer? It's almost too frightening to consider.

Yes, it is an exceptional case. No question about that. But at least here, a less astute buyer might have paid $10.5m or more. And neither that buyer nor Kathleen would *ever have known* of their gigantic mistake! How many ordinary homebuyers have overpaid in this way? Uncountable. But far too many, in my view. Most do not buy at the seller's lowest acceptable price or get best terms.

This case study signals an important caveat. Every unrepresented homebuyer (you) competing in a field dominated by professionals is at risk. History is filled with tragic accounts of buyers acting on impulse and blind faith in all kinds of markets — real estate, stocks, commodities, stamps, coins, tulip bulbs (yes!) and others.

When the time comes to buy, you'll need to manage a mix of pressures: time, fear of loss, money, your excitement for the home, your level of professional know-how, and the negotiation itself, if you are to stay in control.

The Importance of Control — and What Exactly it Means

My first objective here is to clarify what I mean by *control*.

When buying a home (or anything) you can never dictate *all* the elements affecting any single transaction or negotiation. Nor do you need to.

However (and this point is emphasized throughout this book), there are *always* actions, tactics, decisions and elements over which you do have power. Focus on these and you will take charge of any negotiation.

- Control is about having a plan, a strategy, and sticking to it when confronted by persuasive people and situations.
- Control means not allowing yourself to be pushed, talked into or frightened into believing you will 'lose out' or have to agree to the seller's price or terms.
- Control means knowing that 'No' is often just a reaction or a ruse and seldom means 'NO!'.
- Control means vision, being able to see through and see ahead.
- Control is presenting as a reasonable buyer who is firm and definite while not totally inflexible.
- Control is pulling your own strings and knowing which and when to pull.
- Control is non-aggressive, and not needing to look or sound like an expert.
- Control is being comfortable with the fact that your negotiation skills sit behind your personality; they are not out front and should not be.

Let's make a few contrasts to further emphasize this critical point.

Control is subtle rather than blatant; empathic rather than arrogant; respectful rather than argumentative; genuine rather than cynical; resourceful rather than impulsive; and persistent rather than submissive.

By maintaining control you guard against two insidious traps: being intimidated and being manipulated. They go hand-in-hand, typically, which we'll explore as we look at specific examples of control in action.

To understand control better you might need to challenge your current thinking. For example, if you have a clear definition of *negotiation* I suggest you put it aside. By the time you finish this book that definition will be different. At that point, the negotiation skills you need will be familiar and accessible to you.

Right now, let's kill some common misconceptions. To negotiate a successful home purchase, here's what you *do not need*.

What You Don't Need to Pull Off a Good Deal

Contrary to what you'll hear, getting a good deal does not depend on having a buyers' market, low mortgage rates, low inflation, or declining home values. Successful deals are framed by you and how well you negotiate.

If you fear sounding like a negotiator, you can stop worrying right now. That's not how it will be. You won't look or sound conspicuous in any negative way. In fact, nobody but you and those sharing your aspirations will know you are applying what you learned here. You'll come across as a genuine buyer, but one who is not easily led, superficially influenced, or pushed or tricked into disclosing what is not in your best interest. Your skill as a negotiator is subtle; it does not draw attention to itself (that's why I coined the term *invisible negotiation*). You act as natural as possible: courteous, respectful, a serious buyer.

However, beneath these outer qualities lies conviction, confidence, awareness of what goes on behind the scenes in real estate, and your pledge that this is one game you are not going to lose.

As you prepare to handle the real estate salesperson, it's time to start forming a mental picture of yourself as a resourceful negotiator. This sounds hard but it's not. If you examine your day-by-day communications you'll discover that to some extent you are negotiating all the time. You don't call it negotiation, of course, because you have no need to label your interpersonal exchanges; no need to intellectualize what comes to you naturally; no need to identify the skills you have developed for dealing with an infinite variety of personalities, people with whom you live, work, teach, talk, trade, and play. You do, indeed, possess many of the negotiator's characteristics.

Consequently, the principles and tactics in the following sections will feel familiar, like you've encountered them before. In fact, you've been using many unconsciously throughout your life.

But unconscious skills are not enough. Not when you are buying real estate. Your task now is to act *consciously*. To understand and apply effective negotiation tactics when they can save you money or make you money.

For many people (you may be one) home buying is a somewhat unnatural activity, like entering a foreign domain in which you must rely on the direction of others. Feelings of anxiety, insecurity, amateurishness, uncertainty, vulnerability, even fear, are normal. When negotiating, such emotions tend to close down many of the resourceful, natural, intuitive traits that guide you through other interpersonal engagements. Outcome: you feel needy and vulnerable.

Let's change that.

How Thick Is Your Armor?

We've already seen that the salesperson will be making a detailed assessment of you from first contact. She will be assessing you against a list of criteria:

- Your personality and temperament
- How financially qualified you are
- Your level of conviction and capability

- Your astuteness or innocence
- How urgent your need is
- How well-informed you are about the market
- What impresses you, what impresses your partner
- How much money you might be persuaded to part with (not the figure you give her).

It's in the salesperson's interest — and not at all in yours — to be able to predict as much about you as possible. In particular, she'll try to rate your susceptibility to influence, how impressionable you might be to the tactics, logic and emotion she uses to close sales.

Back to the analogy I mentioned earlier: The salesperson wants to know, in short, how thick is your armor. Your task is to disclose no exploitable weaknesses and provide only information that will assist your cause (more on this shortly).

The Agent Sells to Live and Lives to Sell

The skills of even the most congenial real estate salesperson are many and varied. These are professionals who survive based on their ability. They sell to live, and if they're really sharp they live to sell. Their techniques are subtle and refined, not easy to detect. A flashing smile and bright eyes can cause you to lower your guard. If you do, you lose. Because their job is to get the highest price and best terms for the seller.

Does this seem like someone who might become your friend? Someone to invite to your family barbecue or Christmas party? A godparent, perhaps, for your new arrival? Hardly! What you are experiencing is a cultivated persona designed first to disarm, then win your trust.

They're not wolves in sheeps' clothing. Not in a malicious sense. They're simply professional sellers, measured and rated by the number of sales they produce.

To make a successful sale on behalf of the seller, the salesperson sets out to learn as much about you as might be useful in influencing your decisions. Before he can do that he'll need to sell you on his genuineness and credibility. You might hear stories of thankful buyers 'just like you', or unfortunate buyers who didn't act fast enough. He might even mention in passing the credentials and awards he has won.

Behind all that, to him, ultimate success is a quick no-hassle sale at a price for which the seller will be delighted and will refer more business his way. All the while, the average buyer is none the wiser about whose best interests are really being served.

The more delighted sellers the salesperson acquires, the higher his standing in his profession and the wealthier he becomes. Your aim, starting now, is to make sure his success is not achieved at your expense.

Four Traps and Phony Buyers: Five Major Buyer Mistakes

Here are five costly mistakes I've seen far too many homebuyers make. In truth, homebuyers are usually their own worst enemy. Not only do they fail to defend themselves against misrepresentation, tricks and deception, they hurt themselves through what they do and say. Many buyers make the cardinal error of treating the real estate salesperson as a confidant to whom they can reveal their most personal thoughts and circumstances.

The kind of relationship that facilitates this openness is cultivated by salespeople, usually in the guise that it will make for better service. Yes, there are good reasons to communicate your needs and desires. But it is foolhardy to disclose anything that can be used against you, even when it is requested by the salesperson.

Once again, keep in mind that the salesperson is contractually compelled to report to the seller *all information* — including any details revealed by you — that could affect the seller's ability to sell at the highest price and best terms.

The following four traps ensnare unwary buyers, and buyers who naively believe they are prepared. Never communicate these to anyone hoping to sell you anything, especially real estate:

1. *Anxiety.* This is a common side effect of searching for, financing, and buying a home. Typically, it is caused by the loan process, inspections, deadlines, the difficulty of finding the right home, fear of losing the home to another buyer, making the buy decision, negotiating, and all the leg work and scheduling required.

2. *Urgency.* This type of stress is felt by most homebuyers. They believe they are under money, time, family, or emotional pressure to act quickly. Unless your urgency is potentially disastrous, it is never in your interest to reveal it to a salesperson or seller. You'll learn here how to hide these feelings to preserve your negotiation power.

3. *Budget.* Money, in all its forms, is a major concern for homebuyers. What you reveal about your finances can walk you into costly traps. When you follow my earlier advice, you alone will know the maximum loan for which you qualify, a figure best kept in your head or tucked away. Your notebook will remind you of two other figures: your upper spending limit and your comfortable spending limit. Which, if either, do you reveal to the salesperson? We'll go into this in a moment.

4. *Emotional Attachment.* This is one rule you should never break, no matter how strongly you feel about a home. Do not tell an agent or salesperson that you have fallen in love with a home they would like to sell you. Or that a home is 'just perfect' or 'ideal' or 'exactly what we were looking for' or anything remotely similar. Never!

Let's take a closer look and see what can happen. We'll then look at the fifth trap separately.

Trap One: Anxiety

Regardless of what you are negotiating for, anxiety is a liability, significantly threatening when it is obvious to the other side.

First, it diminishes your ability to negotiate the best deal possible. Second, as your anxiety increases the power and options normally open to you decrease.

It's natural to feel a degree of excitement and nervousness while going through the process of finding and buying the home you want. Such feelings can be controlled and disguised with a little practice and self-management skills you already possess.

The kind of anxiety that threatens to overtake you despite your best efforts is particularly hard to conceal from a sharp salesperson. When the salesperson suspects there's a seller advantage to be gained — and there always is in these circumstances — he will be more obstinate in the negotiation and more challenging all round.

A classic, non-real estate example of buyer anxiety happened to me in New York City. I surrendered two of every negotiator's best weapons, power and options. Here's the story.

I landed in Manhattan with three busy days of meetings ahead of me. At the end of the third day, when my business was over, I stayed one extra day to indulge my passion for photography. For over a year I had wanted to buy a particular camera and this was the perfect opportunity (New York photo stores have everything a camera enthusiast could want, and good prices).

At 1pm the clerk at the first store I visited confirmed he had in stock all four items I wanted. His *best* price, he said, was $1,800. I told him I'd check around and, if his price turned out to be the best, I'd be back later in the day. After some hours I'd seen enough. The first store was the cheapest by $68, so I returned, arriving at 5:45pm. The clerk's earlier indifference was now an air of conceit. I could live with that. At this stage all I wanted was my new Mamiya RB67 camera and a cab back to my hotel.

The clerk placed the four items on the counter. We both checked the contents of the boxes and confirmed all was OK.

'That's a total of $1,887,' he said with a whiff of arrogance.

'Hold on,' I replied. 'Earlier today you told me $1,800. You even wrote the prices on my list.'

He floated his gaze into the distance. I was certain then that integrity was not his strong suit.

'Well?' I said. 'How about it?'

'You want them or not?' he responded.

'You told me $1800.'

'That was four hours ago,' he said. 'The best I can do now is $1887.' Then came the sting. 'Take it or leave it, you won't get a better price.'

I'd been taken for a ride. He knew it and I knew it. It was now close to 6pm and my options were two: I could walk out, in which case my whole day would have been in vain, or I could hand over the extra $87 and consider it a lesson well learned. The clerk judged that I'd probably go along with his scheme. He knew I wanted what was sitting in front of me and figured I didn't have time to get to another store. And although he didn't know it, my options were even more limited since I was flying out at dawn the next day.

You guessed it. I paid the extra $87.

Let's try answer a few questions about what happened here, such as who had the advantages, and why.

Well, clearly, the seller had the advantages. I lost because I returned late to his store, obviously anxious to close the deal. Recall that I said earlier that *behavior* communicates more strongly than words — this is a good illustration of that. My behavior shouted messages like:

- *You have what I want most*
- *Your price represents good value*
- *It's late in the day, I'm in a hurry*
- *I'm tired searching around the city*
- *I want to buy now*
- *I have the money*
- *I'm motivated and eager.*

If that's not anxiety I don't know what is. The same trap is there when you are buying a home, make no mistake about it. You must ensure that your behavior does not communicate signals that damage your chance of a successful outcome. When you feel pressure to buy impetuously, perhaps because you are frustrated or weary or because you feel the chance won't come again, summon up every ounce of control you can find and hide those feelings from the salesperson.

Because unless you control it, your anxiety will show itself in speech, exclamations, gestures, actions, and facial expressions. The slightest sign can give you away. Negotiators, experienced salespeople and poker players know to conceal the giveaway signs.

Your best safeguard is to be forewarned, stay aware, and then to do everything in your power to stop what's going on inside you from showing. Bite your tongue, if you must, but manage the emotions threatening to get out. Later, in private, you can release your anxiety in whatever way that brings you relief — but never in company with a salesperson or seller.

Trap Two: Urgency

Urgency, unlike anxiety, is not communicated primarily through gestures and emotional expressions. It's more in the details of your circumstances that you disclose. Some examples:

- *Our house is already sold; we have to find a new one within two months.*
- *We have very little time, my husband's job starts August 5th, we need to be settled in a new place before the end of July, before the kids get back.*
- *Our money is coming through in three weeks; we'll need a place of our own to move into almost immediately.*

 • *I'm too stressed by all this. Find me something. What can you show me today that might be suitable?*

Of course, feelings of urgency also find their way into how you behave, especially when the pressure rises. Normally, you might be a composed and confident type but when you have no place to move into by the end of the month, edginess can overtake you. When your urgency is obvious you start surrendering control, weakening your power to negotiate effectively.

To recap, the following states of mind cause homebuyers to reveal the urgency of their situations and hand advantage to the other side:

1. You make it clear to the salesperson that the whole process of searching for and inspecting homes is one you detest, and that you can't wait until all the hassle is over, if you don't go crazy before then.
2. The deadline by which you must vacate your current accommodation is hanging over you like a ton of bricks. As each week passes your stress level increases, and you caution the salesperson that you are becoming desperate.
3. You are getting married soon (or divorced) and desperately need to have a place of your own — today, if possible, you tell the agent — so that your life can proceed in a sane, private, and orderly manner.

These and other urgency predicaments are potentially damaging to your financial health. Yet this happens every day, in every real estate agency. It traps the buyer with one million to spend just as it traps the starter-homebuyer. Your first defense is to notice it, then control what you reveal; following my suggestions will help you do both.

I find it ironic that homebuyers who efficiently manage other types of professional buy-and-sell transactions can be lulled into dropping their guard when facing a formally attired real estate salesperson who drives a comfortable sedan and behaves benevolently.

So, remember, even if you feel unnerved or a little out of your depth, nothing is gained through passive compliance. Unmanaged anxiety and urgency will only make you feel less secure. Your remedy is to notice what's happening, break away if necessary, and assess how you might handle things differently. Don't doubt for a moment that your state of mind affects your decision making and limits your opportunities, and could cost you serious money.

Trap Three: Budget

Once you have completed your preliminary research you'll know your upper and comfortable spending limits, the type and quality of home you can afford, and general home price information. Now it's time to prepare for one of the first questions the real estate salesperson will ask:

How much do you plan to spend?

What do you say? More importantly, what do you *not* say?

First, don't divulge your upper spending limit. And don't reveal your comfortable spending limit either — at least not yet, if at all.

Before we delve deeper, you'll need ready a description of the type of home you want, being clear about the elimination factors (see your notebook). But don't be surprised when the salesperson encourages you to consider a home not quite matched to your description, or suggests that you exceed your stated budget for 'an opportunity'.

Remember, your budget is based on what you know about prices and values in your selected area. Tell the salesperson that you have details on a number of homes that have recently sold, along with their selling prices and length of time on the market. If she asks you to identify specific properties, don't; say that the information is in another notebook you don't have with you, or something similar.

It's not in your interest to discuss details of the homes on *your* list. The salesperson has plenty of homes to talk about; you can discuss those as much as you wish. All you want the salesperson to know is that you are informed; you have done your preparation. But don't make it seem you are employing a strategy. The comments I'm suggesting should be made matter-of-factly in the course of normal conversation.

Here, you are painting a picture in the salesperson's mind, a picture of a logical, intelligent buyer who won't be easily persuaded, misled or convinced.

Now let's go back to the question the salesperson wants answered: How much do you want to spend? I recommend that you provide a figure 5-10% percent below your comfortable spending limit, perhaps adding that you might be able to increase it slightly for the right home.

Let's take two examples.

1. If your comfortable spending limit is $400,000, deduct 7% ($28,000), making a figure of $372,000. You can then turn this into a budget range $365-380,000.
2. If your comfortable spending limit is lower, say $200,000, I'd suggest using the 10% figure (making it $180,000), and give the agent a budget range of $175-190,000.

This approach will enable the salesperson to select appropriate homes. Almost invariably you'll be introduced to homes with list prices in excess of your stated range.

In the $365-380,000 range, few salespeople would pass up an opportunity to introduce you to particularly suitable homes with asking prices up to $420,000. Naturally, you would then negotiate for a meaningful reduction to bring it within your $400,000 budget.

Had you declared $400,000 as your comfortable spending limit, chances are you'd be introduced to at least a few homes listed at $425-460,000. The logic of declaring a budget slightly lower than your comfortable spending limit should be obvious.

If the quality of homes you're being shown is below the standard you expect, you may need to review your figures — *but only if you have similar experiences with two or more agents.* This is important because list prices of essentially similar homes can vary from one agency to the next (some agencies price homes higher), and even between comparable homes within the same agency (usually due to sellers' believing their homes are worth more than they are).

But there's also another reason. In every geographic area you'll find at least one agency that brags about getting the highest prices for their sellers. Naturally, they won't brag about this to you, the buyer they hope to extract that 'highest price' out of. You'll know how on-target your declared budget is once you've spoken with a couple of local agencies.

Still, you can run into problems. If you're working with just one salesperson and are seeing homes of a lower quality than you expect, the explanation could be, first, that you are being shown hard-to-sell homes or homes in which the salesperson has an extra incentive to sell (all real estate companies have these). Or, second, that you're seeing all the appropriate homes that salesperson can show you. To find out, ask a direct question:

Is that all you can show me in this neighborhood around my budget?

Another word of caution: Be careful your emotions don't get in the way of a good deal. This has to do with *you,* not the salesperson. Occasionally a homebuyer's purchase decision is predicated on winning the admiration of their spouse, partners, relatives, friends or work associates. The human need for approval is the culprit; it's natural, of course. And it's the reason some homebuyers frown on negotiating; they see negotiating as being beneath them. Others doubt themselves or feel otherwise inadequate in challenging or questioning the salesperson. Such mistakes make losing money easy.

My point here is that as a smart buyer you need to protect yourself from your own insecurities, impulses and ego. Because far too often non-negotiators buy the wrong home, or exceed their budget and overpay for what they buy. And they get trapped in mortgage repayments too high for their circumstances. In home buying, decisions driven by anything other than strategic intelligence usually result in loss, meaning that you hand over too much of your money, you get poorer terms or nasty late surprises, or a mix of all three.

Prevention lies in your preparation and in your notebook! Return to both when the heat is on; let these guide you. Leave impulse, passivity, urgency, anxiety, emotionality, ego-buying and such mistakes to those less astute. You don't live there. You are a smart buyer; see yourself that way!

Trap Four: Emotional Attachment

Every professional who sells real estate has heard the sweetest and most dangerous words a homebuyer can speak — sweet for the salesperson, that is, and dangerous for the buyer:

- *Oh, this is absolutely perfect.*
- *I just love this; I love it.*
- *I must have this; Can I make an offer right now?*
- *What an exceptional home! We've seen nothing to compare with this.*
- *I really, really like this. I don't need to see any others.*
- *This is for me, exactly what I've been looking for.*
- *What a wonderful home; how much will they accept?*

These are words you should *never* utter, nor reveal through gesture or expression. When you *must have* something someone else is selling, and you communicate this, you dig a big hole for yourself. You'll pay top price, not to mention settle for less than the best terms. It's called throwing money away, probably thousands of dollars, possibly tens of thousands. *Not* because you fell in love with the home, a common occurrence, but because you *let it be known* that you did!

The key to your success, which I'll continue to emphasize, lies in controlling what your competitor perceives. This is an age-old principle of negotiation. You'll encounter it often in these pages, and soon you'll see it used here in actual case studies and buyer-salesperson exchanges. For now, keep in mind that it's not wrong to feel you *must have* a particular home. But if you reveal this to a salesperson or seller you all but destroy your power to negotiate the best deal, and you risk losing a chunk of money.

Here's one of the oldest 'guarded' secrets of expert negotiators:

It is not what's factual or true that helps or hurts you but what your competitor believes to be factual or true.

In other words, hold back any information that weakens your power and present only that which supports your power. This applies to all discussions with salespeople. If a salesperson's courtesy or affability threatens to lower your guard, remind yourself that *only you* are working for you; the salesperson is working for the other side.

To bring this point alive, let's do a role switch:

You are now the salesperson. You have an older home you badly want to sell. You've been advertising it without any bites. In fact, try as you might, you haven't sold anything for two weeks. Today, things are starting to look better. You've succeeded in interesting not one but two couples in this older home, the Taylors and the Goldbergs.

You call each couple and invite them back separately to view the home a second time. Here are the responses you receive:

Mr. Taylor:
Yes, of course. We can't wait. We don't want to lose it. I told my wife that if we kept looking we'd find the right house for us. Now, it looks like our

search is over. Do you know what price the owner would accept? And could we move in within nine weeks, when our current lease expires?

Mrs. Goldberg:
Well, that house is comparable to two others we're looking at with another agent. We might be interested, but not at the price the owner is asking.

Remember, you are the salesperson. Now try to answer these questions:

1. From which couple are you likely to get the higher price?
2. With which couple are you likely to adopt a tougher, less compromising stand on price?
3. With which couple are you likely to wrap up the deal quicker?
4. Which couple are sitting ducks?

Sorry, no award medals; the answers are obvious. There isn't a snowball's chance in hell of the Taylors getting the home at the best price or best terms. Why? They unwittingly told you of their huge attachment to the home. Call it naivety, if you wish, or simply lack of know-how, but it's unintelligent buying. Sadly, it happens all the time. It's extremely costly. And it's avoidable!

It's why *I wrote this book*, and why *you* are reading it.

The Taylors smashed the rules smart buyers succeed by. They showed anxiety, urgency and emotional attachment. Buyers rarely recognize they are making such expensive mistakes.

Let's continue with our buyers and introduce a shock development (you are still the salesperson, eager to sell the home).

To your horror, the Taylors call to tell you the money they had earmarked for the home is delayed; they're postponing for a year. Now, you have only the Goldbergs. All your hopes rest with them. Does it seem like you'll have to work harder to create a deal and earn a commission? Bet your last penny on it!

Are you in as powerful a position as you were with the Taylors? Clearly, no; you have lost power. Will you be as uncompromising in your negotiation as you would have been with the Taylors? No chance. Will you need to try to get the sellers to accept the Goldbergs' lower offer? Probably.

We could go on but the point is clear.

The Goldbergs, if they continue to negotiate as well as they began, might be able furnish the home with what they'll save on this purchase.

But here's one more key question worth asking:

Who wanted the home more, the Taylors or the Goldbergs? The answer seems easy, doesn't it? If you said the Taylors, think again; you are overlooking the likelihood that the Goldbergs are smart buyers. As the salesperson, you cannot in fact answer my question because you simply don't know. The Goldbergs might have wanted or needed the home *more* than the Taylors. But they didn't show that.

The Goldbergs remained detached and discriminating, no anxiety, no urgency, and none of the emotional attachment of the Taylors. These are the cues salespeople note.

Cues that determine how they'll manage you, cues that dictate the level of stubbornness or accommodation they'll adopt in negotiation. In this hypothetical but realistic case study, only the Goldbergs had any chance of buying at the seller's lowest acceptable price or best terms.

We saw earlier that perception *is* power. And that power can be retained or given away. The Taylors gave away power. The Goldbergs retained power by staying in control of what they communicated while still displaying interest in the home. Re-read the two dialogs above to note how they differ, and to re-embed the core lesson in your thinking.

We've just seen four of the most common traps that will steal your money no matter what price range you are shopping in. Stay aware of these and you will negotiate more confidently and more profitably than ninety percent of buyers.

But there's another trap used every day, in every agency, which you need to be able to manage.

Trap Five: The Phony Buyer

Before you get involved with a real estate salesperson you need to learn how to deal with the phony buyer.

In the Taylor-Goldberg case study we saw two buyers interested in a particular home at the same time. That isn't the norm. Salespeople are delighted to have a single interest in a property. So, it is far more likely you will *not* have competition from another buyer for the home you want.

Expect the salesperson to try to convince you the opposite is true, that if you don't act quickly with a full price offer (or close to it) you risk losing the home to the 'other buyer'; and that the home could be snatched out of your grasp. Most such claims are outright deception, a ruse designed to put you under pressure to 'save' the home. (We want most that which others want to take from us — we are all potentially susceptible to this.)

In any particular instance, it is hard to be certain if the 'other buyer' is real or phony. Regardless, offer a nonchalant response, not quite indifference but unemotional curiosity. After mentioning the 'other buyer' the salesperson will probably suggest that you put 'an offer of some kind' on the table, or words to that effect.

But, before deciding your next move, do this: Ask the following questions and note how the salesperson responds; you're fishing for clues as to whether the 'other buyer' claim is credible or not:

- When did the other buyer first inspect the home? (if there is another buyer, that buyer may be working through a different agency, but still ask this question).
- How many times have they inspected the home?
- Is it a family or a couple?
- Is the other buyer with your own agency?
- How many kids are there?

- Are they local or from out of town?
- Is there an offer in writing at this point? If not, why not?

You are testing the salesperson. Look for specific or at least plausible answers. Be suspicious of vague responses like: *I'm not certain,* or *I'll have to check on that,* or *I don't have that information.* And watch the eyes. If the other buyer is real the salesperson should have some facts, or offer to find them quickly, even if the buyer is not with his agency.

If it's a case of *phony buyer,* the responses you hear will sound less convincing. Watch for the universal giveaways of deception: fumbling, generalities, stalling, averted eyes, diversions, answering a different question, too many uncertainties, an abundance of trivial details, unwillingness to seek out factual answers. If you see a mix of these behaviors, chances are you have a phony buyer for a competitor. Nonetheless, it's a judgment call on your part, time to trust your intuition.

When the salesperson's phony buyer tactic backfires, things turn in your favor. You can capitalize on your advantage with a statement similar to this:

Buyer:
Well, I am interested in the home, but I'm not interested in competing against another buyer. Let me know if the sale doesn't go through. If I haven't bought another home I'm looking at, I might think about making an offer. But if it sells, don't worry about contacting me.

If it's a ruse, you've turned the tables. Not only have you not fallen for it, you've told the salesperson she might lose you as a buyer! You put a picture into her head of her commission dollars slipping away — the last thing she wants to let happen.

Don't expect an immediate about turn, of course, but do expect a call soon after to let you know the good news, that the other buyer dropped out, and an invitation to re-inspect the home or even make an offer (this time without competition).

Then, proceed to negotiate. No triumphalism on your part, no change of attitude, no sign that you know you have just laid the phony buyer to rest. And no letting your guard down.

Reminder: Control! When you make it work you gain benefits measured in dollars and peace of mind.

How to Fine-Tune Your Basic Strategy

You're now almost ready to enter the real estate arena, so let's review briefly the protection you've built up.

1. You have researched your selected area, including sales and prices.
2. You have a clear picture of your needs and wants; your must-haves; and the factors that will eliminate any home from consideration.
3. You understand that anxiety and urgency must never be communicated to the salesperson. Nor must any emotional attachment you might develop for a property, regardless of how ideal it seems.

4. Your budget figures are in your notebook: your comfortable spending limit and upper spending limit. You also know that the figure you give to the salesperson should be approximately 5-10% below your comfortable spending limit but that you are free to increase this figure if need be (if the homes shown to you by *two or more* agents are below the standard you desire). Also, you know the maximum loan for which you can get lender approval and a 'qualifying letter' or equivalent.

You now have what negotiators refer to as a *basic strategy*. It's not yet complete, but it's taking shape. We'll add a few more safeguards before you stride into the real estate professionals' domain.

One of the most important principles of negotiation is building the quality of relationship with the other side that is conducive to your success.

Although they do not and cannot work in your best interest, real estate salespeople do assist you. Yes, they represent the other side; nonetheless, they merit your courtesy, respect, and an appreciation of their position and concerns. This in no way weakens your power. In fact, the opposite is true.

How does your courteous attitude assist you? As humans we all prefer to deal with people who allow us to feel good about ourselves; we'll often go the extra mile for these people. But when courtesy or respect are absent we'll rarely be so helpful.

You also need to accept, however, that when you give out good feelings they won't always be returned. Does this mean your efforts are wasted? Certainly not. Your end goal is to save as much money as you can and get an otherwise good deal. Stay focused on that. Courtesy is always your ally in negotiation, and it does not preclude you from taking a firm stand on price or any other point.

How else might you prepare for meeting and dealing with the salesperson on her own turf? Let's see.

Information is a Double-Edged Sword

Your greatest assets are information and know-how. The information you gather and the insights and skills you learn from this book help you form your strategy.

But, be warned, because information and know-how also work for those who want to sell you your next home. Agents sell for a living; expect them to be smart. But, what they *don't* possess is the personal data that pertains only to *you*, which they'll seek every time. Expect this! Don't they need all that information, you ask, in order to help you? That's what you'll hear. But it isn't so. *They need just the basic details*, which we'll revisit and illustrate frequently as we proceed.

Summary: The more personal data anyone has on you the more they'll be able to predict your behavior. In negotiation, being predictable makes you vulnerable.

Emperors and generals have known for eons that a predicable opponent is a weakened opponent. Information is so powerful a weapon that governments routinely leak *disinformation* in order to deceive, confuse and control. Often, the aim of disinformation is to make the other side think they possess facts when all they have is fabrication (lies). Billions of dollars are spent to eavesdrop on other nations, using satellites, drones, spies masquerading as diplomats, data interception systems, code deciphering departments, and so on. All for information on what the other side is thinking. We use politically correct terms when speaking of such things: *reconnaissance, counter-intelligence, surveillance, psychographics, security monitoring* and so on. It's an insidious game when it involves hostile nations. But that just proves the power of information and why in particular circumstances *you* must guard it.

Your goal is not to withhold necessary personal details from the salesperson. She'll need to know certain things to be able to help you. Guidelines for what you can safely reveal are covered in this and other chapters — your needs and preferences, for instance, and other details from your notebook and research.

Understandably, you will also be asked how you plan to finance your purchase. As I've already advised, make sure your home loan is guaranteed before you start your search (see chapter *How to Save Big on Financing Your Home* for more money-saving tips). Then, you can respond simply with:

The money situation is fine; we're in a position to buy when we find a home we like.

Notice, you are providing the minimum required information, no unnecessary details, and no figures except your preferred price range, which we covered earlier. This will assure the salesperson that you aren't inspecting homes just out of curiosity, or because you're planning to buy a year down the road, that you will act if a suitable home is found. The salesperson wants to know this before investing time with you.

You don't need to follow my wording exactly, here or elsewhere in this book. But be particularly careful you don't fall into being impulsively revealing. Reveal only what is necessary and in your best interest, no more.

Now, let's go over a few reminders before we wrap up this chapter.

Recap: What You Must Never Forget About the Salesperson

As you get set to put into practice what we have covered so far, you'll greatly increase your chances of making and saving money by keeping in mind the following:

Whether the title is agent, broker, realtor, consultant, associate, or salesperson, any individual whose job it is to sell real estate is a professional. They are courteous, respectful, friendly and disarming. But they are not your friend, nor your confidant, nor your advocate, nor your agent. You don't need to view them as your enemy, not in the usual meaning of 'enemy'. However, they *are* your competition, your opposition, because their financial and legal duty, their allegiance, and their fiduciary responsibility, are all pledged to the seller, to getting the best deal for the seller and *exclusively* the seller. Not for you.

If you begin to doubt the salesperson's loyalty to the seller, snap back to reality by asking yourself, or the salesperson, these questions:

1. Who is the salesperson's client, who is she working for?
2. Which party has this salesperson promised to get the highest possible price and best terms for?
3. Whose exclusive best interest is the salesperson legally and contractually obligated to serve?

Keep in mind here that it is not OK if the salesperson tells she is on 'neither side', or on 'both sides'. This means you are on your own! You have *no* advocate working for you in probably the biggest financial transaction of your life. These salespeople are referred to as dual agents or transaction brokers, or similar. We'll return to this point later.

Note: You can be sure the salesperson won't have come up against more than a handful of buyers as well prepared as you — smart buyers. By virtue of what you have learned to this point, you are already significantly ahead of the average homebuyer.

In the following chapters you'll learn further tips that can save you more dollars than you probably ever imagined — in two main areas: 1) negotiating the best home price and terms, and 2) using simple but largely unknown strategies in financing your home.

When you secure a genuinely good deal, the salesperson will remember you. Maybe as stubborn, or strong, or opinionated, or even difficult. That's entirely irrelevant! The salesperson will still earn a commission, though not as much as if she had convinced you to pay a higher price. She'll soon get over it. For you, the deal you get is the deal you'll live with. You won't quickly get over the extra cost of a bad deal, *even if you were never to discover what you left on the table!*

Remember this too: *You* risk more than any salesperson. You have more to lose, more skin in the game, more to protect — nothing less than your long-term financial and emotional health and peace of mind.

Allow no distractions, bluster, sweet-talk or personality traits to distract you from your goal of buying the home that's right for you, for the fewest dollars possible, and on the best terms, with no nasty after-purchase shocks.

If you need it (you shouldn't), here's an interesting consolation. Real estate salespeople harbor genuine respect for smart buyers, admiration often, unimportant as this is.

Now let's meet the salesperson.

CHAPTER 6

The Initial Encounter: How to Handle the Real Estate Salesperson

All the professions are conspiracies against the laity.
— George Bernard Shaw

So far, you've gained know-how and insight, acquired some basic negotiation skills, and you know more about how the game of real estate is played. It's time now for your initial face-to-face encounter with the salesperson.

How best to begin?

Here are my recommendations: Call the agency that seems best for your selected area and say you'd like to drop in for a chat. Don't get trapped into a detailed conversation at this point.

Something like this:

Buyer:
My name is Jane Smith. I'm considering buying a home in the area, possibly within the next 3-4 months. Could I come by on Wednesday around 5pm?

If your call is taken by a salesperson he's likely to want to know more:

Salesperson:
Certainly, Ms Smith. Is there a particular home you've noticed? Or can you tell me what you have in mind, and what price range?

I believe it's best to have that conversation face-to-face, so:

Buyer:
No, it's just a general chat at this stage. I do want to buy but haven't made decisions yet. We can go over details when we meet.

The salesperson might suggest that by knowing your needs and budget he'll be able to select sample homes and have material to show you. Sounds good but it's not the start I recommend.

Just repeat that you'd prefer to meet first. Remember, *everything you do now is painting a picture in the salesperson's head.*

When you speak with anyone on the sales team, you can be sure an impression of you is being recorded and noted, both as a person and a prospective buyer. It's in your interest to manage that impression and maintain it throughout, starting long before any offer or price negotiation arises.

Let's flash forward. As expected, you find the salesperson welcoming and courteous. You provide details of your needs, including elimination factors and your budget range (consult your notebook if you need to). Remember, you arrived at your budget range by first subtracting 5-10% from your comfortable spending limit.

You might say it like this:

I'm planning to spend $138,000 to $148,000 for a suitable property.

Two Keys: Stay Calm and Alert

If you feel nervous, it's just the normal pressures connected with home buying, which are the same for most buyers. No need to worry, on its own a little unease won't mark you as naive or vulnerable.

In your initial discussion, remind the salesperson that you are prepared to buy when the home and the price feel right. As long as that goal seems achievable, the salesperson will remain attentive.

However, after you have said no to four or five of his properties his enthusiasm might wane. If you detect this, offer a 'conferred expectation'. That is, assure him that you appreciate his time and assistance and look forward to him finding a home that interests you.

If complimenting the salesperson like this seems patronizing, give the task to your spouse or partner. Negotiation is business. It requires a willingness to use tactics that serve your ultimate goal. It might help to see it as a drama in which you have the leading role. When the show is over, you can revert to the everyday you. Of course, the salesperson too is playing a role. Courteous, friendly and charming he no doubt is, yet he remains pledged to get the best price and terms for someone other than you — the seller. Despite the cordial exchanges, never ignore this fact. And do your best to remain clear-headed.

With thousands of dollars at risk (it's *all* your money!), stay aware that you are engaged in negotiation from the first contact. After decades of work in psychology and business fields, the greatest thrill I still get is when I hear how a non-professional homebuyer saved serious money or avoided a costly mistake. As I see it, homebuyers have never before been given a how-to guide like *Not One Dollar More!,* devoted *solely* and unapologetically to helping them succeed and stay safe.

Taking the Inquisitive Agent in Your Stride

We've looked at how to respond to the usual probing of the salesperson. But how do you handle a question that catches you off-guard?

Answer: Take a pause, a time-out, and gather your thoughts. It's not possible to take back what you let slip out. Be especially on guard when driving with a salesperson; physical proximity can cause you to feel less in control. If the salesperson presses on matters you don't wish to discuss, here's an old trick: Instead of avoiding his questions, switch roles! You become the questioner. Most people like to talk about themselves; exploit this. Mix personal questions with research questions. Some suggestions:

- How long have you been in real estate?
- What's good and bad about it?
- Do you live locally?
- What changes have you seen in the neighborhood?
- What problems should buyers new to the area watch out for?
- What are the most common reasons owners are selling?
- What plans are in the works for the area?
- Why did you choose your present home location?
- How has the cultural make-up of the neighborhood developed?
- Which neighborhoods are in decline?
- Where are the best stores and schools locally?
- How is transportation locally?
- What are property taxes like here?
- Which are the most popular amenities?

The salesperson will want to live up to your confidence in him. He'll share useful information you might not find elsewhere.

Despite this, he will not tell you anything that will turn you off buying in his area. Neither will you learn confidential details about a particular seller or property. And keep in mind that his stories and statements will be intended to influence your thinking. Nonetheless, as I said above, these exchanges are opportunities to pick up good local information.

Also, let the salesperson know you'll be seeing homes with other agents. If he questions the benefit of this, tell him you believe it's in your best interest. Then add encouragement, such as: *But I do hope we'll be able to do business with you; we appreciate your interest.*

If you feel you are being insincere or manipulative, remember three facts:

- You are on your own, without an advocate.
- You are protecting your money and peace of mind.
- You are dealing with a professional who is trying get the highest price and best terms — for his *seller*.

Tip: Stay focused! And when an opportunity arises, pay him a sincere compliment, but keep it light. Payback might be a small gesture later that pushes a deal over the line. At this point you are being viewed as a serious buyer with a mind of your own — not a captive or passive hopeful.

In all your contacts with salespeople, refer to homes you've seen with other agencies; don't identify specific properties but mention that there are one or two homes you plan to re-visit. No salesperson enjoys losing a motivated, qualified buyer to the competition; he'll want to stay the course.

Why and How You Should Stay Unpredictable

Ironically, human beings are quite predictable in specific circumstances. If we weren't, the structure of society would collapse. In fact, in many life situations you need to demonstrate your predictability, when applying for a loan, for example, or taking on a responsible job.

In negotiation the opposite is true.

The foundation you establish from your earliest exchanges with a salesperson will come back into play when you decide to make an offer (you'll see this in action shortly). When you manage yourself in the ways covered here, rest assured that at no point will you be seen as an anxious, impressionable, or predictable buyer.

Here's a revealing account of an actual incident in which the effectiveness of unpredictability was amusingly illustrated.

A Toast to Unpredictability: I had been engaged to negotiate an expensive media production contract. I helped screen interested production companies and selected one. My main task was to achieve agreement on technical standards and deadlines, and negotiate a budget that was competitive. I had experience in media production but did not know the principals with whom I was negotiating. After protracted discussion we ironed out a deal.

A celebratory dinner was organized for the evening the contracts were signed. After some light-hearted toasts to everyone and everything, and just as the meal was about to be served, the managing director of the production company, now somewhat inebriated, struggled to her feet. She dismissed the troubled waiter and demanded silence. Something more important was on her mind. She grabbed her cocktail glass and thrust a toast in my direction. A little too strenuously, it turned out. The cocktail ran over her hand, down her sleeve, and splashed onto the linen tablecloth. For a few seconds she stared at the spreading damp patch, then seemed to recover.

She lowered her chin, fixed a sniper's stare in my direction, and began:

Want to give this toast, toast to Mr what's-his-name. When we thought we had him figured out, he said something, something that showed we didn't, we hadn't got ... got him figured out, and he did something ... something ... what was it ...

An embarrassed *ssshhh* came from her partners, concerned in part because the event was being filmed, but she continued:

> *... he did something we didn't expect. No, I'll say this, each, each time, all the time, the one thing we could predict was that he'd, Mr what's-his-name, be unpredictable, like the last time. The deal's good, good for, good for everybody. I'm glad it's over, and that we're not, I mean I'm not, I'm not married to him!*

With that she sat down to hearty laughter and applause. What's interesting about this from our point of view is that, although unaware of the fact, she identified that key strategy of professional negotiation: Never help your competitor know how you will respond in decisive circumstances. For homebuyers, that is especially critical when it comes time to talk dollars, a topic we'll get to soon.

Using Your 'Quiet Power'

Here's a piece of advice I cannot over-emphasize. Don't sound like you know it all. I stressed earlier that negotiation is a subtle skill. The power you have built so far is *quiet power*. It's not something to beat the other side with. Such actions only work against you.

From the start, you have been building a relationship that will motivate the salesperson to assist you however possible. Tap into his experience and specialized knowledge. Listen well. Using quiet power brings many advantages onto your side.

Conferred Expectation

Conferred expectation, a term I used earlier, means openly attributing status or value to another person; this sets a standard that person will generally try to live up to.

We strive to please those who place confidence or trust in us. Try to engender this in salespeople but, once again, do it subtly; less is usually more. Benefits to you will typically follow.

Conferred expectation applies universally. It's something you are already familiar with. Let's see:

- Parents use it with children: *I know you are going to be very good while daddy watches the game on TV.*
- Or, perhaps: *Daddy and I love you, and we know you mean it when you promise you won't ever again push your three sisters down the stairs when we're not home.*
- Teenagers hear it a lot: *We'll allow you more freedom because we trust you and because we know you wouldn't do anything that would hurt us.*
- Or, maybe: *This grade D in English is not really you. I know you are capable of getting a B or better next time.*
- In the military, conferred expectation is practiced by putting people in uniforms and giving them behavior codes, ranks, and weapons.

- And, of course, lovers do it too: *Even though I'll be far away, I trust you. I know you'd never be unfaithful.*
- Or even: *I'm saying yes because I know you'll always be there for me when I need you.*

Here's a related tip: Ask for help!

It works because the other person feels elevated, even a sense of *responsibility.* This is more direct than conferred expectation but can deliver similar advantages.

Two examples:

- *Using your expertise, could you help us figure the total monthly repayment on this home?*
- *I can see your agency is very resourceful. Do you think you could find a solution to this?*

Keep in mind that the effects we're looking at in this section are almost entirely *unconscious;* they happen under the person's radar.

At seminars, I get asked by salespeople: What is the best way to get past the secretary when you want to talk to the boss? My answer is always the same: *Ask for help!* This acknowledges the secretary's authority, which is likely to reduce resistance, and you're showing respect for the person's importance and position.

Real estate salespeople are no different. They react to appreciation and acknowledgment as positively as you and I do.

Before we move on, one final caveat. In asking for help and complimenting the salesperson, you are using a tactic to extract maximum benefit from the association. Do not indiscriminately trust the recommendations, suggestions or advice you receive. Nor disclose more personal information than you decided.

Of course, asking questions is not your prerogative alone. The salesperson has one or two you should be ready for. Let's take a closer look.

The 'Why' Question You Need to Know How to Answer

All real estate salespeople set out to discover each buyer's *dominant buying motive.* Consequently, you'll be asked in one form or another why you are buying.

Salesperson:
Do you mind if I ask, Ms Smith, what is your reason for buying at this time?
Why have you decided on a three-bedroom home in this area now?

Sometimes it's more blatant, as below, which should trigger cautions in you for reasons we've already outlined:

The more I know about you, Ms Smith, the better I can help you. Tell me why you decided to buy at this time, and in this location?

First, you *don't,* in fact, mind being asked this question — because you are prepared for it and won't be caught off guard.

Here's the response I suggest (or something similar):

Buyer:
We were planning to buy later in the year (or, three months, six months). But we like the neighborhood. So if we can find a home that's suitable, and that represents good value to us, great; we'll bring our plans forward.

Just a few simple sentences. Right? Maybe not as simple as they appear. What have you communicated?

To start, you said loud and clear: *no anxiety, no urgency, no desperation.*

Next, you put conditions on your purchase. You'll buy *only* if a suitable home is available, and *only* if the price is right — and *you'll* be the judge of both. Here, you are 'setting terms', and projecting an impression that will serve you well all through the buying process. Make no mistake, the salesperson picked up what you intended. You still need to watch out, though, because a salesperson's demeanor and reasonable sounding enquiries can catch you napping. Potential weak points are:

- When the salesperson has a warm endearing style
- When you are enthralled with a home he's showing you.

Your ultimate goal must never be absent from your mind; otherwise you risk saying or doing something that will disadvantage you — worst of all, you could spill sensitive information the salesperson will be obligated to pass on to the listing agent and seller.

And remember, if the relationship is not working, there is no shortage of sales-people eager to sell you property.

Note: This advice assumes you are working with a traditional real estate salesperson, not an Exclusive Buyer Agent. An Exclusive Buyer Agent would handle most of the exchanges on your behalf, a very good idea. More on this later.

The emotions and the risks are about to ramp up. You are prepared. Ready to inspect homes with the salesperson — next chapter.

PART THREE

WINNING: KEEPING THE ODDS IN YOUR FAVOR

CHAPTER 7

Viewing Properties:
Your Chance to Move Ahead

The power of accurate observation
is commonly called cynicism by those who have not got it.

— George Bernard Shaw

We've looked at how to prepare and what you should not reveal when you are with the salesperson. Let's turn now to what you can do and say that will *benefit* you when you are inspecting homes.

I said in the opening pages that my aim is to teach you how to buy the smart way, but not to tell you what to buy or where to buy. Here, I will deviate from that to offer a note of caution.

Some agents like to drive you to a selected property, others let you make your own way. Regardless of how you arrive at a home, and however attractive you find it, you must not buy any property until you have checked its environment! You are also buying the neighborhood, not just the house and the scenic route you took to get there. Here are just some things you'll need to find out:

- What's behind it?
- Two blocks down the road?
- A mile to the east and west?
- What development plans are in the works?
- Are there problems only locals know of?
- What's happening of note in the closest neighborhoods and towns? and so on.

The Latin phrase *caveat emptor* applies: let the buyer beware. In other words, you buy at your own risk. Check out the environment thoroughly.

According to various surveys, homebuyers look at between six and eight homes before selecting one to buy. If your average is higher (mine is) don't worry. By purchasing this book and reading this far you make clear that you are anything but average.

Buying the Right Home:
Six Questions You Should Always Ask

When you find an appealing property you'll want to ask lots of questions. That's natural. But, here's the problem: Your intense questioning signals that you are keen to buy, maybe even in love with the home — a potentially costly message to be sending out, for reason we've already seen. And if you've quickly dismissed previous homes, your attachment will be even more obvious.

But you cannot hide your interest, you need answers. How do you not let the cat out of the bag? It seems like a catch-22 situation, doesn't it? You need answers but don't want your excitement to weaken your negotiation position.

So what can you do?

Here's the best solution I know. *Don't* summarily dismiss *any* property, even those in which you have zero interest; ask serious and relevant questions about each home you inspect. No need to engage the salesperson in long conversations about the no-hopers, but don't show disdain either, and show you are listening to her responses. Later, your curiosity about the appealing won't appear so unusual, at least not right away.

So, when that special home comes along what initially should you ask about? The questions below are intended to elicit specific information you will need. These same questions can be asked with the no-hopers; the answers then will be irrelevant, of course. But for the reason just explained, the exercise is not.

1. What price is this listed at?

Or, *What is the asking price on this one?* Notice that the way the question is worded shows that you see the price as an *asking price* only. It implies also that buyers, including you, don't pay asking prices.

This is similar to a car ad that reads: *BMW 2012 325E, exc cond, asking $9500.* There are hard prices and soft prices; you can be sure this $9500 is a soft price. You might have to hand over $8500 or $9000, but not the *asking* price. Unfortunately, far too many homebuyers fail to discover the *degree of flexibility* in list prices, asking prices, and even 'discounted' prices.

Although residential homes are seldom promoted with an 'asking price' (except in a depressed market), the 'list price' on virtually every property is exactly that, an asking price.

2. Why is the home being sold?

Think about it. Homeowners don't sell without reason. Usually a compelling reason. Here's one of the most important points you'll read in this book:

Most sellers need to sell more than most buyers need to buy!

Sellers need your cash, for any number of life plans. The saying that *cash is king* really is true in real estate, more than in most areas of commerce. By discovering why the owners want to sell — the true reason — you'll be more able to determine how strongly motivated they are. For example, sellers are strongly motivated if they need a sale in order to close on the purchase of another property. Similarly, sellers moving out of town are usually motivated.

More often than you might think, the underlying reason for selling is to clear debt. However, this is difficult to discover because even the salesperson may not have been told. Indebted sellers often present a made-up reason, which is passed on to the buyer. But telltale signs sometimes show through, if you probe.

Real estate salespeople always try to learn the seller's *dominant selling motive*, just as they try to learn each buyer's *dominant buying motive.* If the salesperson offers a vague response about the reason for the sale, press for details. Any time you ask a specific question expect a specific answer. When one is not forthcoming, dig further, be watchful for clues, and move cautiously.

3. How soon does the seller wish to close?

In effect, what you are asking here is how quickly the seller needs your cash. If the salesperson responds (which is likely if she's good): *Well, what suits YOU best?* she might not be saying what you think!

Your first thought will probably be that the seller is flexible. But it could be that this is not true at all. What if the salesperson knows that her client stands to lose out if they don't close within forty-five days, and that they will consider any reasonable offer from a buyer who can meet that deadline?

Then, you declare: *Forty-five days, sooner even; we're under time pressure.*

You've just shot yourself in the foot.

Why? Because the salesperson will *not* then respond: *That's wonderful; the seller badly needs to close within forty-five days.* Not a chance. Most salespeople will play a little game. Like this:

Salesperson:
Unfortunately, I can't give you a yes on forty-five days. But I'll tell you what I'll do. If everything else is all right, I'll do what I can to get them to agree to your time requirement. As I said, I can't guarantee it. I'll do my best.

That's the game. See how you surrendered a big potential advantage? Where did you go wrong? Lots of places!

Your first mistake: You asked a specific question: *How soon does the seller need to close?* But you failed to insist on a specific answer. You fell for one of the oldest tricks in the book: You allowed the salesperson to answer your question with a question. From her perspective that was a clever move. For you, it did no good at all. It led you down a dark alley where you lost a major negotiating point. Here's the warning again: *Insist on specific answers to your questions!*

Your second mistake: You revealed vital information, which was then used against you. You said: *Forty-five days, sooner even; we're under time pressure.*

When you are asked what timeframe would suit you to close or move in, use either of these two responses:
- *We haven't determined that yet.*
- *How soon does the owner wish to close?*

Even better, combine both in a single answer. Use the same trick we saw earlier — answer a question with a question. Now *you* are in control.

When the salesperson asks routinely about your timeframe (when no property is under consideration) your best response is usually: *No urgency. Let's see what happens.* Or something similar, unless you have a hard deadline, in which case you need to reveal it.

4. How long have the owners been living here?

In some cases it might be appropriate to ask: *How long has the home been vacant?* Or: *How long has the seller owned the home?*

Don't underestimate the importance of this question. What if the seller bought the property just six months ago? Would you be curious? Even suspicious? Why would someone sell after six months? Or three years? You'd better find out, particularly (but not just) when the owner is living in the home. If the response you get is not convincing (assuming you are interested) knock on a few neighbors' doors. That might be all you'll need do to fill in the missing pieces.

Asking this question is important even when the seller has owned the home for many years. Such a seller is usually sitting on substantial equity (potential profit) due to home price rises. So, any reasonable offer might look attractive compared with the original price paid. Knowing this could signal an opportunity for you to negotiate strongly and be a little more stubborn.

Here again, fifteen minutes of friendly chat with neighbors can be more informative than all the details the listing agent provides. In fact, this is sometimes the only way to get really useful answers; I recommend you do this before buying *any* home. You'll also get a glimpse of the neighbors you might soon have.

5. What repairs or upgrading have been carried out by the current owner on plumbing, electrical wiring, heating/cooling system, roof, and so on?

The salesperson may not have the answers to such questions. Generally, she'll respond in one of four ways:

1. Tell you what she knows.
2. Tell you she doesn't know.
3. Tell you she will ask the listing agent or owner.
4. Give her opinion (which is not what you want).

If work or repairs has been done in any of the areas you ask about, it may have been to fix a significant problem. The seller will offer assurances that the problems have been remedied. Still, the way most people think, something that has needed repair has decreased in value. In fact, the opposite is often true. A house that has had a new roof would almost always be worth more than before the work was done, even more than a home of similar age and design that still has its original roof (assuming the repair was age related).

Nonetheless, repairs mean problems, and there are seeds of advantage in that.

6. What problems or faults has the owner made you aware of, or have you noticed yourself?

This is related to the previous question. But ask *both*! And listen carefully to the response. Every home has faults, things that could or should be upgraded, replaced or repaired. I'll have more to say about this in the next chapter.

For now, keep in mind that with a home of any age, necessary repairs could mean poor construction, ground problems, premature deterioration, physical damage, poor design, and so on. If you suspect a problem, tread cautiously; tell the salesperson you would need to be convinced of the soundness of the property before you'd consider making an offer. (In an upcoming chapter we'll look at getting a Professional Home Inspection and what you need to know.)

Maybe the repairs or upgrades don't really cause you serious concern. But that's only for you to know. Remember, it's *perceptions* that count. When the seller and salesperson know you have reservations they'll start thinking of how to make the purchase more attractive for you. This can lead to concessions as the negotiation goes on.

You might say: *The home seems fairly OK. If it wasn't for the repaired chimney and smallish kitchen I might be tempted.*

Here's what the salesperson is hearing: *Seems obvious she doesn't have to buy this home. She could be interested though if the price and terms were right.*

Only *you* know when you are using this tactic. It might be the home that's perfect for you. Maybe you've even fallen in love with it. But the salesperson should *never* hear such sweet words from your mouth, or notice even the slightest hint in your behavior!

Let's now delve into the thinking of the salesperson.

Knowing How the Other Side Thinks

Along with the questions above, there are many others you might ask, whether you are interested or not in a particular property. Here are just a few examples:

- What's the quality and extent of insulation?
- Has the home been extended?
- When was the electrical wiring, roof, furnace, boiler last inspected? (Any negatives or delays are points for you.)
- Why is the water discolored?
- Why is the water pressure so low?

- When was the plumbing last checked?
- How come there are so few (or so many) electrical sockets?
- Is the floor sloping on one side?
- Is it cold in here (or hot)?
- What faults has the owner made you aware of? (Ask this at any time, but *always* of a home that interests you.)
- What faults have you noticed yourself? (Ask this at any time, but *always* of a home that interests you.)

When the salesperson you are working with is not also the listing agent (the agent who put the house on the books and who communicates directly with the seller), make it clear that you don't want to be kept waiting for answers.

Notice that you *do not* compliment or praise a home, no matter how positive you feel. A bland *Yes, I noticed that*, or, *Hmmm* in response to the salesperson pointing out a positive feature is enough.

Tip: Never sound enthusiastic! And never ever sound thrilled! You've been asking questions about each home you've inspected, even those you disliked; so your questions, at least initially, won't signal your true level of interest.

Nonetheless, expect the salesperson to point out special features in each home, comments like: *Notice the 10-foot ceilings giving a sense of space and style, and the solid timber doors.* You might love high ceilings and have a passion for fine timber, but your reaction should be *blank, bland,* or *contrary.* Like this:

Buyer:
People seem to like high ceilings but it's really not something that's im-
portant to me. The doors are nice, though, but I feel flush doors would
have been more in keeping with the style of the house.

The salesperson will respond with a comeback that takes your attention in another direction (remember, a professional seller is not easily deterred). Here's what you might hear next:

Salesperson:
I see your point about the doors. But look at this; when have you seen
gardens as well maintained, front and rear?

You know your response by now; you might feel ecstatic about the gardens, but that's only for you to know:

Buyer:
Yes, very good condition. My problem is the amount of time gardens re-
quire. I just have never been able to devote time to garden work, much as
I'd like to.

The salesperson's enthusiasm might drop, but she'll keep trying. When there are no more features to compliment, she might add:

I believe you are making a very wise decision buying in this neighborhood. It's great for families and it's developing all the time.

To which you might respond:

Yeah, the area is nice. We've seen (or will see) *a couple of homes in an area we really like just ten minutes south of here. It's more settled, and the homes seem very good value for money.*

You have the idea. But, be smart. If you dismiss or counter too much, the salesperson will lose interest in you. When you cannot deny a feature, you can be bland or neutral. For example: *Yes, I noticed that,* or, *Yes, the ceilings are high.* Such responses don't give away your true feelings, and they stop you sounding like a cynic.

Reminder: Your true excitement must never show through!

When you pull off a successful purchase, throw a house party, dance a jig, let your hair down. But when you are buying a home *you are a negotiator every moment!* The 'normal' you is separate and should not intrude.

It's clear now, I'm sure, that the negotiation process is continuous; it begins *before* the first contact with the salesperson and ends when your purchase is concluded. In negotiation, as in life, you are *always* communicating, whether you mean to or not. The verbal and non-verbal messages you transmit are interpreted by others to form perceptions of you that can work against you.

We categorize and classify people based on the messages we pick up, even over the telephone. From these messages we predict others' behavior, then act on this — it happens this way in every home buying transaction.

When predictability threatens to disadvantage you (in any endeavor, not just home buying) you have one safe response: selective control of the messages you transmit. Your goal as a smart buyer is to safeguard your wealth and peace of mind while acquiring the home you want at the lowest price and best terms possible.

What are the Real Estate Salesperson's Real Needs?

Let's take the salesperson's strategy of learning as much about you as possible and turn it about face. What makes *them* tick? What are their strongest needs and wants?

Need 1: **To Sell Homes**

First and foremost, they need to sell properties to survive. Their job is stressful; they are required to manage anxiety and urgency. Sometimes even desperation. Ironic, isn't it? Shows how alike we all are.

Need 2: **A Supply of Willing Buyers**

They can never have enough buyers on their books. Very frequently they're short of serious, qualified buyers. At times, they might have just one or two. But if you procrastinate in making an offer they are likely to suggest that another serious buyer is waiting to pounce.

Need 3: **A Monthly Quota**

They have monthly sales quotas to meet, even if self-imposed. Fifty percent of the time they are behind their desired target. When they're ahead they are anxious to have their best month and the extra income. Occasionally, one more sale can mean winning the salesperson of the month award. In a nutshell, they need a continuous flow of commission dollars.

Need 4: **Fresh Properties**

Time is money to salespeople. Devoting their time to fresh properties is how they generate income. Stale properties, homes that have been for sale longer than normal, are harder to sell and they drain enthusiasm. A lack of fresh properties can lead salespeople into a kind of vicious cycle: no sale, no enthusiasm; no enthusiasm, no sale. To be successful they must remain motivated, psyched up. Fresh properties and serious buyers (you) give them that.

Need 5: **To Get Sellers to Be Flexible**

Despite their commitment and loyalty to the seller's best interests, which real estate salespeople take seriously, their ultimate objective is to achieve a sale. Which means they will use their persuasion skills *on the seller*, when necessary. It becomes 'necessary' when they risk losing the sale, their commission, and a serious buyer (you). Your task is to keep the salesperson believing that this is precisely what's at risk — the sale — unless they can persuade the seller to agree the price and terms you require. We'll see more of this in action as we move forward.

Need 6: **To Achieve Reward**

When salespeople invest time, energy and effort in a homebuyer, they feel a bigger need to earn a reward. Consequently, as time is taken up in presenting, discussion, negotiation, clarifying issues and managing offers on a particular home, your chance of getting a better deal improves. In almost every property negotiation, this time investment is in your favor, provided the salesperson sees some likelihood of a sale. That's what keeps salespeople motivated, the reward.

Why the Salesperson and the Seller Need You More Than You Need Them

As we've seen, the seller and salesperson have compelling needs that are satisfied only when a sale occurs. Their need for money and income is typically more urgent than *your* need to purchase a particular home.

Has anyone selling real estate ever told you this? Unlikely. Why would they! These facts shift power to *you*, the buyer.

Understanding what we've covered in this section means you are no longer the low-man on the totem pole, hoping they'll deem your offer worthy. Instead, you're now the problem solver, you are providing needed cash to the salesperson and seller, money that will solve *their* financial needs and facilitate *their* life plans. *They need you more than you need them!*

If you are feeling new power, count yourself among the smart buyers, a relatively small cohort of consumers. And keep in mind that the lessons in this book also work outside of real estate. When you are exchanging money for assets of any kind you will generally be in the stronger position, despite what others try make you believe. You can choose to hand over your money, or choose to hold on to it. You have choices because you have cash. You have what financial people call *liquidity*. The fact that your money is coming from a lender does not change a thing.

On the other side, a home seller has much less flexibility and few options *until* the property is turned into cash. When a home is passed over by one or more qualified, interested buyers due to price, the owner's perceived value of the home (and the asking price) must be questioned.

Quite simply, the value of real estate is dictated by how much homebuyers pay. Not by the asking prices put on them by owners or listing agents. This is why homebuyers overpaying leads to inflated house prices.

What we have discussed here puts power and control in your hands, and guarantees you a stronger negotiating position.

Time to move on. Let's assume all has gone well. You've inspected a selection of homes, asked a series of questions about each, and divulged no potentially damaging information.

Then, that special home shows up. It grabbed you the moment you saw it. Now, how do you take those next critical steps toward buying this home at the lowest price and best terms? That's the subject of the next section.

KEY POINTS TO REMEMBER

Now that we are into the negotiation phase, you'll find a Key Points feature like this at the ends of selected chapters. This will help you re-learn and retain critical points covered in the chapter and embed these in your thinking.

- Ask at least five important questions about every home you inspect.
- Stay in control of the verbal and nonverbal messages you transmit to the salesperson or seller.
- Even when you are very excited about a home, never openly praise the property. Keep your enthusiasm to yourself while in the company of any salesperson or seller.
- Real estate salespeople have sales quotas to meet, and other personal and **professional** needs they must strive constantly to satisfy. Their biggest ongoing needs are to find serious buyers and make sales.
- Real estate salespeople and home sellers, in almost every case, need you more than you need them. They need your money, and they need the sale guaranteed and wrapped up as quickly as possible. Until they achieve these goals they get no reward. You are in the strongest position of the three parties, but not until you realize it!

CHAPTER 8

When You Find the Right Home

It takes two to make a bargain, but only one gets it.
— Anonymous

In this section you'll learn how to navigate your way around common mistakes and traps that arise when it's time to buy. At the first sign of interest from you, the salesperson will encourage you to make an offer and will emphasize why this would be a good move.

However, it's not yet time for chat. It's time to bid farewell. With not a word about the home that is exciting you so much. Your parting comment might be:

Thank you for your help. We have other homes we plan to look at. If anything you've shown us feels like it's worth another look, we'll call you.

If you haven't already done so, your next step is to drive slowly around the neighborhood. Make sure the immediate environment has the characteristics and amenities that are important to you. Check the standard and condition of neighborhood properties. Note the roads that carry heavy traffic. Locate schools and parks and whatever else is important to you.

If all seems satisfactory, let at least one day pass before re-contacting the salesperson. Then, mater-of-factly, tell him you'd like to have a second look, making sure to sound as unexcited as you can. Here's what I mean:

We don't remember some things about that house on Martello Court. Could we take another quick look?

Of course, the salesperson will recognize this as an indication of interest. What he won't know unless you tell him, which you won't, is just *how* interested you are.

As you go through the home again you'll notice a lot more than you did the first time. Take notes of features, color schemes, and anything else that grabs your attention (we'll see later how these written or mental notes can give you an advantage during negotiation). Mention that your notes help you in comparing homes that interest you.

It is never a bad idea to ask the same question twice or even three times. If it makes you feel better, say that you are trying to keep details straight on two or three homes that you like. Now it's time to *re-ask* the questions you asked on your first inspection. Add your own questions to this list, and ensure you get clear answers:

- What price is this listed at? (Or what is the asking price?)
- Why is the home being sold?
- How soon does the seller wish (or need) to close?
- How long have the sellers owned the property?
- How long have the owners (or tenants) been living here?
- What repairs or upgrading have been carried out on plumbing, electrical wiring, heating/cooling system, roof, insulation, and other areas?
- What problems or faults has the owner or listing agent made you aware of, and which have you noticed yourself?

Note that last question: *What problems or faults has the owner or listing agent made you aware of, and which have you noticed yourself?* This puts pressure on the salesperson to reveal what he knows, yet it's one question most homebuyers *never* ask. Ask!

Every home has faults. The salesperson will feel pressed to tell you what he knows. If he says he is not aware of any faults, he'll probably sound uninformed, which he knows can give rise to suspicion in a buyer. Be careful to phrase the question similar to how it appears here; it is most effective in this form.

When you ask this type of question, stay alert for the unexpected. For example, you ask when was the electrical wiring last inspected, anticipating that this has not been done in recent years. Then the salesperson surprises you with: *That's an excellent question* — he's complimentary of you because he has a good answer — *there are receipts showing that the home was completely rewired just six months ago.* Suppress your pleasant surprise! You have an ace up your sleeve that might reverse this seller advantage. In fact, you have two choices in responding.

A disinterested *OK* is appropriate but doesn't gain any advantage. What advantage? How about this:

Clearly, the old wiring was a problem. Was any damage done internally, in the walls or insulation? Were wires burning? Do you know?

That's reversing the salesperson's perceived 'gain'. See how the tables can be turned? Remember, *opinions don't come with receipts or guarantees.* The salesperson can't give assurances about the conditions inside the walls. Can he say definitely there was no spark or burn damage? Of course not. You'll hear something like: *No, not that I am aware of,* which is a lot less than certainty — now it's a point for you.

This tactic can be used with almost any repair. Even a repaired or replaced roof could be construed as work that became necessary not simply to stop rain getting in but to halt damp, treat mold, or prevent further damage to internal timbers. How much damage was done before the repair was carried out? For how long? Ask such questions. The salesperson won't have answers to most, as we've seen, which turns a point in your favor that looked like a point for the other side.

Prepared, Always Pleasant, Never Naive!

I'll stress again here the importance of having developed an amicable relationship with the salesperson. Otherwise your questions could be taken by some as testy. When the relationship is right, your concerns will be seen as genuine and understandable.

Behind all this, the negotiator inside you never sleeps, never forgets that the salesperson, by virtue of two facts, is your opponent. Fact One: He has pledged to sell the home at the highest price and best terms possible — to you. Fact Two: The more he gets *you* to pay, the more dollars he keeps for himself.

Remember too that what you *know* and what you *do* are not the same. You *know* the salesperson is always working to get the best deal for the seller. But what you *do* is deliberately avoid creating an opponent relationship. This is good negotiation. Your armor is in place, but it's quiet. The other side need never know they are dealing with a smart negotiator. To them you're *just* a discriminating buyer; this makes your task easier.

Your motto: Always prepared, always courteous, never naive!

Time: Making It Work for You

On your second or third inspection you'll decide you want to own the home or that it's not right for you. If it's right, your thoughts will race to how much you might offer and what price you might eventually pay. Here again, you need to slow down. And keep these two points in mind concerning time:

1. Allow at least one hour for your inspection. Move slowly room to room; look from ceiling to floor, *not just at eye-level*. Look behind doors, look at things twice, three times, then go back and look again if you need to. If this is going to be 'home', you'll want to take in as much as you can.

2. If you decide to make an offer, wait until you have *left* the property before discussing this with the salesperson.

As a negotiator, you gain advantage when you get the other side to invest time. The salesperson's job is to give time to serious, qualified buyers — you.

The longer he spends showing you the property, finding answers to your questions, getting his own questions answered, and generally working to bring about a sale, the more he stands to lose should you decide not to buy. Naturally, as a smart buyer you made clear earlier that one or two *other* homes also appeal to you. No salesperson must *ever* be allowed to know that this is the only property you are considering buying.

As you move around the interior and exterior of the home, the salesperson might shows signs of anxiety or even impatience. That's fine. The anxiety comes from anticipating a sale. The impatience might be due to a pressing appointment. None of that need concern you. Your aim is to control time — in a way that serves *your* best interest.

Should the salesperson have an 'important engagement' and want to cut short your scrutinizing inspection, suggest he get a colleague to stand in for him. If that's not feasible, tell him you'd like to come back to continue your assessment. He's likely then to ask what is causing your indecision. A number of things, you tell him; then list the items you questioned: asking price, wiring, plumbing, noise, traffic, lot size, location, too few windows, small kitchen, etc. Make comparisons with the other home, if only in talking out loud to yourself, that it is priced lower and has special features. So, yes, you are interested in this current home, you say, but you have concerns.

This 'cautious' approach benefits you all the way through the negotiation proper. The salesperson still believes there's a good chance to make the sale, but only if your concerns are satisfied. This 'buyer uncertain' message will be carried to the listing agent and seller, along with any offer you might make.

Throughout this exchange, stay focused on the fact that the salesperson is eager for the sale, the seller needs to unload the home, and the listing agent is keen to get his commission. But none of these parties gets what he craves until the home sells. Meanwhile, time is going by for all three, while you are making time work for *you*.

No matter how the salesperson deals with your request for another close inspection, the moment will come when you decide to make an offer. But it's better if you let *the salesperson* initiate this step. Here's what I mean.

Crawl and Stall Before Making an Offer

When your interest is obvious, the salesperson will encourage you to make an offer. That's how it should be, rather than *you* suggesting it. By hesitating, even expressing doubt, will add value to your offer. The salesperson's 'success' in obtaining the offer takes emphasis off the size of the offer (you'll see this shortly in action).

Most salespeople encourage an offer with something like this:

It's a beautiful home and definitely won't last. I'd strongly recommend you put an offer on it today . . .

Or maybe:

I'll be speaking with the owner tonight. What kind of offer had you in mind?

In either case, respond with comments like this:

We're really not sure what we'll do. Very hard decision. Maybe we should just think about it.

The salesperson is likely to recap the fine features of the home and how it represents excellent value. You simply listen; showing little emotion and muted agree-ment. The pressure will then ramp up: that any delay by you will risk losing the home to another buyer; it could be gone tomorrow, to one of the other buyers who've shown interest.

There is a risk in procrastinating like this, but it's rarely as big or as real as the salesperson implies, except in a hot real estate market or with a one-of-a-kind home.

You'll recall what I said earlier, that the *other* buyer is very often phony, meant to scare you into making an offer. Sadly, this tactic pressures countless unwitting buyers not only into *quick* decisions but into *wrong* decisions. In my view it constitutes unethical behavior. Our emotional nature makes us vulnerable in such situations. We desire more that which someone is trying to take from us.

Here's another example of the salesperson's 'Don't lose it' tactic:

Salesperson:
If you've got a genuine interest in this home, I feel bound to tell you there's another buyer who could put an offer on it at any time.

Or, a variation like this:

Salesperson:
Look folks, I'd hate to see you lose out on this. You need to be aware there's a young couple keen on it, now checking on their financing. To be safe, I suggest you put an offer on it now.

Like I said, there's a risk these 'other buyer' claims are genuine maybe ten-percent of the time. Most often they expose a salesperson hungry for a sale, one who might be equally resourceful later in getting the seller to agree to a lower-than-expected price.

Here's the kind of response I recommend:

Buyer:
We appreciate you letting us know that. We're the kind of people who make decisions carefully. If someone else buys this home, good luck to them. There are others we like.

And here's an alternative:

Buyer:
If somebody beats us to this one, it sure would make our decision easier.

How can a salesperson respond to such buyer comments? Possibly by:

- Asking if some concession or change would make your decision easier
- Suggesting that you make what you believe is a fair offer
- Saying that the seller might consider an offer below the asking price.

If any such moves occur, you know your crawling and stalling tactic is working.

However, if you hear nothing like this, don't fret. You haven't played any of your trump cards yet. All you've done is dealt yourself a superior hand. And because of the control you've exercised, the salesperson has no idea what's in that hand. Or in your thinking.

How to Make an Offer

Let's assume you have found the home you definitely wish to buy. It has all the required qualities and features and is listed at $178,500.

Let's see some tactics and principles in action.

Below you'll read the story of an actual home purchase I helped my bank manager with. Whether your budget is higher or lower doesn't matter; the principles of negotiation do not change. I'll add comments here and there to make things clearer. Later, you'll see more actual case studies that illustrate different principles (you are likely to get extra benefit from re-reading the case studies). And note that when I use the term *offer*, I am referring to what is often called, more correctly, a *purchase offer*.

Here's the banker's starting situation. He and his wife (we'll call them Mr and Mrs Mellon) had inspected the house just once, two days before seeking my assistance. They told me that this home was one they had admired for some time, and they were ready to move because their present home was now too big.

I asked them: *Is this a home you must have?* Did they *need* to buy this house? They answered No, they'd be very excited about owning it but had some interest also in one other property. Had this been a must-have, their freedom to negotiate would have been lessened.

But first a word of caution: A home that seems like a must-have in the beginning can turn out to be something less on a second or third inspection. Virtually always when you miss out on or decide against a property, you find another that is *more* appealing (though you can't imagine this is possible at the time). New homes come on the market every day. For that reason, my advice on 'must-haves' is this: Be certain that's what it is — it's probably not!

However, if you are convinced you cannot live without a particular home and are ready to pay whatever it takes — don't! Slow down. You *can* still negotiate using the tips in this book. You'll just need to tread more cautiously and be willing to compromise earlier. You might not be able to hold out for the seller's lowest price, but that doesn't mean you can't save a substantial sum of money and get the terms you desire. Just make certain the salesperson doesn't get even a whiff of how excited you are.

Now, let's follow what happened with the Mellons. See if you can spot tactics we discussed earlier. Remember, this is from an actual transaction.

Case Study: Making Money for a Banker

Before inspecting the home, I checked with local real estate sources and reviewed catalogs to get a better understanding of local home values. Then I called a few local agencies and picked up further information. Next, I chatted with the manager of a nearby bank, who gave me details on trends and changes in the neighborhood over recent years.

I discovered that prices had barely moved in the past year. Surrounding neighborhoods had seen slight price decreases and the number of sales had fallen a few percent. Properties were also taking longer to sell because people were buying elsewhere or postponing buying. It was clear that local real estate agencies were not thriving.

Note: Try to get reliable local information like this before you buy.

As I drove to the property, I contemplated the advantages we might have when the negotiation got under way. I instructed the Mellons not to communicate anything, verbal or otherwise, that would alert the salesperson to their feelings. The salesperson duly arrived, and after pointing out features and offering additional details, he left us to wander from room to room while he kept a polite distance.

The house was twenty-five years old and had undergone repairs and alterations. I queried the salesperson about this work and, as expected, he did his best to assure me that he believed everything had been done to the highest professional standard. I then informed him that we'd keep the house in mind, along with another we'd seen, and that we had one or two more yet to see; we'd give the matter consideration over the next few days. Then without any lead up, I asked: *Why are these owners selling?*

He hesitated momentarily. The owners, Mr and Mr Smith, had lived in the home for eight years, he told me, and Mrs Smith was recently promoted to a senior position in her company's head office in another state, where they had *already* purchased a new home. That was more information than I expected, more than he had to provide.

Incidentally, if the answer you get to this *Why are the owners selling?* question sounds vague or unreliable, bring it up with nearby neighbors as you chat about the area; you are likely to learn all you need to know.

I then asked the salesperson: *How soon do they wish to close?* This time he was more guarded: *What would suit you best?* he responded, answering my question with a question. (Remember, when you ask a specific question, insist on a specific answer, not generalizations or rebounding questions.) So, no ingenuity was needed to figure that the sellers would be anxious for a quick close. A definite sale would take a lot of weight off their shoulders and allow their plans to progress better.

My response to the salesperson's question was this: *We're not certain at this stage about closing. How long has the home been for sale?* Again, he gave me a less than confident reply: *Um ... I think about three months.* I suspected it might have been longer, but it made little difference. Even after three months, any seller would be motivated, especially those on the verge of a long-distance move.

As we were leaving, I mentioned again that we were potentially interested in at least one other home, and that we'd be in touch.

The salesperson then used a tactic to close the sale:

*Folks, there's always good homes on the market but 1 think we'd all agree,
this one is unique. It won't be available much longer. I know one of our
offices has a second inspection this afternoon. There's absolutely no work
to do. You could move in and start enjoying it right away.*

Then came a bolt out of the blue. Mr Mellon, the prospective buyer, had been a
good student. Without the slightest giveaway, he said:

*Well, what you say is right. But my wife says we'd need to change all the
drapes and all the carpeting, and completely re-do the masculine decor
throughout the house. Otherwise, it's nice.*

Before the salesperson reacted I interrupted his thoughts with this question:
What did you say is the asking price on this?
This was his response: *It's for sale at $178,500. But I think the owners would
consider an offer close to that.*
We then ended our business for the day.

When the salesperson left, we reassessed the situation. The Mellons now wanted
the home even more than before. The sellers needed a guaranteed sale as soon as
possible. The salesperson had suggested a lower offer and was keen to make the
sale. We had shown no anxiety, urgency, no emotional attachment, and the market
was in our favor. Things were looking good.

Two days later we made a third inspection, at which time the salesperson didn't
seem as enthusiastic, probably because his expectation of a sale had been dampened by
our previous exchange — exactly what our strategy had been designed to achieve. And
now his investment of time was growing. On this occasion he mentioned no other
buyer waiting in the wings (you know why). After about thirty minutes, we decided it
was time to start the offer process, and maybe even close the deal.

Here's what happened. I've kept the exchanges short and readable, though
accurate in important detail.

As the salesperson locked up the home, the Mellons and I stood talking next to
their car. This deliberate 'exiting' tactic is similar to standing up, putting on your
coat and walking toward the door. This is the point at which concessions and deals
start taking shape. The salesperson approached, and this exchange took place.

Buyer:
*In the next day or two we'll buy one of the homes we like. We have no
finance problems. If we make an offer on this home, how soon will it be
presented to the owner?*

Salesperson:
Right away, this evening. What offer do you have in mind?

Remember, he's not expecting a full price offer. During our second inspection
he suggested the seller might consider a reduced offer.

Buyer:
We'll need an answer by tonight. We'll write up an offer for $153,500.

Salesperson:
Thank you for that, but I know the owners would not accept that figure.

Buyer:
What offers have the owners had so far?

Salesperson:
I don't believe there have been any offers. None they could accept anyway. But that's common. It doesn't reflect negatively on the property. It's a top quality home. I know you'll agree.

Naturally, I wasn't about to add to his praise of the home.

Buyer:
In our estimation, the home is in reasonable condition. But, compared with other homes we're considering, it's not worth what they are asking. If it was, we feel it would have sold by now.

By referring to the price 'they' (the owners) are asking, you help the salesperson distance himself (even unconsciously) from the asking price. It's not 'his' price, but 'theirs'; therefore, he feels less compelled to insist on it or defend it. Remember, the home is listed at $178,500.

Salesperson:
Would you be prepared to make an offer around $170,000? I feel I might have a chance of getting that through for you.

What a salesperson strives hardest for is to get an offer of some kind. That initial offer can be worked upward, but without it there's zero chance of a sale.

Here, however, I guessed that the salesperson was fairly sure $170,000 would buy the property. But was it the owners' lowest acceptable price? I didn't think so. We were making good progress, though.

Buyer:
We're not prepared to pay more than we believe the home is worth.

I'd like you to present our offer of $153,500. If they say no, that's fine; we'll consider our options. The owners need have no fear. We're genuine buyers with a deposit we can put down straight away.

The salesperson agreed, somewhat reluctantly, to write up the purchase offer at $153,500. We would close in 120 days, we said, knowing this *was not* what the owners preferred. The Mellons were free to close sooner without any inconvenience. My tactic in looking for this 120 day close was to gain an advantage (a condition) that I could concede later. You'll see how this unfolds.

Another tactic I used here was to have the salesperson insert an expiry clause in the offer. The clause read:

This offer is made at 11am on September 15. If the owners' response is not communicated to us, the undersigned, by midnight on September 15 it will be automatically withdrawn and become void at that time.

This compelled the salesperson to move fast. And it pressed the owners not to sit around thinking it over. Notice that this clause did not say the owners must *accept* the offer, just that they had to respond in one way or another before the deadline, if negotiation was to continue.

Inserting a deadline like this is generally a good idea. This one was unusually tight, just thirteen hours. Too tight for many sellers; twenty-four hours is more reasonable. Occasionally, even longer is justified, especially when one of the sellers is not local (for example, where a divorced couple are joint sellers or where an inherited home is being sold by the beneficiaries).

At 7.30pm the salesperson called and asked if he could come around. The sellers had sent back a counter offer. (A *counter offer* means that the seller is saying no to the price or terms you offered, or to both, but is keen to keep discussions going and is suggesting a compromise.) He then went into an impassioned account of the effort he had expended to get the sellers to be as reasonable as they could be. He assured us that the figure they had sent back was considerably lower than their heretofore bottom price.

Their counter offer was this: They would accept $167,500, an $11,000 reduction from their asking price of $178,500. On the purchase offer, our figure of $153,500 had been crossed out and in its place, for our acceptance, was $167,500. Also, they had changed our 120 days closing time to forty-five days. After speaking privately with the Mellons, I informed the salesperson that *neither* change was acceptable and we'd have to conclude our business. Unless, that was, *he* knew of a way to bring the deal together. We restated our view that the property was overpriced and that was the reason it had sat on the market so long. At $167,500, we said that we felt it was still overpriced compared with the alternatives we were seeing. Here's how the exchange continued:

Salesperson:
Bearing in mind everything this home offers and its excellent condition, what do you believe is a fair price?

Buyer:
Based on the homes we've seen this week, probably $156,000 maximum. Apart from that, it's costly for us to settle in forty-five days. It means a loss of income on term deposits we'd need to cash in, which means we'd be paying an even higher price.

Salesperson:
Folks, as we all know, good agreements are based on reasonable compromise. The owners have been very generous. What do you say we re-submit the offer about halfway between your $156,000 and their $167,500. How about $162,500? I have no way of knowing if they'll accept that low a figure but I'm willing to ask. It's worth a try, don't you agree?

With some stalling and a show of finality, we increased the offer to $159,500, a bigger jump ($6,000) than I advised but what the Mellons decided. Still, we declined the owner's forty-five days for closing and left in our 120 days. The salesperson said he hoped to let us know within an hour.

When he came by, he was looking tired. His investment of time and effort was still growing. But he was a professional, and he sensed a deal.

Note that we still had an ace up our sleeves; we weren't anywhere near the end of our negotiating power. We were certain the owners wanted a closing earlier than 120 days. Perhaps this was critical for them. The Mellons could concede on that point, but they were getting increasingly fearful that they'd lose the deal altogether. I doubted this.

The salesperson laid out the sellers' new counter offer. Our $159,500 had been rejected and in its place was $165,000 (the owners had dropped another $2,500 from $167,500). Our 120 days was crossed out again and replaced with forty-five days.

I wasn't surprised by anything so far. The signs and signals in negotiation don't vary, whether in real estate or outside. They tell you how much to push, when to ease up, when to make a concession, and how likely an agreement is. This knowing comes from life; we acquire it unconsciously and call on it all the time, but we don't fully realize that we possess such capabilities until somebody shows us that we do. I designed this book to give you that awareness.

Despite the late hour, I felt we were close to an agreement. The sellers were clearly anxious and everyone's anticipation was heightened. My experience told me that a deal would have to be struck *now*. If I gave the owners more time, things could cool down; they might easily think themselves out of any offer we left them with overnight. There could be no sleeping on it.

We took the offer document from the salesperson, studied for a minute or two, then I handed it back. And said nothing. Even the Mellons appeared bemused, despite the warning I'd given them about how I might react. Here's how the deal concluded:

Buyer:
We'll write a new purchase offer. This is our final. It'll stay valid until 10.30pm. Either it's accepted as we write it, or we're out. Our offer is $161,000, not one dollar more. And we'll agree to close in forty-five days.

Dare I say it, it was now take-it-or-leave-it time. That's the message I wanted him to bring to the sellers.

Did I mean it? This game of negotiation functions on perceptions, as we saw in earlier chapters. I created the perception that I meant it; that was enough. So what do *you* think?

By 10.15pm, the Mellons had bought the home at $161,000 with a closing in forty-five days. They saved $17,500. Not a fortune, but almost the price of a small car, perhaps. Did we achieve the best deal possible? I'm not certain we did, but I know everybody got a deal they could accept.

Let's look at something different now, a case study illustrating new tactics.

Case Study: Saving $30,000 on a $210,000 Home

Very often, a home purchase consumes most or all of a buyer's life savings. This is such a case.

A couple I'd met previously, Eli and Ben Robinson, asked me to assist them in buying an attractive Victorian house that had recently been fully renovated by the owner. They had arranged to meet a local real estate salesperson at the property, which was for sale at $210,000. I agreed to accompany them. Before the inspection I gave them a brief primer on what to do and not to do, and generally how to play it cool. And I assured them that I knew the neighborhood and was familiar with local real estate prices.

The Robinsons had a maximum budget of $180,000 and were pessimistic about their chances of buying the home. Nonetheless, they liked it so much they felt it was worth trying.

According to the salesperson's data sheet, the home, on the city fringe, was standing on a small lot measuring 42x100 feet. We found the house to be in excellent condition and were impressed. Of course, not a hint of our excitement reached the salesperson, a very experienced woman. She told us she saw no problem in achieving offers at, or very close to, the asking price. And in response to my question she reported there had been no offers so far.

But I didn't see things quite the way she did. I had compiled a list of local homes, some quite comparable, that sold in the previous three months. Everything I knew indicated that the owner was asking $15-20,000 above fair market value, which I estimated was $190-195,000; certainly not the $210,000 list price.

A neighbor confirmed that the home had been for sale for between three and four months, despite the fact that properties were selling well in the area. This gave me an insight into how the owner must have been feeling. We let a couple of days pass before arranging a second inspection. In that time, the Robinsons saw another home they liked almost as much in an adjoining neighborhood. No question, though, they'd buy the Victorian-style home, but only if they could get it for no more than $180,000, which, as I mentioned, was their true spending limit.

From the beginning, the salesperson pressed for an offer. She even suggested 'trying' a figure of between $200,000 and $210,000, and that $205,000 'might just buy it' (remember, it was listed at $210,000). She'd consult with the seller, she said, and let us know, but that she couldn't guarantee anything.

Here's how it continued:

Buyer:
We made a list of homes that sold recently in the area, along with descriptions and selling prices. These details and our familiarity with the area tell us the owner has overpriced this home.

Notice again that the salesperson isn't made to look responsible for the asking price. We want to avoid a defensive reaction. The way my statement was presented, her competence wasn't questioned.

Salesperson:
It might be a tad high. The owner will look at a serious offer. He has purchased a home in the country. It's hard to find a period-style home like this. Similar homes with no updating have sold around the $200,000 mark.

Buyer:
The property is unusual alright. Though a 70-year old renovated home wouldn't be right for most buyers. We're taking a second look at another home after this, which seems good. And there's a third not far from here that we'll also see. Whichever we choose, we'll buy within the week.

Salesperson:
Why don't you make an offer here, now. I'll see if I can get it through for you. Maybe the owner would accept $200,000, I don't know. Would you buy it if you could get it for $200,000?

Buyer:
We wouldn't make an offer higher than what we believe the home is worth. If we were to make a written offer, would you guarantee it will get to the owner today and we'll get an answer right away?

Salesperson:
Certainly, I'll be able to present it to the owner myself this evening. What offer did you have in mind?

Buyer:
We're prepared to pay $168,500. That's what we believe the home is worth.

Salesperson:
The owner would never consider that. I'm sorry; it's way too low.

Buyer:
But you are prepared to present it, as you said. Aren't you?

When a home has been for sale for three or four months, especially in an active market, and has attracted no offers, the listing agent will usually try to get the owner to drop the price. The aim is to prevent the home sitting on the market and looking stale or suspect, which makes it even harder to sell.

The best evidence a salesperson can use in persuading an owner to reduce the price is legitimate offers from qualified buyers. The salesperson tells the seller: *This is what the market is saying; we should listen.* Sticking at the higher price can cause the home to look like it has problems, especially when other homes are selling.

This logic is valid. The more realistically priced a property the sooner it sells, and the sooner the salesperson pockets the commission. In this case, I guessed the salesperson was praying for a sale, which is one reason for our unusually low first offer of $168,500. In a market with homes selling reasonably well, making an offer this far below the asking price (a gap of $41,500) could stop you from being taken seriously as a buyer; a gap this big has a much better chance of working in a slow market and with a hard-to-sell home.

Bear in mind here, however, that we had no expectation of our low first offer being accepted. But as you now know, that's part of negotiating.

Before we return to our case study, here's a critical point to remember:

Whenever you are negotiating to buy a home, the first figure you offer will generally determine the price you'll pay in the end.

The same is true for almost anything for which you negotiate. Let's say you are buying a car with a sticker price of $20,650 and you offer $20,000. What have you *definitely* done? In this one move you have *definitely* eliminated any chance of buying this car below $20,000. It's possible the seller would have accepted $19,200, or $18,500, or less. *But you'll never know!* Because you made too high a first offer. In short, you locked yourself into paying at least $20,000, and probably more.

Principle: You influence, and eventually arrive at, a seller's lowest price *by working up to it!* Keep this indelibly in your thinking. You can never go down from your first offer. Only up. So, start low. And increase your offer by small amounts, each time with a show of reluctance. The seller and the salesperson are in the opposite position: Rarely can they go up from where they start (the asking price). That's why they set the asking price higher than the figure they will accept.

Let's continue with our case study and see how the deal developed. Remember, the asking price was $210,000 and our first offer was $168,500. And my estimate of the home's value was $190-$195,000.

The salesperson's response later that day didn't surprise us:

Salesperson:
No luck. I couldn't get the owner to send you a counter offer. Your figure is far too low. He did say that if you make a reasonable offer he'll give it consideration.

This wasn't a complete rejection. There was no counter offer, but there was a sign of some kind. What did the owner mean when he said he'd consider a 'reasonable' offer? We had to find out.

Buyer:
We consider $168,500 a fair offer based on homes that have sold in this area. We're not sure we'll make another offer. We'll think it over and call you.

Salesperson:
Would you be prepared to offer $198,000, or even $196,000? I think there's a chance he might at least consider that. The home is well worth that.

I was pretty sure now that the salesperson had tried to get the seller to reduce his price. I also felt that an offer of $200,000 would be accepted, not that we had that kind of money; the Robinsons' max was $180,000. And I'd become convinced that my initial estimate of value ($190-$195,000) was even a little high. I consulted with the Robinsons, and here's what happened:

Buyer:
OK, we are prepared to make one last offer. If it's not accepted, we'll let it go. We'd like it written out and presented immediately. Any delay could cause us to lose out on another home.

We made our second offer at $171,500, an increase of $3,000, despite the fact that on paper we and the seller were $41,500 apart ($210,000 less $168,500).

The salesperson phoned later to tell us the owners had rejected our offer. But, this time, they had sent back a counter offer at $190,000. The salesperson insisted there was no more flexibility; this was the seller's bottom price. I surmised that the way the negotiation had gone had built up hope of a sale in the salesperson and the seller. But, for us, it was time for a new tactic.

Incidentally, note the sellers' first price concession: $20,000 (from $210,000 to $190,000). This signaled that they knew their asking price was probably not achievable. It was clear they were becoming more motivated (and more realistic).

Our new tactic was a powerful one — time! We did absolutely nothing for four or five days. In that time, the salesperson, who had worked hard for the sale, phoned a number of times to ask if we planned to respond to the owner's counter offer of $190,000. Each time, our answer was the same: We were considering putting an offer on another home. The salesperson encouraged us to see the home again and make one last offer. This is exactly what we wanted her to do. Here's what followed:

Buyer:
This will be our final try. If it fails we'll walk away from this home. We won't pay more than the home is worth to us. Our final offer is $173,500 and we'll agree to any close that suits the seller, once it's over thirty days. If

we don't hear from you by 4pm, the offer is withdrawn. Our deadline on another home is that tight.

Some hours later the answer came. Another rejection. This time it was a counter offer at $186,500. They had conceded another $3,500. I felt there was more to go.

Despite our earlier threat to walk away, we 'allowed' the salesperson to talk us into making a fourth offer. We stressed again that we would buy the other home the following day (which was a real possibility). I gave the salesperson details of the other home, which she could verify if she wished; this is something I rarely do but the Robinsons' interest was genuine. At this point, our chances of buying the house for $180,000 or less did not appear great. Still, we didn't know what was going on in the seller's mind (you rarely do). We were making progress and had one or two tactics yet to play.

Our fourth offer was $176,000, an increase of $2,500. We told the salesperson we were losing interest rapidly; we weren't even sure of the wisdom of making this offer. Whatever the outcome, it was final. Take it or leave it. We inserted a conditional clause in this re-written offer; it stated that our offer would expire at noon the following day, at which time it was to be considered withdrawn.

The salesperson knew she had to work hard to save the sale. If she failed, all her work and time would have been in vain. It was a genuine climax point, all four of us knew that. So too, we suspected, did the seller.

At 11am the following day the salesperson had this to say:

Salesperson:
I have good news for you. An exceptional deal. I spent two hours with the owners. They are being more than reasonable. They'll accept $180,000, but no less. It's a fantastic price. To be fair, they have come down $30,000. You can't ask for more than that, etc.

The Robinsons signed the papers at $180,000 and bought the property, a full $30,000 below asking price. They were thrilled; they got a good deal on a nice home.

Let's explore that core principle of making a low first offer and increasing it very gradually, as necessary. And let's learn why it worked so well for the Robinsons.

The Importance of Making Your First Offer a Low One

Here's a question to ponder: What if the Robinsons' first offer had been $175,000? How would you have rated our chances of buying at $180,000?

Probably zero, I'm sure you'll agree. Here's why:

The seller's thinking is always conditioned by the size of your first offer!

And so is the salesperson's. Making a low offer and increasing it in small increments engages the salesperson and the seller in a process; this process alters their thinking and re-shapes their expectations. Their focus shifts from the asking price to what they might accept. The seller starts distinguishing between *imaginary* figures (unreality) and *actual* figures (reality). The longer this process continues, the more compromise is achievable.

A low first offer from an obviously genuine, qualified buyer suggests to sellers that they will need to be flexible to get the sale. Conversely, when the first offer is close to asking price, sellers hold tighter to their inflated estimate of their home's value. And while it's true that a seller is free to reject any offer and break off negotiation, in practice this is rarely an easy decision. Sellers need to sell. Usually, more than buyers need to buy. Turning away a serious buyer is a mistake sellers frequently live to regret, realizing too late that it would have been better to negotiate.

Point: Because you hold what sellers and agents need most — cash! — *you* are typically in the strongest position of the three parties. The problem, and it's costly, is that most homebuyers fail to recognize this.

Tip: Don't ever fall for that old salesperson trick, the one where they tell you they 'would not want to offend the seller' by presenting your low offer. This is a ruse to get more money out of you. Insist your offer is presented. And if not, find a new agency.

However, with this tactic, it's not enough simply to make your first offer lower than you believe the seller will accept. You must always *state your justification* for your offer. It might be based on the *selling prices* (*not* asking prices) of comparable homes, or *your own* personal assessment of the home's value *to you*, based on general condition, floor layout, lot size, repairs outstanding, necessary updating, property tax level, neighborhood limitations, and so on. Whatever, you must give a basis for your offer.

Saying that your offer is low because your budget is limited is *not* effective; your spending budget does not set the value of the home. Nonetheless, at the *end* of negotiations, this *No More Money* tactic (as it is known) can work extremely well (more on this soon).

Nor can your early offers be so low as to be totally unreasonable; nothing is achieved by offering $220,000 on a $370,000 home.

When you do agree to increase your offer, do so with a show of uncertainty, even reluctance. Better yet, let the salesperson 'talk you into' it. Never increase without requiring some convincing.

Tip: Don't *ever, ever* make it known that you are planning to make a higher offer if your current offer is rejected. And I mean *never!* Such an admission destroys your credibility and kills any chance of getting the best deal — plus, the salesperson will tell the seller you'll pay more!

Stay aware too that increasing your offer steeply in one move works against you. In fact, it's dangerous. It signals that you are just trying your luck and that further rejections will cause you to make big increases. Significantly, it also makes a lie of the justification you used for your lower offer; you can't say you believe a home is worth no more than $230,000, then later offer $280,000.

Note that the Robinsons' saving of $30,000 on a $210,000 purchase illustrates the principle of creeping with your offers, and the benefits to be gained. Our first offer was $168,500, a full $41,500 below the asking price (this is not the norm). Our second offer closed that gap slightly, a $3,000 increase. Had we increased our first offer by $10-$15,000 or more, we'd have thrown away the advantage of creeping.

But there's another good lesson here. A $10-$15,000 increase, for example, would have set a size precedent. The negotiation might have broken down had we followed that with a $2,000 or $3,000 increase.

On top of that, a big increase screams that you are nowhere near your spending limit, you have finances in reserve. And, as we saw above, when you've used the *No More Money* tactic, only very small increases will preserve your credibility, and your power.

More than any other disadvantage, though, a big increase in your offer marks you as a naive buyer, which makes you vulnerable and will cost you money.

Let's put what we've covered here into two short rules:

Rule 1:
When you feel you must increase your offer, procrastinate, show reluctance, and hint that you might forget the whole idea. The mood you communicate should be one of seriousness and uncertainty.

Rule 2:
Regardless of how far apart you and the seller are, make your increases small. And try to make them progressively smaller. Better not to do in one jump what can be done in three or more smaller jumps.

Protect Yourself Legally

In the first pages of this book I stressed that this book does not provide you with legal advice. It always makes sense to consult an attorney before entering into any contract to purchase real estate. If you don't have one (or even if you do) shop around. Ask for referrals, talk to friends; better still, call an Exclusive Buyer Agent.

You want an attorney who is expert in real estate and is prepared to have a *no-cost preliminary meeting* with you. It might take one phone call, or you might have to search for one that feels right.

It's important to do this long *before* you are ready to make an offer. Ask the attorney if she recommends that you use an Offer and Acceptance form. This form has blank spaces for the details of your offer, and states that you and the seller, on agreement, intend to enter into a full Purchase and Sale Agreement. These forms are not used everywhere, so be guided by a local attorney on this.

Don't rely on the salesperson or broker to provide this offer document. Brokers' documents are generally weighted in favor of the agency and the seller. Some do *not* adequately guarantee return of your deposit if you pull out of the deal. Others bind you to using the broker's Standard Real Estate Agreement if your offer is accepted. So, be guided by your attorney on the recommended procedure to use when making a verbal or written offer.

How to Use Escape Clauses For Protection

If you feel you might be unable, for any reason, to go through with the purchase, you can, and should, add an *escape clause* to your offer. This allows you to pull out of the agreement without incurring a penalty. This clause is in most attorney's Offer and Acceptance forms. If it isn't, ask for it to be added.

An escape clause states that you will go through with the purchase, but only if certain other things happen. For example, you'll go through with it contingent upon your partner or attorney approving it. Remember, this offer document is *not* the full Purchase and Sale Agreement. That will be drawn up (or approved) by your attorney when your offer is accepted, and will contain all the conditions attaching to the agreement.

The escape clause is often called a *contingency* or *contingency clause*. It's there for one purpose, to allow you the right to withdraw in certain circumstances without cost or further obligation. Seek advice on this in your preliminary talk with your attorney. At the same time, get direction on how to put a deposit on a home. And finally, keep in mind that you can withdraw your offer at any time prior to it being accepted, with or without an escape clause.

When it comes to handing over money, my own approach is one of caution. Even when protected by an escape clause, I believe it's wise to give the salesperson the smallest possible deposit (sometimes called an *earnest money deposit* or a *good faith deposit*). In some parts, the salesperson will expect this before submitting your offer. A properly worded escape clause guarantees you will get your money back if a deal is not reached. Without such a clause, you could forfeit your deposit. Once again, practices vary with location; talk to your attorney about this.

Placing Other Conditions on Your Offer

By now you are thinking like a negotiator, a smart buyer. In negotiation, one important reason for placing conditions on your offer is to have something to bargain with (to concede) later. The pros call this *leverage*. When you have conditions you have the power to make concessions, which is how deals come together. And making concessions (judiciously and when appropriate) shows you to be a reasonable buyer, which works in your favor. Soon, we'll consider specific conditions and how they benefit and protect you.

For now, keep in mind that a condition should never be conceded lightly. You hold out until it is to your benefit to concede. Better still, *allow* the other side to work for and 'extract' the concession. Make it appear that you haven't *given it up* but that they have prized it from you. In negotiation, small victories like this for the other side can bring greater advantage later for you.

Let's simplify the psychology behind this, most of which happens unconsciously. When you make a concession too easily, without a show of hesitation, you are *conditioning* the other side to expect more from you. On the other hand, when your opponent has to fight hard to win a concession, he believes he has won a *bigger* victory. The satisfaction this 'victory' produces tends to dull his appetite for battle and disposes him to reciprocate.

Also, when you concede a small victory to the other side (or even a big one, when prudent) you diminish the other side's need to get all they previously expected. In this way, sellers stop holding out for a higher price and ideal terms.

Having conditions you can concede also enables you to control the momentum of the exchange, the pace at which progress is made. And, as you'd expect, how you manage making concessions influences the perceptions of the salesperson and seller, which is precisely your aim.

Stay aware, too, that the conditions you place on your offer may be insignificant *to you*. But only *you* know this. In our case study with the Mellons, we held on to our 120-day settlement condition knowing that this was *not* what the seller needed. Then, very late, to make the deal, we conceded.

This tactic is under-used, and often misunderstood. Let's clarify it further.

On the surface, it seems like the side that wins a concession would push for even bigger gains. In my experience, this is rarely so, provided the buyer hesitates and shows reluctance before conceding. Perhaps the explanation for this has to do with battle fatigue: victory dissipates energy, produces satisfaction, and relieves aggression. Or maybe it's because a small 'victory' moves the victorious side toward a position of balance. We are complex psychological beings!

Whatever the explanation, a small increase in your offer, or a concession of any sort, can keep you on track for a good deal even when agreement seems distant.

Before we look at specific conditions (or 'contingencies'), keep in mind that there are two types of conditions, indispensable and dispensable. The indispensable you never concede. Whereas you can usually bargain with dispensable conditions, in return for the seller being flexible on price, terms, or some other point. However, before you rush to test this strategy, be clear on exactly what is dispensable and what is not, and make certain your partner sees things the same way.

Remember: At any point, if you're in doubt about a legal matter affecting your position, an appropriate 'third party' escape clause will allow you time to get advice from your attorney or other expert before you commit. Often, a quick phone call will deliver the answer you require.

Types of Conditions that Can Protect You

An appropriately used condition improves the value of a purchase to you, or in some way protects your interests. As you'll see, this doesn't apply just to money. Below are common conditions you can use tactically to get a better deal, and better self-protection.

• **Time**

Buyers and sellers work within typical time frames when transferring ownership of a home. As a buyer, you'll get to state the length of time you'll need from your offer being accepted to when you'll close on the home (often called the 'settlement period'). If you can be flexible, you might agree, at the seller's request, to change this.

In return for this concession, you could look for a price reduction or other reciprocal concession (that the seller agrees to leave all the downstairs furniture, for example). So, a designated settlement period (sixty days, 120 days, etc) might be one condition you place on your offer, and possibly alter later to your advantage.

• Feature Related

Let's assume the home you want to buy has an old dilapidated shed in the back yard. You have no use for it. In fact, it's an eyesore and detracts from the home. So you make your offer conditional upon the seller agreeing to have the shed and any residual debris removed before the settlement date.

Alternatively, your condition could state that you will accept the property with the shed in place, provided the owner agrees to compensate you for the cost of having it removed (you might specify a dollar amount). When the owner accepts either condition on your offer you can feel sure the problem will be solved.

• Repair Related

You suspect that the home has a leaky roof, but you are not sure. Waiting for a professional roof inspection might allow another buyer to come into the picture and complicate things. But it would be risky to pay up front for a professional roof inspection. Should you later fail to reach agreement with the seller, you'd be seriously out of pocket.

The best solution in such circumstances is usually to negotiate as you normally would, but to place a condition on your offer that stipulates either of the following: a) that you will go through with the purchase only if the roof is inspected by a professional and found to be in sound condition, or b) that you will go through with the purchase only if the owner agrees to pay for any repairs that are found necessary by the roofing professional.

Of course, this might be only one of the conditions you write into your offer. As the negotiation progresses, you can agree to drop any condition in return for the seller making an appropriate price concession. Be absolutely sure, however, that you get an accurate assessment of the cost of any needed repair. You can adopt this approach with electrical wiring, plumbing, heating/cooling, chimney, landscaping or any feature or system that causes you concern. (More information later on home inspection services.)

• New Homes

Although home builders and their representatives seldom tell you this, you can often negotiate 'extras' when you purchase a newly-built home. Things like better landscaping or higher quality appliances can often be acquired at no extra cost. So too can better carpeting, additional interior painting, fencing, extra power points, security system, and other such items.

Consider making your offer subject to such concessions being granted. In other words, insert these extras as conditions on your offer and continue to negotiate on price. You might eventually have to give up one or two, but you're likely to come away with a better deal than if you sought no extras and therefore had nothing to concede. This can work particularly well when the builder is trying to sell several new properties. Naturally, neither the builder nor the salesperson will volunteer how flexible they might be.

The list of possible conditions is endless. Don't hesitate to use those that are important to you. Ask for what will make you feel better, more comfortable or more secure.

And remember, if your conditions are extremely unreasonable or impossible to meet, you risk killing the interest of the salesperson and seller. The seller can say yes or no to any condition you impose on your offer. In practice, however, sellers are generally reasonable and will go at least part way to meeting your needs.

The types of conditions we have covered here, which serve homebuyers' interests, are not used nearly often enough. That's because there are few people out there honestly helping the average homebuyer to buy safely and smartly.

Points to Remember: Before you go house hunting, ask your attorney for guidance on: 1) Using Offer and Acceptance forms, and 2) Placing conditions on your offers.

Should You Send Information to the Seller along with Your Offer?

This is an interesting tactic and one you might favor. It's common in some parts and not in others. Negotiators, including Exclusive Buyer Agents, frequently use it.

One idea is to attach to your offer basic details of local homes that sold recently. You can include addresses, home description, size, number of bedrooms, etc, along with selling prices (and asking prices, where relevant), all relating to homes comparable to the one you wish to buy. Naturally, you include only details that make your offer look fair and reasonable.

A percentage of sellers will be sufficiently influenced to consider an early concession of some kind. The majority, however, are likely to be swayed more by the negotiation process itself, the home's specific shortcomings, expenses you will incur, the price comparisons you cite, the passage of time, the professional home inspection report, offer and counter offer, and so on. But attaching details that support your offer will rarely work against you. If the idea interests you, try it, but don't rely on it alone.

Tip: Here's a final tip before we leave this section. When you have negotiated price and terms acceptable to both sides, make sure you and the seller sign the agreement immediately. Do this whether using an Offer and Acceptance form or a full Purchase and Sale Agreement. Your attorney will have ensured (or will soon) that there is no 'sudden death' clause in the agreement, which could permit the seller to accept offers from other buyers after accepting yours. This is another reason your attorney should draw up or approve the documents you sign.

If a deal comes together suddenly and catches you unprepared, keep in mind that you can insert a condition on any offer form that will make the agreement subject to your attorney's approval.

When executed correctly, a sale/purchase agreement takes the home off the market and locks the seller into honoring what has been agreed therein. You will also be protected by other regulations and conditions about which your attorney can advise you. One condition most attorneys (rightly) insist on is that the agreement can be voided by you without penalty if the professional home inspection report is unsatisfactory to you. The buyer typically arranges and pays for this inspection after agreeing price and terms with the seller.

Finally, any condition that makes a purchase subject to the approval of a third party (attorney or other advisor, for example) is sometimes referred to as a *weasel clause*. Don't let that stop you. All it does is put protection where protection is needed most — on *your* side.

You'll find more advice on professional home inspections and related matters further on. Right now, let's look deeper into tactics and how to shape 'the deal'.

KEY POINTS TO REMEMBER

- Keep in mind when you buy a home that you are also buying the surrounding neighborhood. Take a long, slow tour of the area and make sure it has the features you want and need, and no nasty surprises (existing or planned).
- While inspecting a home, make notes of significant features and any positive or negative aspects that grab your attention (use your notebook!). They may prove useful later, even valuable, when it's time to negotiate.
- Ask the salesperson specific questions about every home you inspect, even those in which you have little or no interest. Ask important, relevant questions the salesperson will have to find answers to. And insist on clear, definite answers.
- Time is your ally. Learn how to make it work for you, especially when you find a home that captures your interest.
- Crawl, stall and procrastinate before making an offer. Best if you can let yourself be 'talked into' it by the salesperson. When you feel it is necessary to increase your offer or make a concession, do so with a show of doubt and reluctance. And let the other side work hard to 'win' this from you. That way, they'll value your concession or higher offer more, and will be less keen to go through the 'extraction' process again.
- When talking to the salesperson, refer to the price of the home as the price 'they' are asking. Don't make it sound like it is the salesperson's price. If you do, the salesperson will feel compelled to defend it.
- Place a deadline for response on your purchase offer, a time by which the seller must respond or your offer will automatically be withdrawn and become void.
- On your offer, try to have at least one condition you are willing to concede. But don't concede it until late in the negotiation. In return, look for a corresponding concession or final agreement. This is sometimes referred to as the Red Herring tactic.
- Any time you are negotiating to buy a home, the first figure you offer will determine the eventual price you pay. Choose it well.
- The best way to influence and arrive at the final price the seller agrees to accept, is by inching up to it in small increments, no big jumps.
- Shop around for an attorney who is expert in real estate (not all are) and consult with him or her before you begin your search. Get guidance on putting an offer on a home and placing conditions on the offer. Preliminary consultations of this kind are usually free.

CHAPTER 9

Deal Time:
Tactics, Concessions and Credibility

The pure and simple truth is rarely pure and never simple.

— Oscar Wilde

By way of introduction to this chapter, let's first restate a key principle of negotiation we mentioned earlier.

Any time you increase your offer, the increase should be based entirely on the last figure you offered. It should not be dictated by or based on what the seller expects. Or, by how far away you are from the seller's position.

Here's the example I'll use to illustrate key points. Assume I am the seller and I want to sell you my home. Through the real estate salesperson, I tell you it's worth $243,000. You offer me $215,000, which I reject. However, I tell you I will accept $238,000. That positions us, right now, $23,000 apart ($238,000 minus $215,000).

You say you can buy a better home for less money a couple of streets away and you act like you are ready to cancel your interest in my home. Then the salesperson comes up with a stroke of genius, what he claims is a fair compromise, that you meet me halfway. That we should 'split the difference'.

Should you go ahead? No!

Let's see why. And how you might proceed.

Why You Should Almost Never Agree to
'Split the Difference' and Other Buyer Mistakes

By agreeing to meet me halfway, you allow me, the seller, to dictate the size of your new offer. My figure of $238,000, wherever I got it from, becomes the *benchmark*. It dictates where the price will go from here. It also determines *how much* you will eventually pay. Any figures you had in mind, such as your estimate of the value of my home, or the price you might be able to get me to accept, lose their meaning right away.

Consider also that I (or the salesperson) might be employing a tactic to get you to pay a higher price. I might have hiked up my asking price to well in excess of what I will accept. Maybe I had one appraisal significantly higher than two or three others and that's the figure I'm using. Now *you* are using *my* figure to set *your* offer. Maybe I hiked up my price with just this kind of 'compromise' in mind. (Even if my asking price is close to what the real estate salesperson says my home is worth, this is still *not* a guarantee of value; appraisals on the same property often differ widely.)

For now, let's assume you agree to meet me halfway (we're $23,000 apart). This means you will add $11,500 to your first offer of $215,000. The salesperson then brings me your offer of $226,500. But now, I start thinking, particularly about your willingness to add so much, $11,500 to your first offer. And I wonder:

- Is your willingness to pay $226,500 based on the value you see in my home?
- If so, what does this tell me about your first offer of $215,000?
- Am I to assume your $215,000 offer did not reflect the real value you saw in my home? That you were simply bargain hunting, or employing your own idea of 'negotiation'?

You see, now I know you believe my home is worth $226,500. At least! I figure you believed this all along, that your $215,000 offer was just a try-your-luck, feeble kind of bargaining. Now I start wondering how far you might go. You're clearly no negotiator. Maybe I'll push hard and see what I can get out of you.

Do you see what is happening between us? Your credibility has evaporated. And with it your power to influence my price. Perhaps you'll pay $232,000, or $235,000, or more. After all, I got you up a huge $11,500 in one jump. I figure you'll go for another few thousand. Clearly, I, the seller, am controlling what you'll pay, not you.

What's more, there is no obligation on me to accept your new offer. I might instruct my salesperson (after all, he is working *exclusively* in my best interest) to tell you I'm *not* prepared to sell for $226,500, that it's just too low. My home is worth $238,000, and that's what I expect. And, by the way, other buyers have come by and one may be on the verge of submitting an offer.

You see, I figure you are very keen on my home. Maybe you've fallen in love with it and want it even at my asking price. I'm smug and confident also because the salesperson told me how much you can spend and how perfect my home is for you, and a whole lot of other things you told him about your personal circumstances (his loyalty is pledged to me 100%, not to you).

Who would you say is in the stronger position now — me or you?

You might protest when I reject your halfway offer. You might even accuse the salesperson of misleading you. In response, he pleads innocence, telling you he acted in good faith and did his best to help you buy the home. Then he adds that in his professional opinion, anything less than $238,000 would be like giving away the home. He reminds you that you can still have the home if you act quickly, and of course he'll present your new offer immediately. Pay $238,000 before someone else steals it. (Were you expecting wings and a halo?)

Obviously, you've lost control. What can you do? You scratch your head. You know you've been outmaneuvered. Your expectations were falsely raised. But now you've become committed emotionally to the home; it's disheartening, to say the least, you can't think of pulling out. You've been seeing the home as yours, even visualizing how your furniture would look and which rooms family members would occupy. Unlocking yourself now is impossible.

But you're still $11,500 away from my price ($238,000 minus $226,500). So you begin rationalizing. You tell yourself it's only $11,500 and, after all, the original price was $243,000. And $11,500 mortgaged over a number of years won't increase your monthly payments that much. Inside, it gnaws at you. But going ahead sure beats starting your search all over again tomorrow. It would be foolish to lose it for $11,500 (so, too, says the salesperson with an air of conviction). And on and on the thoughts roll. Until, eventually, you think yourself into paying $238,000. I win.

How about you, do you win?

In the end, only I and the salesperson know that I would have accepted a lower price. I might have accepted $220,000 or $225,000, if you had negotiated well. And there really wasn't any other keen buyer. But you'll never know these things. You failed to set, or even influence, the price. What were your biggest mistakes? Let's run a check.

Your ability to negotiate successfully was wiped out by a range of mistakes. These are common mistakes that make ordinary homebuyers vulnerable. Take a look at seven costly errors:

1. You accepted my asking price as the basis to work from.
2. You were too quick to compromise, too quick to split the difference.
3. You were too extravagant with your second offer, an increase of $11,500.
4. You were too willing to believe you risked losing the home.
5. In your mind you 'owned' the home much *too early* in the negotiation.
6. You interpreted the salesperson's 'meet half-way' suggestion as a way to make the deal, when it was nothing but a ruse to get you to pay more.
7. You gave up control; you thought yourself into acting desperately, prematurely and extravagantly in agreeing to pay my figure of $238,000.

These and similar buyer mistakes are dealt with repeatedly and in different ways throughout *Not One Dollar More!* These are some of the worst mistakes I've seen buyers make. Soon, I will illustrate six simple tactics and money-saving techniques you can use in almost any situation. Right now, let's look at some basic moves you could have used in this home purchase.

A Few Self-Defense Basics

First, to negotiate successfully you must be seen to be genuine and credible.

You accomplish this by letting the salesperson and seller know the justification or logic your offer is based on. *Only two* justifications are acceptable, and you must be able to defend both. So, make it clear that your offer is based on one or both of these:

- *Your* estimate of the value of the property, what *you* feel the home is worth *to you*
- Your spending limit, your inability to pay a higher price; best used toward the end of the negotiation.

Both, of course, will typically be tactical positions. What I mean by that is they won't reflect your true thinking. Stating that your offer represents what you believe the home is worth, is by far the stronger of the two arguments. It can usually be combined effectively (later) with the claim that your budget just can't stretch any further (more on both soon).

For now, remember this: An offer to split the difference should never be entertained in the early or middle stages of the negotiation. Never before a stalemate seems likely. Nine times out of ten it results in you paying a higher price. The single exception is in the final stages of the negotiation, when only a small amount separates you and the seller.

For example, splitting the difference or 'meeting halfway' can be justified where your 'final' offer is, say, $220,000 and the seller is stuck stubbornly at $225,000. This compromise could be the making of a good deal. But even here, procrastinate, act like you are at your limit or over it and on the verge of pulling out.

In our home purchase illustration above, major problems started when you agreed to meet me halfway (I wanted $238,000, you offered $215,000 then you increased to $226,500). Your second offer should have been made with a show of doubt and stalling, and kept between $3,000 and $5,000. Your third and fourth offers, if you had to make them, could have added from $1,000 to $3,000 to your previous offer figure.

Incidentally, it's a good idea to make increases progressively smaller. By that I mean a $5,000 increase should be followed by an increase of $3,000 or less. It is *most important* not to go in the opposite direction, from smaller to larger. An increase of $2,000 should not be followed by an increase of $5,000. Only in very rare cases, can this rule be broken. One instance might be when it is *certain* to close a deal. Progressively smaller increases have the added advantage of signaling to the seller and salesperson that your budget is running out fast.

Another error is to assume that what the seller or salesperson says is factual. Or fair. The only opinion of what is *fair* or what is *good value* that is worth trusting is your own. Certainly not the salesperson's or seller's; surely that's too much to expect seeing how they're on the opposite side to you.

Listen as long as you choose, but try to follow these suggestions:

- Read between the lines

- Question relevantly and specifically
- Challenge what you are told
- Ask for evidence (not another opinion)
- Get hard facts, and verify them
- Rely on your *own* intuition
- Act on your *own* logic
- Apply your *own* tactics
- Dictate your *own* pace
- Base your decisions on your *own* feelings and impressions, and on your *own* needs and objectives.

This is how you stay in control! If you have an Exclusive Buyer Agent working for you, this will be easier.

When making a first offer, whether it's verbal or written, communicate clearly and emphatically that your offer represents the fair value of the home *to you!* Later, you might state that you have reached the limit of your budget. It is totally irrelevant what evidence the salesperson offers to dispute your opinion of the home's value. Your offer represents what the home is worth — *to you!* You explain that it's based on your personal judgment, on the selling prices of homes you've seen and, on the current asking prices of one or two other homes that could interest you. Don't be dissuaded from making the first offer you have in mind, even though you know you might later agree to pay more (only you should know this, of course). Then move slowly and be patient. In negotiation it's the tortoise, not the hare, that wins in the end.

Let's go back to our example and analyze further.

In trying to buy my house at the lowest price possible, had you emphasized that your first offer of $215,000 was all you believed the property was worth and that you'd have no interest at a higher price, the salesperson would have acted very differently with me, the seller, in trying to get me to compromise. As it was, you jumped $11,500 with your second offer, indicating that you believed all along that my home was worth more than you first offered, at least $11,500 more — if not, why would you make that second offer? That move made it easy for me and my salesperson to figure you out as a buyer and eventually outmaneuver you. Consequently, you paid a lot more for my home than a smart buyer would have.

Another mistake: You failed to control the momentum of the negotiation. Instead of slowing up and showing signs that you might buy another home at better value, you speeded up the momentum. You jumped at splitting the difference when you should have made a slightly increased offer and stretched things out in preparation for a possible third offer.

What you said, in effect, was: *The home is worth $215,000.* Then you said: *Yes, I'm prepared to pay $226,500.* This worked against you because your actions contradicted your words. Naturally, your actions spoke louder — actions always do. Your goal is to ensure that your words and your actions remain in sync and reinforce the impression you need to make. Only then are you in a position to negotiate and concede productively, because you are in control and dictating the momentum.

Introduction to Six Powerful Tactics

Tactics. Think of them as jewels in a crown, elements in a performance. They are not the crown, nor the performance. But they are potentially your most powerful asset.

I'll explain here how to apply six of the most effective tactics for use in home buying, whether you are negotiating through a salesperson or with a private seller. In the next chapter we'll look more deeply at buying, whether it's from a private seller or a real estate agency. Keep in mind that these six tactics, when you grasp them, will help you defend your interests in many life situations.

Having said that, tactics on their own are relatively ineffective. To work well they need the disciplined approach this book teaches you, and your willingness to apply them when your money and security are at risk.

Caution: Be careful not to overplay any tactic. State it (or apply it) once or twice confidently and clearly, then repeat it only when it fits naturally into the discussion. This will be enough. Unnecessary repetition, or pregnant pauses as you search for what to say or do, will make you seem 'drilled', and will weaken you as a negotiator. In short, act the part! Your behavior must establish your credibility and support your strategy.

Here is a preliminary introduction to six practical tactics the smart buyer can use in negotiating the best deal.

The Attractive Alternatives Tactic

From the beginning, before you find the home you wish to buy, casually let the salesperson know that you have seen at least one home elsewhere that interests you. Later, when the negotiation process starts, refer back to this other home; make comparisons out loud, to your partner or yourself, as you inspect the various features of the house — you have an attractive alternative!

If the salesperson asks you to identify the home (she'll want to look it up in her book), say it's being sold privately, or that you feel it would not be in your interest to disclose that information. Or both. By the way, either of these responses is good generally when the salesperson pries.

Of course, your attractive alternative does not have to mean another home. It could mean you'll hold on to your present home and not buy anything. Or that you'll keep renting and buy next year. Both positions work particularly well when combined with a that's-all-I-can-afford tactic. For example:

I'm giving it my best shot, I'm at the end of my budget. If they say no I'll just put off buying for a year.

The Stall And Jolt Tactic

This is where, in the negotiation, you back off to 'think over' the proposition that has been put to you. There's just the slightest hint in your tone that your response will be favorable, that you'll agree to the other side's price or terms. Although your hint is clear, you give no guarantee of what you will do.

Then, in your next contact, you deliver the jolt. With a show of disappointment, even inevitability, you reject the price or terms you've been offered. This shocks the salesperson's optimistic expectations. Now you stall again and you wait for the other side to try rescue the situation. You re-state your 'final' price or terms calmly and your genuine interest in the home. If further concessions are possible from the other side, this tactic will often extend the negotiation in that direction.

The Comparative Value Tactic

You inform the salesperson or seller up front that the price they are asking is higher than a number of comparable homes that sold recently and others you've inspected, one or two of which you have some interest in. You might state also that you believe your offer is fair and consistent with prices of homes that are largely similar.

Don't let the salesperson draw you out by getting you to identify the homes you refer to. Just let her know you've kept all the relevant details in your notebook, including asking prices and selling prices, and have a good feel for what your money can buy (which is what you have been doing, isn't it?).

The Third Party Tactic

This tactic enables you to prolong the negotiation while keeping the other side involved, if that's what you wish to do. It's the ultimate safeguard against making a bad decision. You indicate your interest in owning the home but say that the decision rests with another person (spouse, advisor, attorney, lender, or even parent). Unfortunately, that person believes the price is too high or the terms are wrong, or they prefer another home or have some other reservation you are finding difficult to get around.

Much as *you* would like to buy the home, your hands are tied, at least at the moment. The only thing that might enable the deal to go ahead right away, that you can think of, is if the seller resolves the problem or makes the deal feasible in some other way. Your third party might then give the green light. This tactic is best used later in the negotiation, as you stretch out the communications with the other side.

The No More Money Tactic

You've negotiated well but have reached a point where the seller refuses to reduce the price any further or change the terms. You say matter-of-factly that your offer is genuine, your finance approved, you're ready to go ahead, and that you believe you've offered a fair price for the home. You are already over your spending limit (here's one good reason to never reveal your true budget details to the salesperson) and, aside from next month's salary, you simply have no more money.

If you suspect the seller might still not accept, even after you have increased your offer, you can pull one 'last' trick out of the bag. You somehow 'find' or 'borrow' a few last minute dollars that you say you hope will close the deal (your brother-in-law gave you a loan, for example, or you cashed in part of your pension). Your budget is, in fact, now over-spent, you say. And after this, you have no more money. You can then consider applying the 'walk away' tactic (below).

The Walk Away Tactic

Your position here is that you are keen on the home and have made a very fair offer. Your new slightly increased offer is the last one you'll make, it's your best shot. If the seller doesn't accept it you'll be satisfied that you went as far as you could. You'll forget the idea of owning this home. Instead, you'll probably just buy the home you saw on Sunday, which is your second choice but it's very attractive, represents better value for money and is within budget. If asked, you say this other home is being sold privately, or just that you feel it's not in your best interest to disclose details at this point (if word got out someone could beat you to it — perfectly reasonable).

You tell the salesperson that it's now up to the seller. If the salesperson persists in trying to get you to increase your offer, act like you're ready to cancel your interest immediately. Begin making your exit, head for the door or your car. This is the ultimate 'walk away.' If the salesperson makes no attempt to stop you, *don't lose your nerve!* Keep going. You're probably being tested. If the salesperson believes there's any chance of saving the deal, you won't get far, or you'll get a call later suggesting a possible solution. Act on what you hear, knowing that your position is now stronger than before.

I could add to this list but what's here is sufficient, especially when you combine tactics. For example, your advisor or partner (third party tactic) is not enthusiastic because they feel the 'other' home is brighter, bigger, more modern, has a better kitchen or bigger lot or is in a better location (attractive alternative tactic) or costs less (comparative value tactic).

And you also have the stall and jolt tactic to add into the mix. The seller re-asserts his price and terms and says he is through compromising. You re-confirm that you are definitely interested in the home, and that you'll go away and 'think it over' (the stall, in advance of the jolt). Later, despite the protests of the salesperson, you reject the seller's price and terms (the jolt). But you add a small amount to your last offer and state with finality that you are offering a fair price (comparative value tactic) and if the seller doesn't accept, you'll cancel your interest and buy another home (walk away tactic).

Which of these tactics you apply, and when, are judgment calls on your part. Trust yourself, trust your life experience, it's almost certainly richer than you believe.

And when inspecting homes that are *not* of interest to you, try out any tactic that seems appropriate to the situation, a dry run for the real thing.

Throughout your association with the salesperson, and indirectly the seller, and especially during the negotiation phase, *you are trying to influence their thinking* with subtle skills of which they are unaware. Years ago I named this *Invisible Negotiation* for that reason; when done well it goes largely unrecognized by the other side.

From the start you intentionally build an impression of you that will work to your benefit as the negotiation progresses. In effect, you are shaping the salesperson's and seller's perspectives, shaping how they assess your confidence as a buyer, your seriousness, your circumstances, your spending power, your temperament, your definiteness, your poise, your toughness under pressure, and your level of desire for the property in question.

As a smart buyer, it will pay you (literally, many dollars) to make certain the impression you create is one that empowers you to buy the home you want at the lowest price and best terms. The steps explained in these chapters help you do that.

We'll move now to invisible negotiation in action, common buyer-seller-salesperson exchanges and see the six tactics being applied.

If negotiation sounds like a conditioning process, it is exactly that. It will happen either *by* you or *to* you. That's the difference between a smart buyer and a naive buyer. The smart buyer controls, the naive buyer *is* controlled by others.

KEY POINTS TO REMEMBER

- Splitting the difference or meeting halfway is rarely a good idea, unless the gap is relatively small and splitting the difference will close the deal.
- Any time you increase your offer, the size of the increase should be based entirely on the *last* figure you offered. Rarely should it be influenced or determined by the figure the seller expects or is demanding.
- Any offer you make must be seen to be based on one of two factors: 1) what you believe to be a fair price for the property, or 2) the fact that you cannot afford to pay a higher price. Combine the two, if you wish, but make the 'fair price' argument your principal justification for the amount you offer.
- When you increase an offer, it is always better to do it gradually in small increments rather than in one or two big jumps.
- When a home interests you, ask specific questions and look for specific answers. Verify what you are told and accept only hard facts rather than opinions, guesses, generalizations, or estimates.
- In negotiation, it is usually the tortoise, not the hare, that wins in the end (momentum).
- Your tactics are your defense against, and best response to, the tactics of the other side.
- Along with your research and the professional advice you receive, tactics enable you to expose and counteract tricks, fraud, and deception.
- Tactics on their own are relatively worthless. They need to be part of a strategy (an overall plan) to be effective, and be executed convincingly.
- Always let the salesperson believe you are also interested in another home (or homes) with a different agency or private seller.
- Needing a third-party's approval (real or not) gives you more options, particularly in the later stages of a negotiation.
- When you have claimed your budget is already used up, you can later, if you have to, make a slightly higher take-it-or-leave-it offer by 'discovering' an overlooked, but believable, source of limited funds.
- When you have stated you will have to 'walk away' if your offer is rejected, follow through! Say your good-byes courteously and with an air of finality, and leave. Give the other side time to contact you. If no contact follows, contact the salesperson 'out of curiosity', then ask if they have any new listings you should know of. And be ready for what happens; the negotiation may not be over.

PART FOUR

INVISIBLE NEGOTIATION

CHAPTER 10

Tactics in Action: Influencing Salespeople and Private Sellers

Honesty is the best policy — when there's money in it.
— Mark Twain

Just about everything you learn from this book will help you whether you are buying directly from a private seller or through a real estate agency. With a private seller you'll make just minor adjustments, which we'll cover in this chapter.

In both cases, your preparation needs to be diligent; relevant information is vital. You should know something about what has sold, and selling prices, in your area. Also, what is currently on the market and the prices being asked. You can get this data easily from local real estate offices and various online sources.

What the Neighbor Knows — Ask!

Often, a nearby neighbor will know more about a home, its history and the neighborhood than you'll learn from anyone else. If the first neighbor isn't keen, try a second and a third until you develop a feel for the situation. What you learn will help your decision making, and perhaps provide information that will be useful in negotiating with the seller. Let's face it, sellers don't always reveal their true reason for moving. What if there's a problem with the home or the area? If you don't find out, it could become yours.

The sellers are possibly in debt and under pressure to sell. Maybe a quick sale is to your advantage and theirs. Or there could be a neighborhood issue. Is a new highway to be built within view or earshot? Are undesirable changes happening close by? A new airport being planned for where green pastures now exist? Is crime a problem?

These are the types of questions to which you need answers. If the owner isn't likely to tell you, who is? A chatty neighbor! Cultivate conversation, and listen; your mission is to absorb. But keep your own details confidential; you can't be certain what you say won't get back to the seller. And bear in mind, you could be talking to your future neighbor.

Some people find it difficult to knock on a stranger's door. Others don't know what they should say. It's much easier when you have prepared your opening remarks. First, smile! It gets the connection off to a good start. Then, try a simple introduction:

> *Hi, my name is Chris Smith. I'm thinking of buying the home across the road. I'm new to the area so I thought I'd ask your views on the neighborhood. You know, what's nice about living here and what you'd like to see change. Would you recommend the area?*

Get down to specifics rather than allowing an unfocused conversation. You know the questions you want answered, make sure you ask them. And be prepared to learn things you hadn't anticipated. When you've established rapport, say that you hope to meet later with the owner and add a comment like this:

> *I guess you know the owner. You've been neighbors for a while?*

You're trying to learn critical relevant details. This informal approach will usually succeed provided you focus on key questions. Previous to this you'll have explored the neighborhood and have a good feel for the wider area. And you'll have your earlier research to call on.

Tip: Particularly when buying from a private seller, leave your best clothes and fancy car at home. Appear as ordinary as possible whether talking with neighbors or the seller. People can develop a stubbornness on price when the prospective buyer looks like a *money person*. This applies whether you are spending $90,000 or $900,000.

A Strange Story of Perception and Legitimacy

Before we look at how you might manage a face-to-face meeting with a private seller, let me remind you that your task will be to shape that person's perceptions. You'll do that by various actions, some overt, others subtle, some verbal, others visual. All strategic. Your aim will be to communicate messages and impressions that lead the seller to think in a specific way.

I'll break here to tell you a remarkable story about the power of perception. This true story is not about real estate but it's an ideal introduction to the following sections on using tactics effectively.

One of my best friends in college was an eccentric character, Peter G, who came from a wealthy Dublin family. His field was psychology, but he was no typical student. Peter had become consumed with devising his own practical experiments and recording the evidence and proofs these delivered. Academic theories, he argued, were for those afraid of *real-world* testing. Freud had his place, of course, but he was fascinated with Pavlov and Skinner and the ways in which people's behavior can be programmed. Over the often intriguing few years I knew Peter, he spent most of his time working on these experiments. He learned his most valuable lessons, he claimed, not in the classroom but in the 'world laboratory'.

One warm August day, sitting in an outdoor cafe in Manhattan, he and I became engaged in a conversation about perception, as we often did. A short while later we were joined by three strangers, two girls and a guy who had been listening in on our animated exchanges. All three were students at a New England university and were intrigued with what we were saying. They joined us and the five-way debate went on.

At one point, Peter claimed that by using his knowledge of how humans react unconsciously to different signals, he could program hard-to-believe outcomes. In defense of his assertion, he accepted a glib challenge put to him by our new friends. Yes, he could sleep in New York City for an entire week, at a top hotel each night, with just $20 spending money. The other three scoffed. But I knew Peter well. And I knew something about psychology and conditioning.

This was not an attempt to cheat the hotels. It was an odd but genuine experiment in psychology, which no amount of theory could prove, that would be tried out in the real world.

The only possessions Peter would have, we all agreed, were the following:

- A set of casual clothes (jeans, sneakers, shirt, etc.)
- His best business suit, white shirt, tie, dark shoes, and a short bowler hat (the type you might see on an aristocratic banker, which we had to find)
- His diamond tie pin, gold watch and pen, and a conservative looking briefcase
- A pair of dark-rimmed spectacles (borrowed)
- A large Bank of New York envelope with a fictitious name, Walter C. L. Sykes, typed on it.

That was it. Everything else he needed would come from within, or so he said.

On the day the experiment began, our friends and I gathered casually in the lobby of the hotel, close enough to see that Peter adhered to the rules, and to watch him apply his theories on the power of legitimacy, perception, and persuasion.

Peter arrived on schedule. His chin was slightly high, his walk brisk and deliberate, and his gaze never left the direction in which he was heading. Although only 23 (and prematurely balding), he looked as impressive and important as any corporate executive the hotel regularly accommodated. A distinctive aura surrounded him, his demeanor exuded confidence, superiority, his shoes even squeaked on the marble floor, and he carried an aloof, slightly displeased look in his face. As he reached the desk he was far from the picture of a relaxed hotel guest.

The female desk clerk greeted him with: *Good morning, Sir.* That's when the fun started. To the best of my memory, here is the essence of what happened next.

Peter (in a detached, perplexed tone):
Hmmm, I wish it was. I'm Walter Craig Sykes. If you wouldn't mind, I need the quietest single room you have. I don't wish to be above the fifth floor and my preference is for the rear of the house.

Clerk:
Certainly, sir. If you'll just fill in some details here. May I see some identifi-
cation, your driver's license?

Peter had no license, of course, not on this adventure. He ignored the clerk's request, pulled his gold pen from his inside pocket, and made like he was about to write
on the card. But then he stalled, reached up, removed his bowler hat, and placed it on
the counter between himself and the clerk. And with a deep sigh he removed his
(borrowed) spectacles and rubbed his eyes. A grimace stretched across his face. He
looked directly at the clerk, and for a moment, said nothing. Then this followed:

Peter:
What an airline! It's not enough that they lose my case and overnight bag
but they leave me with these darn driving spectacles.

He handed his gold pen to the clerk:
Do this for me, please. The lines are fuzzy. I'll be staying two nights, possi-
bly longer.

The desk clerk did as instructed, writing the information Peter dictated. He
then removed his gold watch, checked the time with the clerk, and re-set it. He
reached for his bowler, picked his banker's briefcase from the floor, and said this:

Peter:
My bags should arrive within the hour from the airport. Have them sent to
my room immediately. If I'm at dinner please ensure my overnight bag is
placed in your safe right away and send someone to inform me. I'll be in
your mezzanine restaurant. What room am I in?

The clerk did nothing for a moment, then she motioned to the porter, to whom
Peter presented his briefcase and bowler hat. As they marched to the elevator I know
Peter was chuckling inside. But he certainly didn't show that. It was a mighty perfor-
mance.

Peter slept well that night and did the same the following night in an equally
good hotel. We all agreed there was nothing left to prove, so we called off the
experiment. At the two check-ins his performance altered only slightly to fit the
circumstances. Both times he acted the part, he talked the part, and he looked the
part. No one he dealt with doubted the character he presented.

You might be wondering why he wanted the Bank of New York envelope. This
was a fall back, he said, in case he needed the smallest piece of 'proof' that he was
who he said he was, Walter C. L. Sykes. In neither case did he show it.

And what about the twenty dollars? Tips. He conspicuously placed money in
the porter's hand before presenting him with his hat and case (ironically, as a
student, Peter was usually broke). Both hotel bills were later paid by Peter's father,
who viewed the experiment as fascinatingly as we did and considered it a valuable
contribution to his son's education.

Why do I tell you a story like this in a book on how to buy your next home? Primarily to illustrate how human perception can be influenced when you learn how to program the responses you desire. You influence people's perceptions by sending the right messages. Some messages are verbal, most are *unspoken*. With Peter, his clothing, demeanor, personality, body language, speech, and assurance all worked together to give him credibility and, consequently, the power to shape how the hotel staff thought and behaved. He programmed their thinking without them being aware of it.

He had the 'power of legitimacy' because he looked and sounded and acted legitimate. To the hotel staff, he was an important business executive, upset, mildly cantankerous, demanding and quite stressed by the events to which he alluded. His demeanor demanded superior service. In both cases that's what he was given. Without money, without identification, without a credit card or check book, without a job even, or a business card.

You don't have to become a Peter to get the best deal on your next home. Your task is more simple. Once you have the basic know-how (this book gives it to you), all you need add is the key ingredient that wins negotiations, the courage to put it into practice. You have that, too. Channel it correctly and you'll achieve what others cannot.

Let us now apply some of this to dealing face-to-face with a private seller.

Face to Face with the Owner

Let's assume you are meeting with the owner, Mr Clinton, at his home and are about to make your first inspection. Keep in mind that it makes no sense to talk money at this early stage, particularly if you are already very keen on the home. If the owner goes on about how fair he is being with his price, don't agree or discuss, just nod and move on to something else. Talk of money will come.

After you've made a thorough inspection, then ask the price, *even when you already know it*. Ask the question in such a way that it seems part of your list of routine questions and doesn't indicate particular interest on your part:

- What age is the home?
- What type of tree is that growing in the back yard?
- How far is it to the nearest convenience store?
- What property taxes do you pay?
- What schools are close by?
- What is the asking price?
- Where does the public transportation pick up?
- How long have you lived here?

Also, consider making at least one or two notes of the owner's answers in your notebook, and mention that you always do this.

If you like what you see and hear, wander slowly around, going back over the areas you've already looked at, saying as little as possible without seeming impolite. A cursory acknowledgment here and there is fine but, as we saw before, don't praise or compliment the home. And even though you are inspecting closely, don't show signs at this stage that you might consider making an offer. Nonetheless, ask all the questions you need answered. When an answer is impressive, subdue any feeling of delight or approval. For example, let's say you have asked about the heating system:

Owner:
It's the top model on the market. Solar powered from twin roof panels. Cost me $6,000 just eight months ago. It's under warranty for five years. It's economical, efficient, clean.

Despite being impressed, you are not there to add to the owner's estimation of the value of the home. Instead, switch to an unrelated matter, maybe a slightly negative remark about some aspect of the home, but don't overdo it. Here are a few examples of what I mean:

Buyer:
• *The fencing around the property looks like it's ready to be replaced.*
• *Why did they design the kitchen so small?*
• *I noticed the siding is split in places. Some of it would need to be replaced. Have you had any estimates done?*

You get the idea. You don't want to seem overly critical, but neither do you want to play up the value of the home. Whether you bring them up now or later, make a point to note faults or negatives about any home you might buy. Apart from their potential strategic value when the negotiation proper begins, you can point out these 'faults' any time the owner over-states the quality of the home.

If your question about the heating system (or any aspect) brings a less than glowing response, you do the opposite. Here's what I mean:

Owner:
It's the original oil burner we put in when we built the home twenty-two years ago. We've had it checked and cleaned regularly. It works fine.

Some ways you might respond:

Buyer:
• *The whole system might have to be replaced soon. Have you had any cost estimates on having a new one installed? It's very expensive.*
• *I find the older systems, oil or gas, get less reliable and more and more expensive. The new systems are much better but they cost an arm and a leg. It's expensive either way.*
• *I always worry about the safety of older systems. The new systems are safer and more economical but they are prohibitively expensive.*

I used the heating system here to illustrate this tactic. The same approach can be applied to plumbing, wiring, fencing, brickwork, chimney, timber, foundations, paint work, windows, landscaping, roof, decor, and so on. Pass quietly over the positive features and focus on those things that will cost you money to replace or repair or upgrade, or that will cause you worry.

Owners with emotional attachment to their home sometimes fret at it being criticized. So, no empty criticism. Whenever possible, base your negative comments on issues that genuinely concern you, even if the concern is minor. You'll be more convincing this way.

However, even more productive than what you say is the amount of time you spend discussing the items that concern you. Let time rather than criticism put the desired impression into the owner's thinking: that you are potentially interested but have reservations. Even when a property is difficult to find fault with, you still have 'negatives' that will work for you, *your* perception of the home: its location, lot size, floor area, floor plan, style, orientation, and so on — things that cannot be 'fixed'. Be careful not to come across like you are criticizing the home, you are just voicing concern over one or two limitations.

The house, you say, or a special feature, is nice, just not quite what you imagined. It looked bigger or brighter online, or newer or different in some other way, and prettier from the outside. The owner cannot refute your opinions, and so has little defense against them. As this proceeds, you are affecting the owner's expectations, though you won't necessarily notice any signs yet.

Do You Know the Owner's Real Reason for Selling?

This is a question you should ask the owner directly, even if you have learned the reason from a neighbor or some other source.

If the owner's answer corresponds with what you have learned, you probably need investigate no further, unless something arouses your suspicion. Stay alert, trust your judgment and intuition, and check out anything that doesn't sound or look right. If you are still not satisfied, probe deeper. A neighbor's account could be gossip. Or, maybe the owner isn't being up front. It's in your interest to find out.

Owners in debt sometimes protect their pride with a made-up reason for selling. If you suspect this, your lawyer may want to take additional steps to ensure you can get possession of the home free and clear, so make sure you mention it.

Knowing the owner's reason for selling might also influence the kind of offer you will make, which we'll see shortly.

How to Respond When the Seller Offers to Reduce the Price

The Attractive Alternatives tactic is adaptable and useful; it can be applied in almost any negotiation. Like all tactics, it must be presented in a sincere-sounding way, never in a way that could be offensive to the owner. This would be counterproductive.

To get the outcome you desire you must be convincing in your application of any tactic. Tactics have no inherent or automatic or magical power. They are just ideas. The power is in *you*. What you achieve comes from how well you apply the tactics you select.

Let's assume you are completing a slow second scrutiny of the Clintons' home. You've conducted two careful inspections, followed my recommendations with regard to your conversations and comments, and got satisfactory answers to all your questions with the exception of a few minor issues.

And then it happens.

The Clintons make you a reduced-price eyeball-to-eyeball offer. You're super interested! Excited! What should you do? What should you say? How should you react?

Most unprepared buyers in this and similar situations react impulsively, and wrongly. Because they lack a basic strategy and tactics.

Here's one thing you *don't* do. You don't accept the offer. In fact, you do *nothing* quickly, regardless of how you are feeling. There is some chance, a small one, that you will later accept this offer. Not now! But neither is a blunt rejection appropriate. So, if you are not accepting and not rejecting, what are you doing?

In the quiet moments following the Clintons' offer, and in light of what has gone before, consider your most appropriate response. This will usually be obvious from the exchanges you've been having with them up to this point. Stay in pause mode a few seconds; this will be noticed by the sellers. Your aim is to avoid implying or hinting that this is a price you are willing to pay (had you decided to use the Stall and Jolt tactic, you'd be responding differently — more on this shortly).

Here's how you might respond using one or more tactics:

- You remind the Clintons of another home you are very keen on (Attractive Alternative) and that you find it hard to choose.
- You tell them, or remind them, that your partner (Third Party) likes both homes but prefers the other one (you can use this even after you've made an unsuccessful offer on the Clintons' home).
- You respond that even at their new reduced price you believe their home is still priced higher than comparable homes you've seen (Comparative Value).
- You inform them, or remind them, that you have overstepped your budget with the 'fair value' offer you have *already* made for their home (No More Money).

Or choose another tactic, or combine two or more tactics that dovetail into the discussion you've been having with the Clintons.

No matter what comes into your head, even (especially) if you feel it's a bargain, you must not jump at their offer. But don't attack it either. Just pause. Get your head clear, take a few deep breaths, then respond in a courteous tone that communicates non-acceptance or, at least, serious reluctance or doubt.

As I said, you have choices, you are not stuck for options. Your most appropriate response will come from the context of the situation, from the conversation you've been having with the Clintons. Continue where you left off, and add a tactic you haven't used, if you feel that will help. Convey your understanding of their situation (don't get sloppy) but don't thank them for offering you the home at a reduced price. You are preparing the ground for your next move — closing the deal.

What follows are more ways to apply the potentially powerful tactics introduced in the previous chapter. These can be applied and re-applied at almost any stage in the negotiation, not just to close the deal.

How to Apply the Attractive Alternatives Tactic

In your initial contact with the Clintons you'll have mentioned that at least one other home has captured your interest. On your second contact, mention the home again, commenting on similarities and differences. Try work this into the conversation in a way that sounds natural (examples below), then refer back only occasionally to the other home. It won't go unnoticed. At all costs, avoid making it appear as a ploy, which would make your task harder.

Here's what I mean by making it a natural part of the conversation:

- *We have to rush away, I'm sorry. We've arranged a second inspection on that townhouse and I don't want to keep them waiting.*
- *It's quite a coincidence. Your home is almost identical in layout to the rancher my wife and I will be seeing for a second time tomorrow evening.*
- *Rather than making things easier, finding two homes you like at the same time makes deciding almost impossible. My husband favors one of the other homes we've seen. I'm not sure I agree with him, though.*

Another option is to pick a feature that the Clintons' home does *not* have and incorporate that into your comments. For example:

- *My wife is keen on a bigger home we've looked at a few times, just south of here, but yours is quite big enough for me.*
- *We've seen a couple of homes with a spacious sunroom, which is nice to have; it's a feature my husband really likes. Personally, I think we'd do fine here without one.*
- *We're looking again at a nice townhouse with beautiful big windows. We love how bright it is, but the hallways feel too narrow, and it's a tiny bit smaller than yours.*

Each of these last three comments puts the Clintons' attention on features that are important *to you* but *not* offered by their home. This indirectly diminishes the value of the Clinton home, but you are doing it inoffensively and with subtlety.

By letting it be known that you have attractive alternatives, you are laying the foundation for a successful negotiation.

How to Apply the Stall and Jolt Tactic

I added this phrase to the lexicon of negotiation because it describes simply the two stages of the maneuver and is easy to remember.

Here's the situation: You've been engaged in negotiation with the Clintons; eventually they make a reduced price offer to you of $362,000. You are prepared to buy the home at this figure. But you think $355,000 might be achievable. You are not through negotiating. You'll use the Stall and Jolt tactic.

As we saw earlier, when a reduced price offer is put to you, you pause. But with this tactic, you let your expression and body language suggest that you *are* thinking, assessing, and seriously considering the offer. Your demeanor and averted gaze hint that you might be on the cusp of agreeing. Forget what you learned about eye contact; in negotiation it's often the absence of eye contact that makes things work.

Allow this pause to continue, even if the atmosphere grows tense, as it should. Fifteen seconds will seem like sixty. If you can stretch it further, even better. The tension might compel the owners to interrupt to justify their position, or even improve their offer. Regardless, you react in the same way, a glance of acknowledgment and eyes averted again. This is the stall. Its duration can be stretched well beyond the pausing you use with other tactics. Generally, it will be interpreted as positive by the other side, a prelude to acceptance.

To end it you bring your attention back to the owners. It's time for the jolt. You reject their offer gently but definitely, and you present a new lower offer with a reasoned justification (and possibly a small concession on some non-financial point).

> Buyer:
> *We could be interested in buying your home from you, we like it a lot. But, considering other homes we've seen, one in particular, and the expenses we'd have here, the highest we can give you for your home is $348,000, or possibly slightly more if you can agree one or two inclusions.*

In the Clinton camp the pressure is on. You are probably their only solid prospect right now. And you're in control. Despite this, expect an initial rejection of your figure. But it's very unlikely they'll pull out, in part because you left room for further discussion; you might make a higher offer if one or more conditions can be agreed (what you called 'inclusions').

Still, tread carefully. The trap you can fall into here is acting hastily (excitement can cause your emotions to overtake your intellect). If necessary, say that you'll go over your figures again to see if there is room to cut back on repairs and refurbishing expense. And that you'd like them to include the garden furniture in the agreement. Then open your notebook and start checking and scribbling, looking like you are doing some difficult figuring.

In the following second option, the jolt is less gentle:

Buyer:
I'm sorry. The very best we could do would be $348,000. Why don't you think it over and let us know later tonight or in the morning. We'll definitely buy one of the two homes, yours or the other one, tomorrow or Wednesday at latest. Our financing is guaranteed, so we can go ahead immediately, if we agree.

Rather than stopping bluntly at *The best we could do would be $348,000*, you increase your chance of getting this deal if you sound less urgent, inviting no immediate response from the owner but making clear that any delay creates a risk for them. Plus, your words emphasize that you are bankable and ready to act.

If the Clintons are prepared to compromise further they won't let you leave, or they'll contact you soon after. As already noted, the seller usually has a more urgent need to sell than buyers imagine. Sometimes, that need is desperate. The moment you walk out the door, the sellers' opportunity lessens. Because within the next twelve to twenty-four hours anything could happen to kill your interest in their house. If they are going to make you a better offer this is their moment to act, or face losing you.

You might hear something like this:

Owner:
Listen, we want to be reasonable about this. Can we meet halfway, and we'll agree the garden furniture stays? That would be 362 less 348 equals fourteen, divided by two. We can agree $355,000. But that's our bottom line. You can't ask for better than that.

But you can. You can negotiate for whatever you want. Where you go from here is up to you. If you choose to push it, the strongest tactic now is to motion to leave. That's the last thing the owners want. They're getting used to having you around; for a while they've been on the brink of a sale.

This scenario is hypothetical; in the real world things don't happen this quickly. Nonetheless, it is typical of a big percentage of transactions when there's a smart buyer involved, one who knows how to negotiate.

How to Apply the Comparative Value Tactic

Let's stick with the same example. The Clintons have just reduced their price to $362,000 and are waiting for an answer.

You decide to use the Comparative Value tactic:

Buyer:

Your home is our first choice. Our problem is that two other homes we like compare very favorably with yours. To me they seem to offer us more, with virtually no repairs or expense in either. But we'd like to see first if we can buy your home. To us, $348,000 is a fair price. We're willing to pay you that, and our financing is 100%. But that's our limit.

As before, immediate rejection of your offer shouldn't frighten you. In negotiation, No rarely means No! It's often an instinctive reaction. But just as often it's a calculated response by the owner to press you to make a higher offer. Whichever you suspect, hold your ground. As the negotiation continues, the risk of losing you and the sale looms larger in the owners' thinking.

Then, proceed as before. You say you are willing to go over your figures. You consult your notebook, a tactical exercise. It is important for you to understand the reason for this 'refiguring'. When you increase an offer, your power will depend to a large extent on the justification you present for doing so. The exception is when a small increase is likely to close the deal. Otherwise, making a higher offer without a justifiable reason (see examples below) damages the impression you've tried to build in the mind of the seller; it marks you as naive and makes you vulnerable to over-paying.

Here are some useful justifications for increasing your offer:

- Openly re-figuring your costs, as we've seen here, to squeeze the expenses you will incur and save dollars (updating, repairs, improvements, neglected maintenance, fencing, landscaping, etc)
- Saying you will phone your bank (spouse, attorney, parents, etc) to see if you can borrow additional funds. Best used with the No More Money tactic to close a deal.
- Having the owner agree to pay for repairs, replacements, landscaping, etc.
- Having the owner agree to include 'extras' in the sale. For example, cabinets and interior furniture, extra appliances, motor mower, outdoor settings, chandelier, etc.
- Saying you'll sell an asset or cash-in an investment to free up additional dollars to add to your offer. This works best to close a deal at the end of the negotiation, when you have 'spent your budget'.
- Getting the owner to agree to pay a larger part of the closing costs.
- Saying you are prepared to spend a little more than you believe the home is worth because your spouse thinks it is worth 'one last try'.

Rely on your own feel for the situation in deciding which of these (or others) is appropriate. If you claim you believe your offer reflects what the home is worth (a 'fair market value' argument), it would be inappropriate to base a higher offer solely on being able to free up more money. You must indicate that a higher offer would mean you'll be paying above the value of the home. Your position should be definite: either your offer is based: 1) on what you believe what the home is worth, or 2) on the fact that your budget is spent, and you have no more money. One of these positions must explain your offer. Otherwise you risk not being believed.

Nevertheless, a spouse's preference for the home in question is a legitimate basis for making an offer above what *you* personally believe the property is worth. This is a variation on the Third Party tactic and can be quite effective.

It is nearly always better to claim your offer is based on what *you believe* is the fair market value of the property. Saying that your offer is based on the amount you have to spend (no more money) is rarely as persuasive, though it is entirely appropriate at the *end* of a negotiation, as we covered earlier.

One of the best demonstrations I've seen of this notebook 'refiguring' tactic occurred when my then fiancee and I went shopping for our wedding rings. I asked the clerk what discount I could expect as we were buying not one but two expensive rings. After checking with his boss he told me he'd allow 12.5% discount on the less expensive ring, no discount on the other. I rejected that, so off he went and soon brought back a marginally better deal, which I also rejected. This happened a third time. As you'd expect, I was working to a strategy. When we declined his third offer, we stood up, thanked him, and said we'd think about it.

My hand was pulling open the door when the owner stopped us (a man we had not seen before); he asked us to come back, said he'd look after us himself, and promised he'd 'work something out'.

To cut to the chase, he made us two slightly better offers, both of which I rejected. He arrived at each new reduced price after copious refiguring on a yellow legal pad (which he never let us even glimpse) and a calculator. His final price, the one we accepted, took him a solid five minutes of mathematics and muttering to 'work out'. We got a deal few others did, much better even than I anticipated.

He was a very good tactician and ran two high-profile stores. What he *never* realized was that he was dealing with a buyer who knew how to negotiate.

That's *your* big advantage; this is a *quiet* power that should never be revealed to the other side after you have forged a good deal. Egotism has no place in negotiation of this sort.

Incidentally, this jewelry store owner confided, just before making us the offer we accepted, that he was going to 'bend the rules' to find a way to get us an 'exceptional price'. That was a ploy, of course (and a smart seller tactic) put to good use by an astute businessman. Did he make a profit in the end? He certainly did, or he wouldn't have made the deal. Both sides did well!

So far, we've seen the Attractive Alternatives, the Stall and Jolt and the Comparative Value tactics. How else might you say no to a reduced price offer from a private seller or salesperson? The next one is a classic.

How to Apply the Third Party Tactic

Look at the statements below; they all cite a third party who seems to be guiding the decision.

- My *bank manager* won't go for that.
- I understand, but my *wife* has her eye on something else.
- My *lawyer* isn't comfortable with that arrangement.
- Personally, I'd like to, but my *husband* just doesn't see it that way.
- My *kids* prefer to be close to the beach; I can't disappoint them.
- I talked to my *accountant;* he feels I should hold off on this.
- I would, but the *architect* says we'd need to spend $10,000 here.
- The *roofer* is adamant there's less than two years left in the roof.

Clearly, unless this third party is satisfied a deal is unlikely. The Third Party tactic is simple and comfortable. And it works. Like all tactics it requires good judgment in its application. It's also one of the most difficult tactics for the seller to refute or navigate around. One reason is because the third party is often absent or not real. And even when real, he or she may be an unchallengeable *expert* — architect, lawyer, banker, spouse, roofer. It's a powerful tactic also because when the third party is remote from the negotiation the seller has no opportunity to argue face to face.

By distancing yourself from the final decision (as the seller perceives it, the third party will control the decision), you reduce competition between you and the other side. This allows you to offer the seller more understanding, when appropriate, without necessarily agreeing on viewpoint or price. These types of situations can also cause sellers to tell you things they would not have done had it been a head-to-head negotiation.

However, be careful here not to create a too-friendly connection with the seller. Your behavior should not differ from that which I've described throughout this book. The Third Party tactic is simply that, a tactic you may choose in response to the seller making you a reduced-price offer (or at other points in the negotiation).

Comfortable as the Third Party tactic is, it still requires you to research and prepare as you would for any negotiation. It's effectiveness stems in part from slowing the momentum while fostering a less competitive association with the seller. Since the seller usually can't talk directly to a remote third party, you move closer to the role of go-between. You can agree to discuss the seller's perspective with the third party, but if the third party is not keen on the price, or the neighborhood, or the outstanding repairs, or the lack of landscaping, or the kitchen, the answer is unlikely to be acceptance of the seller's current offer, regardless of *your* opinion.

A spouse or partner is a useful third party. A parent or son or daughter can also fill the role effectively, as can your plumber, architect, lender or attorney. If the third party is a real person (your spouse, for example), try to arrange for that person to take a quiet, *secondary role* in the discussions and negotiation, particularly as a deal gets closer. The best way is to have your spouse (or other third party) stay out of the negotiation exchanges with the seller. As noted earlier, it's difficult for the seller to sell his position, or the value of the home, to someone who is remote either physically or in engagement level.

Generally, the more time a seller invests in negotiating with you (even prior to the negotiation proper), the better chance you have of achieving a good outcome.

Still, you do need to recognize the best moment to introduce the Third Party tactic. This will come from your feel for the situation. Usually, it's best during the offer-counter-offer stage. Up to then, everything proceeds in line with the strategy you adopted from first contact, that of an astute, informed homebuyer. No tactic requires you to change this demeanor.

When you introduce this or any other tactic into the price negotiation, allow that tactic (or combined tactics) to reflect your position. For example, it's OK to mention the third party (professional home inspector, architect, roofer, attorney) at any stage in your discussions but don't introduce the third party's opinion until you are in the offer stage, when it will support the figure you offer or the terms you look for.

Let's return now to our example and apply the Third Party tactic. You are interested in the Clintons' home and are making a close inspection. You had your sister-in-law, an architect, inspect the home on your behalf. She told you that the property is in reasonable condition but requires quite a lot of updating, repairs and outstanding maintenance:

Owner:
Look, if you're seriously interested in the home we're willing to take $362,000 for it.

You know that the owners are feeling the tension. They want a sale. Today, if possible. They want to wrap things up and move on, and right now you are probably their only serious prospect (seldom are sellers so lucky as to have two or more buyers competing for their home):

Buyer:
We do like your house. I'm taken with the flower garden out back. But my husband seems certain we can get a roomier house closer to the shore for less money. He likes a condo we've already seen that's quite similar to yours but less expensive. I know he prefers yours but he's not convinced about the price. We are willing to pay $348,000, and our finance is in place and ready to go.

Then remain silent, even if the pressure inside you spikes up. The owners are feeling it too. Let this push them to respond first. Whether it takes five seconds or twenty-five, it is decidedly to your benefit that the owners speak next.

Note: The comment about liking the flower garden adds nothing to the strength to the seller's position, but it carries a subtle degree of endearment, which can pay dividends (as I said earlier, we are complex psychological beings).

Here's another way to use the Third Party tactic:

Buyer:
I appreciate you are keen to sell. And we both would like to buy your home. But our concern is the expense for the work we'd have to do here. The architect said allow $10,000. We didn't count on that. We're willing to pay $348,000. If we can agree on that, we'll buy it. As you know, our finance is approved, we can move ahead right away.

Your position is clear. You are ready to buy, but not at the seller's reduced price of $362,000. And, as always, when you put your position to the seller like this — shut up!

How to Apply the No More Money Tactic

Don't be deceived by the apparent simplicity of this tactic. It's powerful for closing deals. However, when applied ineffectively or at the wrong stage in a negotiation it can do more harm than good.

Almost never should this tactic be used alone. It is persuasive only when used in combination with another tactic. And, equally important, no matter what combination of tactics you use, No More Money should be one of the two final tactics introduced into the negotiation (the Walk Away tactic, when used, will be final). The No More Money tactic is always most useful when you are nearing your spending limit (or the limit you have set for a particular property) and the gap between you and the seller has reduced. It is rarely effective as a beginning position (your initial offer).

We saw earlier the benefit of creeping with your offers, making a series of small increases. This hints that your budget is tight, maybe close to its limit. The seller starts suspecting he'll soon be flogging a dead horse, that there's no more money to be squeezed out of you. This is the perfect foundation for introducing the No More Money tactic.

But first, in every negotiation, you must make clear that you believe your offer is fair, based on your extensive research locally, and reflects this home's value *to you*. You can never claim, not even with the No More Money tactic, that your offer is based *solely* on how much you can spend. I mentioned before that your budget has no direct relationship to the value of a home; the two are distinct entities.

If the seller asks (some will) how you arrived at your offer figure, you say that your 'estimate of fair value' is based on: size, age, condition, style, decor, layout, brightness, lot area, location, local selling prices (value for money) and other such factors.

When you apply the No More Money tactic, the impression you are trying to communicate in your words and behavior is along these lines:

- I'm convinced my offer is fair and reasonable and that the home is not

worth more than I've offered. I'm concerned now because the figure I am prepared to pay is already stretching my budget.
• Even if the house was twice as large and had an ocean view, I simply wouldn't be able to spend more than I've offered, which I believe is entirely in keeping with local property values. I just have no more money.

No need to speak these exact words, but work this message into your verbal exchanges and your behavior (remember, negotiation is a performance). This is what the seller should be hearing and inferring from what you say and do.

Note: Earlier, I explained the importance of keeping your true spending limit confidential whether buying through an agent or from a private seller. If you break this rule you lock into a position from which you cannot escape, you lose the opportunity to claim 'no more money' except at the figure you disclosed. Here's what I mean: If the other side knows you can spend $250,000 (because you told them), you cannot claim 'no more money' at $225,000. They already know you can spend more. Consequently, you have severely limited or eliminated your ability to use No More Money. Take note!

When you apply the No More Money tactic and it appears to have failed, you still have a couple of options, even if the seller has rejected your last offer.

The first option is to appear to accept that you will *not* be buying the home. Act like you are sadly about to conclude the discussion. Thank the sellers, compliment them *lightly* on their home and wish them luck in finding another buyer. Then, make one or more distancing comments such as:

• *It's a pity, because we both like your home. But there are others we like, too. That's how we've got to look at it, I suppose. In one way it makes our choice easier.*
• *Well, I think we both tried our best. That's all we can do with anything in life. Thank you.*
• *Well, thank you. I'm sad that we won't be buying your home. I wish we could have reached agreement. Good luck in finding a buyer. You have a nice home.*

The idea here is to start pulling away from the closeness and hope you built up during the negotiation. To the seller it will feel like everything that was warm is getting cold, not a good feeling. Let this play. Delay as you prepare to leave, but make it seem you are simply having one 'last look', that you are resigned to letting it go. Write your name and phone number on a card and hand it to the seller (even if they already have it). Then pick a few trite questions out of the air; for example: *How did you get the roses to grow so well?* These seem like parting remarks before you leave for good.

Show no sign that you believe a deal might still be possible. You have accepted defeat. Now let the great warrior go to work for you — time.

Your exiting of the negotiation is pressure-filled for the seller. Often it will trigger a concession, sometimes even acceptance of your offer. Because if you leave, the seller faces the uncertainty of a no-buyer situation all over again.

And if no concession emerges, all is still not lost. Take it all the way. Get into your car and drive off. Whatever new offer you might decide to make you can make tomorrow, or the next day. Give the sellers time; they might surprise you. And if not, you can call them with 'an idea'.

A second option is this: As you exit, or after walking back to the home from your car, make a new, slightly higher offer. This tactic needs all the conviction you can muster, along with a credible explanation of where the extra dollars are coming from. Just a few moments ago you claimed persuasively that you had no more money. How do you now avoid being disbelieved?

Well, it could be that while talking in the car your husband reminded you that he is due holiday pay or an annual bonus soon. Or that your tax rebate check is due within the month. This is what I call 'discovered money'. When you 'discover' this extra money you can make it part of your offer. The chief requirement is to be believable.

Another source of discovered money could be borrowing from your family. Just a little, of course, *and only*, you tell the seller, if it will clinch the deal. When you seem to be bending over backwards like this, it endears you to the seller (though not openly) and often pulls a decision in your favor.

Whatever extra money you discover, it must appear understandable why it didn't occur to you earlier. So, make the source credible. A few more examples include withdrawing money from your retirement fund, even if you'll be penalized for doing so; selling the 1966 Mustang you are restoring; borrowing from your kids' college fund; cashing in part of your life insurance policy, etc. Say it once; don't overplay it, don't repeat it, and don't over-explain — these mistakes give you away.

You are doing this, you explain, because you want to be certain before buying the other home that you tried your best, you explored every avenue. And even if it should fail, you'll walk away happy.

The seller might still say no, or possibly put a new deal on the table. How much resistance is still in the seller? You can't be certain; that's what you are now testing. Consider the context and trust your judgment. And remember, the more time you invest here, the higher your odds of getting the best outcome possible.

However the seller reacts to your discovered-money offer, you can again use the Walk Away tactic — and mean it. You'll walk away and forget the entire deal, you say, if your new improved offer can't buy the home. If it comes to this, and you have to follow through, there's nothing but pride stopping you from adding another small amount to your offer later, as long as a deal seems within reach and still makes sense.

At this endgame point, how much you add to your offer will depend on the price of the home and how much discovered money you have already added. As a guideline only, an extra $2,000 to $5,000 might work on a $250,000 to $500,000 property. On an $80,000 to $200,000 property, $500 to $2,000 might be a more appropriate add-on to your 'final' offer. It's difficult to put rules on this; the context, the relationship, and the history of the negotiation will tell you. If in doubt, err on the low side. There's no law that says you can't increase a $300,000 offer by $1,000 or $2,000 to edge it over the line.

Caution: Before we move on, I'll repeat this caution. You cannot use the No More Money tactic as the basis for your initial offer. Your initial offer must be presented as representing what you believe the home is worth. Only later in the negotiation do you get an opportunity to use No More Money, and after that, No More Money combined with your discovered dollars. And after that, perhaps a few more discovered dollars. And even then, if necessary, consider any 'sweetener' that might bring the deal together or confirm it is out of reach.

This powerful tactic requires more skill in application than most others. That skill is largely in your timing and performance, particularly in how credible you can come across.

Walking Away — The Ultimate Tactic

We've already seen how acting like you are about to terminate the negotiation is best used in combination with other tactics. The fear that you will walk away is always in the seller's mind. The more genuine, ready-to-buy and interested you appear, the greater that fear, particularly as the gap between your positions narrows.

Sellers must persist until they find a buyer; you can walk away from their home but they cannot. Still, the Walk Away tactic is one you must use *carefully* and with *subtlety* and *courtesy*. Never present it as an ultimatum, but as an inevitable consequence of your inability to reach agreement, an unfortunate end. But one you can live with.

When applied like this it exerts maximum leverage and quite often leads to concession and agreement, especially when there has been an investment of time and the seller accepts you as reasonable and genuine. Even stubborn sellers are tempted to relent at the prospect of a qualified buyer walking away.

As you make your exit, remember that agreement and concessions come late in a negotiation, very often after the deadline has passed or the opportunity seems dead.

So, when the seller makes no attempt to stop you, follow through with your exit. You might get a call later with the concession you wanted, or something close. That's why you invite the seller to call you if he reconsiders. However, if that doesn't happen, you can, as we saw earlier, discover extra dollars, which gives you reason to resume negotiation. Don't allow pride to stop you doing this; a good deal is long term and worth a lot more than a minor slight to your ego.

It is almost always best to conduct this type of negotiation in person rather than by phone or online video. This usually means going back to the home multiple times. *Do it!* You'll increase your chance of getting the best deal.

Keep in mind also that every day the home is on the market the seller faces uncertainty. The worries are obvious: maybe the home will prove hard to sell, maybe it will languish on the market for months, how many of the buyers coming by are genuine, what's the security risk, is the asking price too high, and so on. All this ends the day the house sells, all the hassle turns to hard cash, life and plans can go ahead. Despite the seller's apparent confidence, these factors are always working for you.

Why do I emphasize these homebuyer advantages so strongly? Because, with few exceptions, homebuyers believe the opposite is true, that the advantages lie with the seller. This is seldom the case. Stop for a moment and consider what sellers need. They need to sell to move ahead with their life plans; they need money (yours); they have a deadline of some kind pressing them; they need time for their other interests; they need to get back to normal, and so on. In fact, sellers have more riding on getting a sale and less riding on the price. Accepting less than expected won't abort their plans, whereas holding out too long *could* be detrimental to their hopes and goals.

For these and other reasons, sellers do *not* want to see a genuine buyer walk away from the negotiation. Taking a price cut is often the best solution, better than continuing to deal each day with the terrible uncertainty of it all.

Finally, here's an example of how you might present the Walk Away tactic:

Buyer:
My husband and I both really like your home, you've kept it very well. We'd like to buy it from you, as you know. It's our first choice. It's just that the price doesn't compare well with other homes we can buy. Now it looks like we've gone as far as we can both go. All we can do now is say thank you and wish you well. You have our number if you decide to reconsider. We hope to buy this week.

Remember, find your own words. It isn't necessary with any of these tactics to use my words. Just be clear on the impression you need to communicate.

How to Answer the Question: 'How Much Would You Be Prepared to Offer?'

Often, a seller will respond to the buyer's rejection of his asking price (in this new example $228,000) with: *How much would you be prepared to offer?* Here we'll apply the Third Party, Comparative Value, and Attractive Alternative tactics.

You might continue like this:

Buyer:
To be honest, we hadn't planned on making an offer for your home. I'm sure, though, that I could not convince my wife to pay more than what we

can buy the other home for, it's very similar. They said they'll accept
$196,500. I do prefer yours though.

Once again, *don't* add anything once you've given your response. The owner might dismiss your figure (even though you have *not* made a formal offer). This doesn't necessarily mean rejection, only that the negotiation is under way. If the seller persists that the house is definitely worth more than the figure you mentioned, put on a show of mild disappointment, but empathize with his situation.

Buyer:
I know it isn't easy to sell your own home. You have to be really very care-
ful. It is a fact, though, there are quite a number of attractive homes
available around the price I mentioned. But my preference is for yours,
there are some little things I like better here.
Then, later:

Buyer:
I'll talk to my wife before we decide. Whichever home works out, we're
ready to buy right now. But as I said, I can't see her being willing to pay
more here than we can get the other home for, $196,500. I'd be fine with
either, though she knows I prefer yours.

You've not only re-stated your figure, you've injected an element of doubt into the matter. Maybe you'd be able to get your spouse to reconsider. But maybe not. Yet you've established that you're a serious, interested buyer, ready to act.

There's a subtle but powerful tactic in what you said that is overlooked even by experienced negotiators. You put you and the seller on one side (your preference is for *his* home) and your spouse on the other. It's called *alignment* by the pros. You then strengthened this by repeating your preference; to the seller the job appears fifty percent done. This will keep alive the seller's hope that an agreement can be reached, despite your rejection of his asking price of $228,000.

Your position is now stronger. You know you are unlikely to get this home for $196,500, but you've left the next move to the seller. Expect a concession, or a suggestion of one.

Before that, you're likely to hear a recitation of the virtues of his property. And then maybe a number of statements like: *I couldn't possibly accept $196,500. That's just too low.*

If the seller makes no mention of a compromise, return to your preference for his home over the one your spouse favors, and remind him that you'll buy imme-diately once you decide. Make clear that your spouse's leaning in favor of the other home is based solely on value for money, and that, all things being equal, she *wouldn't hesitate* to buy his home. The phrase *wouldn't hesitate* is an important language key in persuasion. It makes a sale seem certain and tantalizingly close. Also, repeat that your financing is *100% guaranteed.*

But what if a seller continues to give no hint that he is willing to compromise and seems unperturbed by your opinion of value? Let's assume here that you've stretched out the discussion on how his property compares with others, not least the fact that it is overpriced. You've also discussed anticipated expenses a new owner would incur and played down the positives, being careful not to offend the seller regarding overdue maintenance and the inevitability of aging in all buildings. But still you've seen no sign of flexibility.

What options do you have left?

You have failed, so far, to alter the seller's position. So your task continues, to persuade him to accept a different reality — yours, the reality of a lower price but a definite no-risk sale, to a buyer who will act immediately if the deal is right, a buyer he could lose within minutes.

As you proceed along these lines, the statements you made earlier about the other house take on greater significance. And because you referred to this attractive alternative *before* you declared your interest in the seller's home, it doesn't seem like a spur-of-the-moment ploy. From here you move into repeating the offer, which might start with you saying you are willing to put your offer of $196,500 on paper, to make it a formal offer (which always feels more real to sellers than a verbal offer and encourages more serious engagement).

Reminder: Almost without exception, sellers price their homes higher than they are willing to accept. And while most are flexible, some are stubborn, believing that it is not in their interest to volunteer a price reduction. You are forced then to 'win' the concession. You accomplish this through negotiation, the use of tactics, tactical questions, probing statements and actions that influence and alter the seller's thinking. Below are additional suggestions you can use to your benefit.

How to Use a Probing Statement Instead of Making an Offer

Let's assume the seller hasn't yet offered to reduce the asking price of $228,000. A probing statement by you pushes aside a lot of the posturing sellers go through before revealing their flexibility. Here's an example you might try:

Buyer:
Your home is not very different from another home we're considering. But your asking price is higher. In fact, a few we've seen are quite similar and the one we like a lot, along with yours, is also bigger. They'll accept $196,500.

Whether the seller responds immediately or not, add part two of this probing statement:

Buyer:
We hope to buy something immediately, today or tomorrow if we can. If I can get my husband to make you an offer I know it would be at the same

price as the other home, $196,500.

This is an effective probing statement because it forces the seller to respond in a way that will reveal his or her current flexibility. Listen long if you have to but don't help or agree with the seller's point of view. The more the seller talks, the more likely he is to re-think the home's value in light of your probing statement. This shift might not be explicit, but detectable in the tone of what's said. At this point, apply whatever tactic you deem best, while maintaining a cordial relationship.

Note that in your probing statements above you've made *no offer*. Not even a verbal one. So there's nothing formally to accept or reject. Nonetheless, the seller feels compelled to respond. As you wait for the reaction, avoid eye contact. For reasons that have to do with psychology, not generally well understood, direct eye contact in a situation like this usually works *against* you, as I noted earlier, because it can provoke a seller into a stronger defense. What you have presented here is not a challenge or an ultimatum, and nothing you do should hint at such.

The impression a probing statement communicates must be that it is part of a pragmatic discussion. In even mildly adversarial engagements, face-to-face positions and direct eye contact signal a challenge. Here, that would be counter-productive, possibly even putting progress out of reach.

Therefore, when using a probing statement, sound open, genuine, and factual. The last thing you need is a contest of wills. Negotiating from a superior stance, *or one perceived that way by the other side*, rarely leads to the best deal.

Using a probing statement effectively is like any other aspect of negotiation, it requires judgment and a convincing performance. Which also means adjusting to the personality (attitude, temperament, sociability, communication style) of the seller, a life skill you already possess.

When you have made your probing statement explaining your feelings about value for money and your potential interest in the property, start drifting toward the exit. Do this even as the seller is responding. If you get the slightest hint of flexibility, slow up and allow yourself to be sidetracked by a feature of the home, the brickwork fireplace or built-in bookshelf, for example.

Your calmness and avoidance of eye contact communicates your probing statement as just that, a comment, not a disguised offer for which you stand waiting for an answer. Your hope is that your probing statement will throw light on the seller's resolve, and on how badly he wants or needs a sale. Whatever response you get, continue the discussion without showing any stronger interest in the home.

The seller has just two options in responding: 1) address specifically what you have said, or 2) divert to an unrelated matter. Either way, what you learn will guide how to proceed.

Naturally, the point will come when you tell the seller directly how much you are willing to pay. This won't be a probing statement, but a verbal offer to which the seller will have to respond.

Now, let's clarify a common question about 'the market'.

Buyers' Market or Sellers' Market?

In negotiation programs, one question I frequently hear concerns the cycles and trends that occur in all markets. The terms mentioned are *buyers' market* and *sellers' market*, and the usual question is when can you negotiate and when not.

The simple answer, and the correct one, is that you can *always* negotiate. Of course, common sense plays a part in *how* you negotiate. You already know that you can negotiate harder when there are few buyers and many sellers, when homes are not selling well. This is a buyers' market. Sellers find it difficult to turn their homes into cash. Consequently, prices tend to be softer. Sellers who remain rigid find it hard to sell. And homebuyers who can negotiate can expect greater success.

A sellers market is just the opposite. This is when there's an abundance of buyers and a shortage of homes for sale in a particular area. A 'hot' market like this generates competition among buyers, causing homes to sell faster and pushing prices higher. If you are buying in a seller's market, inspect properties as soon as they come available and let sellers know right away that you have loan approval.

Most of the time, residential property markets are at neither extreme. Demand for homes isn't so low that properties languish, nor so high that buyers rush to purchase. Demand fluctuates between being slightly in favor of sellers to slightly in favor of buyers, or, more often, varies between areas.

Homebuyers often fail to appreciate that in every type of market a private situation lies behind each home for sale. This includes anxious, motivated, impatient, flexible, frustrated and even desperate sellers. *At any time,* a good negotiation strategy can save you thousands of dollars. The smart buyer will always have relevant facts and data; stay alert for signs of a seller's true position and needs; consult nearby neighbors to discover problems and potential advantages; and be willing to use the basic negotiation tactics this book teaches.

It is important never to let the opinions of real estate salespeople, or family or friends, dissuade you from negotiating. As a smart buyer, your opportunity to save hard-earned cash is always better than those who don't know how to negotiate or choose not to. Success in negotiation depends much *less* on external factors like market conditions and far more on your willingness to apply the simple tactics explained here. Have faith in them. They work!

Professional Home Inspections

Before moving on, keep in mind that no home should be purchased without a professional home inspection. Before you make an offer it might be sufficient to have a suitably qualified person do a preliminary check of the property for obvious problems that would eliminate it from consideration — structural or foundation issues, infestations, fire damage, etc.

However, your offer should always include a contingency clause stipulating that the purchase is subject to a professional home inspection being satisfactory to you. This is one more thing to discuss with your attorney before you start looking at homes.

Expect to pay $350-$450 for a typical full home inspection (varies with property size, etc). Two well regarded national services you might consider are HouseMaster of America and Pillar to Post. Alternatively, get a referral from American Society of Home Inspectors or International Association of Certified Home Inspectors. Contact details for all are listed in the ToolBox/Resources section at the back of this book. Or, you may know of a local professional service that will do an equally thorough job. Whichever option you choose, look for a comprehensive written report. The services mentioned here provide inspections covering numerous features and systems inside and outside the home; plus, they can often suggest solutions to problems and approximate repair costs.

You should discuss with the inspector the need for additional testing for radon, lead paint, indoor air quality, carbon monoxide, asbestos, mold, furnace, chimney, pests, swimming pool, well, septic tank, and so on. These may not be included in a basic service, and may even require specialist testers. Have this discussion before the inspection begins. An Exclusive Buyer Agent will be able to offer advice and provide appropriate references when needed.

Should You Buy a Flipped Home?

Just a brief caution about buying a 'flipped' home. Flipping is the practice of buying a home, doing it up, and selling it within a year, often within months.

There is nothing inherently wrong with buying a renovated or 'flipped' home. It often makes good sense, but not without a full guarantee that all the required work has been done to bring the home up to code, most importantly in relation to the mechanical, electrical and structural elements.

Legitimate renovators and 'fixer-uppers' have long been part of real estate and typically provide a valuable service. In recent times, however, the word 'flipping' has taken on a negative connotation due to a percentage of home flippers covering over serious problems rather than fixing them, including water and pest damage, and otherwise not complying with regulations.

Before the crash, flipping was very big business. Now it is making a comeback. In 2016 almost 200,000 homes were flipped in the US, with a median sale price of just under $190,000, according to ATTOM Data Solutions.

Some classic nightmare cases have emerged of new owners discovering (often months after buying) that their 'perfect' home lacked mandatory construction permits and had numerous other violations. For buyers in that predicament it is usually too late to walk away, and bringing the home up to code can be extremely expensive.

Once again it's a case of *caveat emptor*, let the buyer beware. Your best defense is to get timely advice from your lawyer on how to make sure the flipper has complied with all required licenses and inspections and has a certificate of occupancy, then base your decision on a full professional home inspection report.

Exclusive Buyer Agents possess 'on the ground' knowledge and can guide you on the practical considerations involved in buying a renovated or flipped property. And that's exactly where we are going now, to take a closer look at EBAs and the many ways they can help you make a safe purchase at the lowest price and on the best terms.

KEY POINTS TO REMEMBER

- Neighbors close to a home you are interested in will usually be a good source of information about the home and the area. Knock on doors, introduce yourself, and ask.
- Salespeople and private sellers form impressions and judgments based on what you do, say, and communicate. This is how they 'assess' you as a buyer.
- Success in negotiation relies on what the other side perceives to be true, not necessarily on what is actually true.
- Don't compliment a home in such a way that you add to the owner's estimate of its value.
- Negative comments you make about a home should relate to matters of genuine concern. However, your degree of concern, even if only minor, can be used to win concessions.
- A professional home inspection is worth the expense; it can highlight hidden defects and eliminate unpleasant surprises that show up after the sale. It can also give you an edge in negotiation by adding the 'power of legitimacy' to your position.
- When you state your position to the seller, don't wait like you expect an instant decision. This form of 'imposed urgency' can be counterproductive, especially when you have put your 'best' price on the table.
- Try to find a credible reason to make an increased offer. One way is to 'refigure' required expenses you'll incur in the home. Another is to come up with additional 'discovered' dollars.
- State that your offer reflects the value of the home *to you*; it comes in part from tracking selling prices (not asking prices) of comparable homes you have seen or know of.
- The Third Party tactic reduces competition between you and the seller, slows up the momentum, and can place you in a (positive) go-between role.
- Silence is a powerful tactic. Recognize when to shut up and let it work.
- Don't use No More Money as a basis for your offer. No More Money is a secondary tactic used to support your 'fair value' offer.
- Whether working through an agency or with a private seller, help the seller see a 'reality' other than the one he is seeing. This other reality makes clear the logic of your position and the fairness and objectivity of your offer.
- Face-to-face positions and eye-to-eye contact can work against you in many negotiation situations.
- When you find a home, go back and inspect it three or four times, and let the negotiation proceed naturally. If it's a flipped property, talk first to your lawyer and a knowledgeable Exclusive Buyer Agent.
- Let no one talk you out of negotiating, regardless of how pointless they say it is. This is either a self-serving move or due to naiveté.

CHAPTER 11

How to Find and Work with an Exclusive Buyer Agent — and Why You Should

I not only use all the brains I have but all I can borrow.

— Woodrow Wilson

Homebuyers who are reluctant to negotiate or who would just enjoy sharing the task, have the choice of hiring an Exclusive Buyer Agent. EBAs, sometimes referred to as *Single Agents* or *True Buyer Agents,* have been working on behalf of buyers for decades.

This whole question of agent types is complex and confusing and is misunderstood by almost all homebuyers. Unfortunately, the traditional real estate industry has shown little willingness to educate consumers.

Let's take a close look at EBAs and clarify a few terms. First, Exclusive Buyer Agents represent only buyers; they do this primarily to eliminate the conflict of interest that occurs any time one agent 'represents' buyer *and* seller in the same transaction. That word 'represents' is an oxymoron and entirely misleading. Because parties on opposite sides, with opposite objectives, cannot have their best interests represented or protected by *the same agent* in the same transaction. It's a fundamental contradiction, like a lawyer claiming he can represent plaintiff *and* defendant. It means that the homebuyer, who needs an advocate in making a major life decision, has none.

But most real estate agencies function this way. They handle buyer and seller in the same transaction. This is called 'dual agency'; it is permitted in most states but usually only when it is disclosed and agreed to by both sides.

When you buy a home through the agency that listed that home, the agency makes a double commission. You can see why most in the industry resist change.

There is irony and danger in this reluctance to educate consumers. Buyers are almost always entirely unaware that their best interests are not being represented. They even talk about the traditional agent as 'my agent', when in fact that agent is

NOT ONE DOLLAR MORE!

not acting in their best interests at all, but is acting exclusively in the best interests of the seller. That's the irony.

See what I mean about confusion? This situation endangers homebuyers. For decades, national consumer advocates have been objecting to 'dual agency' and continue to call for homebuyers to be treated equally. But the wheels turn slowly.

Like these consumer advocates, Exclusive Buyer Agents see 'dual agency' as unfair to buyers. And so it is, in very serious ways. Because homebuyers typically believe they have an advocate to look to for guidance, who they trust with their most confidential information, when that 'advocate' is not an advocate at all. Thankfully, today, more and more ordinary homebuyers are recognizing the safety, fairness and plain good sense of having a true ally in their corner, an EBA.

The EBA will do for the buyer what traditional agents have always been doing for sellers. An EBA will represent exclusively the homebuyer's best interests, will advise comprehensively, will identify *all* suitable homes, will point out potential problems, and will negotiate for the lowest purchase price and best terms. As you'd expect, EBAs give no loyalty, confidentiality, information, fiduciary duty or advice to the seller (which the traditional agent and salesperson are obligated to do).

This way, the homebuyer gets the protection *and* expertise that are badly needed, typically at no extra cost. The agent who listed the home for sale (the listing agent) shares the commission with the EBA, which is how the EBA earns income. One other big benefit is that the homebuyer's interests are fully represented all the way through the transaction, right up through closing, which can be extremely important.

So, in virtually all cases neither the buyer nor the seller pays extra when an EBA is involved. Plus, EBAs can show every home on the Multiple Listing Service, the listing resource all agents work from.

A small percentage of EBAs ask for a flat fee from the buyer, an upfront retainer of 0.5-1% of the buyer's target price. Almost always, this fee is *returned* to the buyer at closing, or is applied against the purchase price.

Although a little less preferable, this retainer arrangement can work equally well, especially where an expert agent-negotiator is available to work on your behalf. Just be clear on all details of fees and responsibilities before you sign any document or engage any agent.

EBA Studies Show Significant Savings

As far back as the 1990s, U.S. Sprint, a large American company, conducted its own independent study into the effectiveness of EBAs. The study focused on 232 of its employees relocating to different parts of the US.

The findings were impressive. Employees who bought using a traditional agent paid, on average, 96% of the list price for their homes. Those who used an EBA paid just 91%. This study proved once again that all prices are indeed negotiable. More importantly, it showed that the know-how of the EBA saved buyers thousands of *extra* dollars on each home.

How much on average? Let's investigate.

The US median home price at the time was $106,000. We'll assume the employees bought just average priced homes. In that case, buyers who used a traditional agent paid 96% of $106,000, which is $101,760, a saving of $4,240. Not bad.

But buyers who used an EBA paid just 91% of $106,000, which is $96,460, a saving of $9,540, an *extra* $5,300! A whole lot better!

Keep in mind that these savings are *not* just cash in the buyer's hand. We saw earlier that over the life of a mortgage any amount borrowed, or saved, multiplies. In this case, buyers who reduced their home loan by the $9,540 (the amount saved), on a 30-year mortgage at 5%, saved an *additional* $9,000 in interest charges alone. That's almost $19,000 in total savings over the full term of the loan!

To many homebuyers, savings like these represent a small fortune. This is power, *the power to save money and make money,* that you can learn from *Not One Dollar More!*. It gives this same power to the EBA acting on your behalf. The methods explained here will work for anyone who uses them wisely: ordinary homebuyer, experienced property investor, or EBA.

Other studies I have come across support U.S. Sprint's findings, showing that buyers working with EBAs see more homes, pay less, and buy more quickly than buyers who are not represented by an EBA.

Every year bigger numbers of homebuyers are discovering that EBAs merit serious consideration. The movement is growing strongly but has yet to reach all who might benefit from it. If you prefer not to negotiate on your own behalf, try to find an EBA in your area who has read this book and has otherwise been trained in representing buyers.

Reminder: You *don't* want an agent or salesperson acting in the best interests of the other side, nor one who tells you they can act for seller and buyer at the same time. Nor do you want an agent or salesperson who tells you they can function as *a facilitator* or *go-between* or *transaction broker*, acting for neither side but just to get the deal done. All these arrangements leave you *without* representation when you have so much at stake, *without* an advocate for guidance, *without* someone in your corner.

So, my best advice is, be safe. Hire an EBA to help you get the right home at the lowest price and on the best terms possible, an ally who will listen well and advise sympathetically, and act faithfully on your instructions.

Engaging an Exclusive Buyer Agent

First, where do you find an EBA? EBAs work in smaller real estate companies and in exclusive buyer agencies. The agencies usually have the words *buyer* or *buyer agency* in their name, and they don't engage *at all* in selling real estate. Along with these, some 'traditional' agencies offer what is called *single agency,* which means they will represent the buyer or the seller but *never both* in the same transaction, and never on one of their own listings; this arrangement can work well when these guidelines are observed.

However, by far the best way to find an expert Exclusive Buyer Agent is to ask the National Association of Exclusive Buyer Agents (NAEBA.org: 800 986 2322), for contact details of members closest to the neighborhoods you have selected. Alternatively, call a local real estate company to identify prospects.

You'll find EBAs thoroughly buyer-focused. An experienced EBA will have accumulated a range of competencies and will offer insights on specific areas, local property regulations, financing options and so on. Almost all will be able to assist you in applying for loan approval and securing the best mortgage. For all these reasons, an EBA is usually your best starting point, before you even select a lender.

Because of the work they must do for the buyer, EBAs will typically possess negotiation skills that are at least as sharp as the competition's, the selling agents with whom they negotiate on your behalf. Even here, when you leave negotiating to the EBA, it's still a big advantage to know the basics of influence and persuasion.

Before you hire an EBA to represent you, even one that comes recommended, have a getting-to-know-you meeting and ask questions. What you've picked up from this book will guide you.

Here are some suggestions:

- Does the company also represent sellers' interests, or is it an exclusive buyer agency?
- Does the EBA, personally, also represent sellers?
- How long has the EBA represented buyers' interests?
- What special negotiation training has the EBA had in getting the best deal for buyers?
- Will the EBA give you specific details of recent purchases in which the buyers benefited?
- Will the EBA give you those and other buyers' names and phone numbers? And permission to contact them?

Then, see what you can find out about the EBA's specific skills:

- How well does the EBA understand tactics and timing?
- What does the EBA know about setting the mood and building credibility?
- Is the EBA aware of the importance of control and the power of perception?
- Does the EBA know how to make use of concessions and capitalize on home inspection reports?
- Is the EBA aware of the power of relevant factual research?
- What type of relationship does the EBA advocate with sellers and sellers' agents?
- Can the EBA pick and mix tactics to make up a good strategy?
- Can the EBA *sell* a strategy convincingly?
- Can the EBA communicate the right impression and create distance when it is necessary?

- Is the EBA aware of the subtlety of persuasion and how it is based on an understanding of psychology, motivation, and interpersonal communication?
- Can the EBA leave his or her ego aside when a good deal depends on it?
- Can the EBA adapt to different agent and seller personality types and select an approach that will get you the best deal?
- Can the EBA use probing statements and read between the lines?
- Does the EBA appreciate the importance of verifying seller information and the power of legitimacy?
- Is the EBA prepared to listen and take specific directions from you?
- Does the EBA understand the value of 'alternatives' and the use of power?
- What is the EBA's philosophy on how offers should be made?
- Does the EBA recommend getting legal advice on particular contractual issues?

Naturally, you won't be looking for answers to all these questions, at least not in an initial meeting. Just pick a selection from this list for discussion. You are looking to be impressed; you are looking for experience and resourcefulness and an earnest commitment to getting you the best outcome possible. The above list also gives you a good understanding of the wide range of critical capabilities an EBA can provide.

And remember, you are still in control. All the strings are still yours to pull. In fact, what you have learned here can be used to your advantage in *any* situation in which you stand to gain or lose anything of value.

Most important, never put your fate entirely in the hands of someone else. You are not a passive buyer, but a smart buyer. Working with an EBA should be a positive, collaborative experience in which you stay involved throughout, one in which your own know-how plays a significant role in securing your objective.

One final caution: With buyer representation now gaining popularity among homebuyers, you'll come across loose and ambiguous use of terms like 'buyer broker' and 'buyer representative'. This can easily mislead you. You need to be certain of the type of agent you are dealing with, or hiring, before you commit to anything.

Put simply, your goal should be to engage an agent who will represent only *your* interests, not any 'buyer agent' or 'buyer broker', but an *Exclusive* Buyer Agent. You should not settle for less, regardless of persuasion from others.

Remember too that agents known as 'true' or 'single' agents also give you undivided loyalty and exclusive representation, and they will never try to sell you one of their own listings.

The language around real estate has always been confusing. So let's recap how you can distinguish between agent types you are likely to encounter (see a fuller explanation in Chapter 2, *When Your Agent is Not Your Agent at All: Who is Really Looking Out for You?*).

The agent I recommend, who will always represent you exclusively, is known as an 'Exclusive Buyer Agent' (EBA), 'true' agent or 'single' agent. Don't confuse any of these terms with 'designated agent'.

Because here's the big problem you can run into. With a designated agent, if you like one of their in-house listings, which is quite likely, who will the agent then be representing — her company? the seller? you? anyone? You see, the designated agent's company has *also* pledged loyalty and exclusive representation to the seller of the home you like. The conflict is that obvious, but largely ignored by the industry. Can you expect the agent to work *for you* and *against* her company's best interest? Or *for you* and *against* the seller's best interest? Such conflict of interest is outlawed or unacceptable in virtually every profession.

On top of that, there's another problem with designated agency. To represent your best interests, the designated agent would need to *refuse* to share your confidential details with her same-company colleagues hoping to sell you the home that interests you — with a *double commission* reward for their agency if you buy, and *zero* reward for their agency if you decide to buy a different home through another agency. Of course, any sharing of your confidential information — things you would never want the seller to know — will almost certainly kill your chance of getting the best price or terms. Talk about conflict of interest — and designated agency lands *you* in the middle of it!

See how messy it gets? In the above situation, if any of your confidential information is shared within the agency or 'leaks out' — for example, how much money you have to spend, what your next offer might be, your urgency, or your excitement about the home — you lose the exclusive representation and undivided loyalty you expected. Consequently, your ability to negotiate is compromised or destroyed entirely. For these and other reasons, I don't recommend using a designated agent.

Solution: Keep it simple, keep it clear and clean, keep it totally reliable. Choose an agent who will pledge undivided loyalty and exclusive representation to you *right through* your entire home buying journey, all the way up to closing — an agent who will *never* try to sell you a home, an EBA.

Make sure this is what you are getting — the key word is *exclusive.*

I interviewed twenty-four of the nation's top EBAs for this book. I asked them to say in their own words why they do the work they do and why it's important to them. The next chapter will give you a fuller understanding of exclusive buyer representation, the principles and values that motivate EBAs, why they never sell homes, and why they choose to represent only buyers.

CHAPTER 12

Why Be an Exclusive Buyer Agent?
Top Professionals Respond in
Their Own Words

Beware of false knowledge; it is more dangerous than ignorance.
— George Bernard Shaw

I added this section to give homebuyers (and consumers everywhere) a close-up look at Exclusive Buyer Agents: what motivates them, why they believe this is the only fair and ethical way to treat homebuyers, and the services they provide.

The following comments are direct quotes from some of the nation's leading EBA professionals. I asked them to say simply why they choose to be Exclusive Buyer Agents when there are easier and potentially more lucrative options open to them in real estate.

Here's what they said:

Tom Wemett, Massachusetts & Florida
As an EBA, I am proud to be part of a highly principled group

When I started as a licensed broker in 1973 sellers were treated as clients and buyers as customers. But in the mid-1980s buyer representation became accepted. This was the only ethical way, I felt, to eliminate the conflict of interest inherent in 'representing' two parties with opposite objectives. So in 1992 I became an EBA and never looked back.

Since then, however, due to pressure from large agencies and their desire to 'double-dip' commissions, buyer representation has been compromised. The traditional real estate industry has used deception and political power to change regulations to create the pretense that it's OK (once again) to 'represent' both buyer and seller in the same transaction. That position is not morally acceptable; in fact, it's damaging to both sides. Homebuyers and sellers have opposing needs, each requires true, independent representation, which is impossible with in-house deals

— one or both parties will always end up being short-changed. I'm proud to be part of this EBA movement, a group of highly principled real estate professionals who give undivided loyalty exclusively to homebuyers.

Tom Wemett
Homebuyer Advisors LLC
Author: *Massachusetts Homebuyers Beware! The Cards are Stacked Against You*
Tel (978) 633-9090; 800-383-8322
tom@tomwemett.com
www.expert-homebuying-help.com

John Rygiol, California
I am happy to provide full loyalty to my clients

Throughout my forty-five years in Real Estate I have always believed that the homebuyer needed professional representation just as much as the seller. So, in 1986 I stopped taking listings and started to exclusively represent buyers.

I tell my clients that I welcome the fiduciary responsibility I give them; I am happy to provide the same loyalty they expect from their attorney or certified public accountant. Not only do I feel better about representing buyers exclusively, I am able to work by appointment only and enjoy a rewarding family life outside of real estate.

John Rygiol
Buyer's Broker Inc, Serving Orange County, CA
300 Spectrum Center Drive, Suite 400, Irvine, CA 92618
Tel 888-700-0110; Cell 949-525-7344; Fax 888-279-4580
John@ebausa.com
www.homesoforangecounty.com

Gea Elika, New York
Buyers need a professional looking after their best interests

I decided to become an EBA twenty years ago to provide unbiased advice and service to homebuyers and investors. I tell my buyer if a property is a lemon. My clients find comfort in knowing this, that I have their best interest in mind and no bias for any particular property, whereas traditional dual real estate agents are tooled for selling.

Undivided loyalty is crucial; buyers are spending an average of $1m for a one-bedroom property in our market. It's obvious that the homebuyer needs a professional looking after their best interests. Buyers make money when they buy the right property for the right price. Helping my clients achieve this is my motivation. A successful EBA needs to be able to communicate effectively, read between the lines and represent buyers expertly.

Elika Real Estate
26 Bond Street, Suite 2R, New York, NY, 10012
Tel (+1) 212-590-0545; Cell (+1) 917-291-1824; Fax (+1) 212-590-0549
www.elikarealestate.com

Stephen G. Carpenter-Israel, Maryland
As EBAs we are all consumer advocates

Some people think we're nuts giving up half of our potential income by not listing and selling homes, until they realize that we are not salespeople, we are consultants to homebuyers. In fact, we are all consumer advocates. We virtually never have a client who doesn't buy a property, so we have a whole different structure for earning a living. Referring our clients listings to the best traditional agents is a big part of our income; needless to say we make a lot of friends in the business because of it.

Primarily, though, I just love what I do. I'm always looking out for my clients' best interests and I'm always on the right side of the deal. Without hesitation I tell my clients all the negatives in every property as well as the positives, something you just can't do when you list and sell homes. I help people find the best homes and evaluate them, then I put on my negotiator's hat to get them the best deal possible.

Stephen G. Carpenter-Israel
Buyer's Edge Company, Inc
4849 Rugby Avenue, First Floor, Bethesda, Maryland 20814
Tel (301) 657-1475; (800) 207-6810; Cell (301) 807-2130; Fax (301) 657-4494
broker@buyersagent.com
www.buyersagent.com

Victoria Ray Henderson, VA, MD & DC
I like being fully transparent in my relationship with buyers

I became an EBA in 2011. While studying for my real estate and broker exams I learned about dual agency and how this very gray area of representation is a bad deal for the homebuyer. If a lawyer can't represent both clients in a legal procedure, why should a single real estate agent represent both buyer and seller? It's not too difficult to see the obvious conflicts of interest that can arise in this situation. And when a buyer and seller have their own agents but the agents both work for the same brokerage, conflicts of interest arise again.

Just because people do business this way, does not make it right. This gray area of real estate is what gives real estate agents a bad name. The fact that agents are encouraged to sell their companies' own listings and gather buyers' names at open houses so they can fill company listings is not the way I want to do business. I like being fully transparent in my relationship with buyers.

Victoria Ray Henderson
Buyer's Edge (Virginia, Maryland & Washington DC)

4849 Rugby Avenue Bethesda Maryland 20814
Cell 301-922-1677; Tel 301-657-1475
www.buyersagent.com

Ronn Huth, Massachusetts
We have saved buyers millions of dollars in home purchases

I'm Ronn Huth of Buyer's Choice Realty. We cover the greater Boston area and specialize on Boston's north shore. I started in real estate in the late 1980s, in an office like all others back then, that worked only for sellers. In 1990 I started my own company, working for buyers as my clients and with sellers as customers. Since then, we have saved thousands of buyers millions of dollars on home purchases.

I chose to be an EBA because of the simplicity of working only for homebuyers, the integrity of never having to compromise my loyalty, and being free to focus on only one side of the transaction. This has given me a love and passion for what I do. I have no vested interest in any property; therefore, I'll show all properties, even those For-Sale-By-Owner and some not yet for sale. I help buyers understand market conditions and decide what to offer, then I negotiate as the buyer's advocate. Buyers often ask me, 'Why would anyone buy a home any other way?'

Ronn Huth
Buyer's Choice Realty (Greater Boston area & North Shore)
162 Main Street, Wenham, MA 01984
Tel 1-800-252-8937; 1-800-25-BUYER; (978) 979-7800
ronn@BuyersChoiceRealty.com
www.BuyersChoiceRealty.com

Ken Reid, Arizona
Doing the right thing, the right way for the right reason

I've been an EBA for sixteen years and never worked as a traditional agent. Previously. I worked for a large corporation who credited their success to consistently 'doing the right thing, the right way, for the right reason'. When I got my real estate license I decided this was the right approach. The traditional practice of real estate didn't fit any of these parameters. But then I remembered a very ethical friend who had an Exclusive Buyer Brokerage. So I became an EBA, avoiding the conflict of interest inherent in traditional real estate, where one brokerage claims to represent buyer and seller even though their interests are opposite.

To do the right thing we must decide who our true client is and provide full fiduciary services. This is not possible when a brokerage claims to represent opposing parties. Doing the right thing the right way earns our clients' respect and trust. Homebuyers know we always represent their best interests exclusively. A traditional brokerage cannot do this. You are either a salesperson or a consultant.

Ken Reid
Buyer's Broker of Arizona (Phoenix and 'West Valley' areas)
22224 N. Las Brizas Lane, Sun City West, AZ 85375
Tel 623-815-5116; 877-815-5116; Mobile 623-433-6188; Fax 866-601-3260
ken@BuyersBrokerofArizona.com
www.BuyersBrokerofArizona.com

Kathleen Baylies, North Carolina
I'm an EBA for four good reasons

1. It's the right thing to do. Homebuyers deserve the peace of mind of knowing their agent really is *their* agent, especially when they fall in love with a home.

2. Being an EBA is an excellent way to be noticed. What sets me apart isn't about me, it's about my clients and providing them with a benefit that has real value to them.

3. It's easier to make money. You've never heard a heart surgeon complain about all the money she's missing because she's not a general practitioner. Everyone except real estate agents know it's easier to make money when you specialize. Plus, EBAs don't 'give up' the seller side of revenue; we connect our clients, friends and family with great listing agents, and receive a welcome referral fee.

4. Homebuyers are fun to work with. Whether they're first-timers, trading up or down, or retiring, almost always they're excited about what's going on in their life, and about buying. I'm fourteen years in real estate, all as an EBA, and I still have zero desire to list properties.

Kathleen Baylies
Just For Buyers Realty (Greater Wilmington & SW North Carolina)
5 Silva Terra Dr, Wilmington, NC 28412, USA
Tel 910-470-3190
kathleen@JustForBuyersRealty.com
www.justforbuyersrealty.com

Andi DeFelice, Georgia
There is never a doubt as to our loyalty to homebuyers

It has never occurred to us to represent sellers. I was talking just yesterday to a prospective new agent about our unique position in the real estate market. We are passionate about our duty as EBAs. We also feel there needs to be more consumer education about agency and who works for whom. None of us wants to work for free, that's true, but the day I am more concerned about my commission than my care for my clients, I will need to change careers.

I truly don't understand how traditional agents do it. I'd never want to find myself in a position of having conflicted loyalty. I guess that is what motivates us as a company, the fact that there is never any doubt as to our loyalty to our homebuyers; we can promise and deliver on this every single time. As EBAs we feel a true sense of accomplishment and joy when the transaction closes and our buyer looks at us and is genuinely grateful for the service we provided.

Andi DeFelice
24 Drayton St, Savannah, GA 31401
Exclusive Buyer's Realty, Savannah, GA
Tel (912) 656-4614; (912) 232-0029
andi@ebrsavannah.com
www.ebrsavannah.com

Alysse Musgrave, Texas
As an EBA, I don't sell, I protect; I don't close, I advise

I became an EBA because I've never been a fan of the hard sale, nor the tactics used by traditional agents. I'd sooner close my doors than make cold calls or knock on people's doors. I'm a terrible salesperson, but I'm a great caretaker. As an EBA, I don't sell, I protect; I don't close, I advise. I like the way that feels.

It's easy to have a career in real estate when you offer a service people need and want. The industry is saturated with agents who mistakenly assume it's better to be a real estate generalist. Instead of becoming a niche expert, they jump into an industry that has 1.7m agents selling the same service. About 88% of these agents are out of business within two years. As a business decision, it's hard to defend. My 22-year-plus career as an EBA is rewarding personally, financially and intrinsically. I'm well-respected as a home buying expert, not a desperate traditional agent begging for clients, and I enjoy training other agents to accomplish the same. I really can't imagine working any other way.

Alysse Musgrave
HelpUBuy America
Dallas-Ft Worth: 820 S. MacArthur Blvd, Suite 105-535, Coppell, TX 75019
Houston: 1707 Post Oak Blvd. Suite 558, Houston, TX 77056
Tel 214-734-3863
alysse@HelpUBuyAmerica.com
http://HelpUBuyAmerica.com

Thomas E. Coler, Florida
Buyers overpay by working with the wrong type of agent

Since 1989 we've been helping homebuyers find the most appropriate home and then negotiate the lowest price and best terms. This goal has always been our motivation; it's why we work with homebuyers exclusively. Oddly, in Florida, buyers are rarely represented, though many Buyers never realize this because they are never informed. Thus, they overpay by working with the wrong type of agent. We think this is unfortunate and wrong. If the right home is out there (and it almost always is) we will find it for our buyers in sunny southwest Florida, home of 'warm weather, low taxes, and active lifestyles'.

In the twenty-eight years since we opened we have never represented a seller. It has been our pleasure to serve so many homebuyers, and we have made many good friends along the way. Our EBAs have enjoyed representing countless buyers who later went on to purchase several hundred million dollars worth of Florida real estate, primarily in the Sarasota, Naples and Boca Grande area.

Thomas E. Coler
Buyer's Broker of Southwest Florida
Sarasota: Tel 800-331-GULF (4853)
Naples; Tel 800-417-GULF (4853)
www.buyersbrokerswflorida.com

Mike Crowley, Washington
I like being free to tell my buyers what they need to know

I've been a practicing EBA since 1997 and a Realtor since 1993. I became an EBA because I knew I was better at one side of the business. I detested working with a seller and a buyer with competing interests in the same transaction. Plus, I've never missed having to list homes at prices that I knew would not be achieved. And neither have I missed spending my weekends doing open houses.

As an EBA I like the control I have in helping buyers. My clients appreciate it when I tell them that the right home may not be out there on a given day. Before I became an EBA it troubled me when sellers could not understand why I wasn't able to create a buyer out of thin air, especially when their home was over-priced or not showing well, or even not open for showing. As an EBA I like to advocate for just one party, my buyers, and being able to tell them what they need to know. A long list of referred clients come from our buyer clients.

Mike Crowley
Spokane Home Buyers
5802 E Sprague Ave, Spokane Valley, WA 99212
Tel 509-951-9710; 509-327-7372
mike@spokanehomebuyers.com
www.spokanehomebuyers.com

Jon Boyd, Michigan
I've documented millions in savings for our homebuyers

We serve the Ann Arbor Michigan market and areas north and east. Our office has been representing buyers since 1988. Before I became an EBA, I was in electrical engineering. At that time, my wife and I wanted to buy single family homes in Ann Arbor as investments, so we hired my father to be our buyer's broker. He was the first buyer's broker in Michigan. In 1993, when our state started requiring disclosure of agency, I left engineering and started full time representing buyers. Since then I've helped buyers buy homes of all kinds and I've documented millions in savings for those buyers. I've also met a lot of really great people in the process.

Being an EBA provides me with a great income, a career with a lot of flexibility, and I feel really good working with and advising buyers. Every day I am thankful we can help ordinary people as we do. I would not be comfortable in a sales position where I couldn't reveal to a buyer reasons to be cautious about a particular home.

Jon Boyd
The Home Buyer's Agent of Ann Arbor, Inc (serving Ann Arbor & areas North and East)
1905 Pauline Blvd. Suite 1, Ann Arbor, MI 48103
Tel 734-662-6240
www.buyersagentannarbor.com

Janine J. Wilson, Tennessee
Our buyers say they will never again buy without an EBA

I've been an EBA for over twenty-one years. Before getting into real estate my husband and I had been purchasers of residential and commercial property. We learned the hard way that our interest was not always well served by 'our' agent, there was always a conflict of interest. I got licensed in 1993, bearing these experiences in mind, but not aware at the time of exclusive buyer agency. I just knew that buyers needed honest advice and unchallengeable loyalty, which I could provide.

I've always enjoyed my work as an EBA, seeing the amazement of homebuyers who did not know their best interests could be represented exclusively. Many of our buyers talk of having been taken advantage of previously; they say they will never again use any other type of agency as long as an EBA is available. We do everything we can on local and national levels to help home buyers learn they have a choice, they can choose to be protected by an EBA. Buyers in every state need to be better informed about this.

Janine J. Wilson
A Buyer's Best Choice Realty, (serving upper east TN & Tri-Cities)
3908 Marable Lane, Johnson City, TN 37601-1044
Tel 423-283-4677; 423-773-3812
www.tnbuyerbroker.com
info@TNBuyerBroker.com

Eve Alexander, Florida
Ignoring home deficiencies and inflating prices felt wrong

In 1991 I got screwed in a property transaction by a real estate agent who was the undisclosed owner. So I decided to get a real estate license simply to be smarter, and one thing led to another. I became a traditional agent (for one year) in an era when being an EBA was taboo. And I hated being a fake. I was good with buyers but lousy at ignoring deficiencies in homes or inflating the price for the seller. That all felt wrong.

Working for the buyer's best interest made sense. In 1992 I opened an Exclusive Buyer Agency in south Florida and for the first time in my career I was excited. That office grew to be the largest buyer brokerage in Florida. Today I'm located in Orlando. I have a smaller office still representing exclusively the best interests of the homebuyer. My buyers thank me for my service and my expertise and I have incredible job satisfaction. I also make an excellent living which proves that you don't have to list property to be successful. I love it.

Eve Alexander
Buyers Broker of Florida, (serving Greater Orlando area)
Tel 407-539-1053
www.OrlandoBuyersBroker.com

Andrew Show, Ohio
We are consumer advocates, advisors and counselors

What distinguishes you from the rest of the pack in your marketplace? What is your measurable 'competitive point of difference' compared with other agents? Everyone claims to be hard working, the neighborhood expert, have the latest technology, blah, blah, blah! If all your competitors say these things then what truly distinguishes you, and at the same time provides tremendous benefit to the homebuyer?

Only being an EBA with an Exclusive Buyer's Brokerage can genuinely distinguish you. You get the best price and terms for the buyer, your fee is paid by the seller or builder, and you guarantee no conflicts of interest, no insider trading, and no double dipping on the commission! This is why a career as an EBA is so satisfying and rewarding — professionally, personally, and deep down at your core. We are not traditional salespeople that flip-flop on both sides; we are home buying consumer advocates, advisors and counselors. The mindset of an EBA is different from a traditional agent, and that's been most appealing to me through twenty-five years as an EBA.

Andrew Show
Buyer's Resource Realty Services, (serving Columbus & Central Ohio)
7100 North High St, Suite 204, Worthington, Ohio 43085
Tel 888-888-4110; 614-888-4110; Fax: 614-839-4110
AShow@BuyersHome.com
http://buyershome.com

Benjamin Clark, Utah
Exclusive homebuyer representation is desperately needed

I started as a buyer's agent twenty years ago. The industry was heavy on sales training; true representation appeared secondary. This benefited the brokerage and often the seller. Homebuyers were more likely to be harmed by this; they were buying without professional representation, often being 'sold' a home, or 'facilitated' through a purchase, while the agent's primary interest was in getting the deal. This bothered me so much that I opened Homebuyer Representation Inc in 2001, offering buyers full and exclusive representation.

Today, I represent home buyers at the highest level. Their best interests are more important than getting a deal done. I'm their trusted resource and advocate from the moment they hire me, through home searching, contracts, inspections, negotiations and closing. When disputes arise I'm there in the room, advising them of their options. A buyer represented like this will fare better than one who goes it alone or works with an agent who also (or only) represents the best interest of the seller. Home buyer representation is desperately needed. That's why I am an EBA.

Benjamin Clark
Homebuyer Representation Inc, (serving Salt Lake & Northern Counties)
PO Box 701481, Salt Lake City, Utah 84170
Tel 801-999-8889
www.hmbyr.com

Rich Rosa, Massachusetts
Consumers appreciate that EBAs conduct business ethically

When I first decided to enter real estate I didn't know what it meant to be an EBA. As an attorney, I felt that homebuyers were not receiving true advocacy from real estate agents. I saw the industry as seller-centric and believed homebuyers needed advocates to level the playing field. It was only after my business partner, Dave Kres, and I researched the industry and started Buyers Brokers Only, LLC that we discovered there was a small group of brokers and agents dedicated to protecting the rights and interests of homebuyers. These consumer advocates called themselves Exclusive Buyer Agents, and I realized that I was one too.

Besides enjoying my work, it is professionally fulfilling to know I am providing representation to my home buying clients exclusively, without the conflicts of interest associated with dual agency and designated buyer agency. Despite what many real estate brokers think, exclusive buyer agency is good for business. Consumers appreciate that EBAs do not try to be all things to all people and they conduct business in an ethical manner.

Rich Rosa
Buyers Brokers Only, LLC, (serving Greater Boston Area)
Tel 978-835-5906
rrosa@buyersbrokersonly.com
www.BuyersBrokersOnly.com
Twitter: @OnlyBuyers; Facebook: Facebook.com/bbollc

Merrill Ottwein, Illinois
Our clients tell the story of our loyalty to their success

The most important reason I enjoy working exclusively with buyers is that I never have to worry about what set of representation standards prevail. I am always representing my buyers, period. There's no switching back and forth. No withholding of any enhancement, no conflicts, no limits to that representation, anything I can do to enhance my services to the buyer is fair and legal. And, in fact, this is what earns the most accolades, doing unexpected things for buyers which often surprise them. That's what really drives exclusive buyer representation and makes practicing it such fun.

Buying a house is a process of values clarification and personal decisions. It is also a rare, high-stakes financial decision for homebuyers. Our model is high on counseling and low on sales. We regularly astound our clients by talking them out of houses that may not work for them. That seems to go against our interests, but it does not. Our happy clients pay us back, ten-fold, by telling the story of our loyalty to their success. And our success flourishes.

Merrill Ottwein
Home Buyers AdvantEDGE (serving mid-SW Illinois)
6100 Center Grove Road, Edwardsville, IL 62025
201 McKinley Avenue, Edwardsville, IL 62025
Tel 618 -781-1822; 618-656-5588
merrill@homerelo.com
www.homerelo.com

Rona Fischman, Massachusetts
Our mission: Get our buyers the best house at the lowest price

Buying a house is a rare, high-stakes financial decision. Our EBA model is high on counseling and low on sales. We regularly astound our clients by keeping them out of houses that may not work for them. That might seem to be going against our own interests, but it's not. Our happy clients pay us back ten-fold by telling others of our loyalty to their success. We work hard to get our buyers the best house at the lowest price; traditional agents strive to get the highest price. We work as a team with our buyers; we share ideas and tactics, we're on their side exclusively, not negotiating against them.

It takes people skills to be an EBA, and cynicism towards sales-hype and advertising. I'm known as an unrelenting consumer advocate and a fierce negotiator. When I opened my office, I found kindred spirits in Dianne Schaefer, Ron Rothenberg, Dave Twombly, and Anna Culmone. I didn't hire people to be 'top producers', I hired people to work to get our clients exactly what they need.

Rona Fischman
4 Buyers Real Estate

2326 Massachusetts Avenue, Cambridge, MA 02140
Tel 617-776-8304
contact@4buyersre.com
www.facebook.com/4BuyersRE

Julie P. Tuggle, North Carolina
I'm an EBA because I want to level the playing field

I am an EBA because I want to level the playing field. In NC it's still 'buyer beware'. Sellers can demand that prospective home buyers pay a nonrefundable 'due diligence' fee for the buyer's right to inspect the property prior to completing the transaction. This concept was borrowed from commercial real estate. But unlike corporate entities, ordinary buyers are at the mercy of the seller's moral compass, which may or may not make for an accurate representation of the material condition of the home.

By the time the buyer finds out that the seller has misrepresented the property (intentionally or unintentionally), the buyer may have lost their due diligence fee, which can be in the thousands of dollars, plus the cost of the home inspections, appraisals, and survey. The seller can 'unintentionally' misrepresent the condition of the property with no consequences. Changes to the NC Offer to Purchase contract are needed to even the playing field between buyers and sellers. These are only some of the reasons my work is dedicated to helping buyers exclusively.

Julie P. Tuggle
Carolina Buyer's Agent, (serving Charlotte Metro Area)
1809 East Barden Road, Charlotte, NC 28226
Tel 800-304-1429; 704-366-0542; Cell 704-408-8791
jtuggle@carolinabuyersagent.com
https://carolinabuyersagent.com

Marge Bish, North Carolina
Helping buyers find their dream home is my greatest joy

While I loved real estate from the beginning I could see what buyers were experiencing when they were not properly represented. At that time no one talked about buyers' rights. When a buyer deals with a traditional agent, whose fiduciary duty is always to the seller, the buyer cannot be represented properly. How can the buyer get the best price and terms when the agent is working for the seller to get the highest price and terms? Many things have changed over the years, with the industry manipulating disclosures and rules, but it has always neglected the homebuyer's needs. From 'due diligence' fees to non-required appraisal contingencies in contracts, the buyer needs true buyer representation today more than even.

Helping buyers find their dream home, whether their first or a retirement home, is my greatest joy. Then seeing them return several years later as changes occur and a different home is needed, is a wonderful reward, and just as challenging once again to make sure they get their new home at the best price and terms.

Marge Bish
Buyers Advantage Group Realty
3737 Glenwood Ave. Ste. 100, Raleigh, NC 27612
Tel 919-796-8513
mbish@nc.rr.com
www.buyersadvantagegroup.net

Dawn E. Rae, Florida
I am happy to serve with integrity

I'm an EBA because I am happiest when serving with integrity the best interests of some person or some cause. As an EBA I make a good living serving both. Every homebuyer deserves to have exclusive buyer representation. Every homebuyer also deserves to have an advocate they can trust one hundred percent to act in the their best interest. This is the cause I serve.

As an EBA, owing loyalty to my clients, I get deeply involved with the search for and acquisition of each client's new home. My buyers receive all my expertise, guidance and years of experience, which makes their entire home buying journey much less stressful and the process more enjoyable. This is how all home buyers should be served. For me, being an EBA is the only way to be in the real estate industry.

Dawn E. Rae
President, National Assn of Exclusive Buyer Agents (2015-2017)
Florida Buyers' Advocate (for all of Tampa Bay)
5849 Park St N, St Petersburg, FL 33709
Tel 888-FLA-DAWN; 727-565-4954; Cell 813-368-3698; Fax 888-352-3296
dawn@FloridaBuyersAdvocate.com
www.FloridaBuyersAdvocate.com

Ashley Dean Wilson, Tennessee
We're driven to perform above and beyond for our homebuyers

Fifteen years ago I became an EBA because I recognized the amazing advantages EBAs bring to homebuyers. This came about through observing the workings of my family's exclusive buyer agency, A Buyer's Best Choice Realty, which started in 1996. I saw there the huge gratitude of clients, the expertise used to ethically protect and assist them, and being able to serve them with no confusion about where our loyalties lay. Having no conflict of interest in a field like real estate is very refreshing. So is helping buyers with mortgage preparedness, home inspection hazard concerns, and so many other facets of the buying process. In 2002 I obtained my brokers license, eventually becoming the managing broker.

You can't do this type of work if you don't care about buyers. Or if your focus is just on the bottom dollar. You can be an EBA only if you value the singleness of purpose, the clarity and satisfaction that only single agency can provide, and if you are driven to perform above and beyond for the home buyers you represent.

Ashley Dean Wilson
A Buyer's Best Choice Realty, (serving upper East TN & Tri-Cities)
3908 Marable Lane, Johnson City, TN 37601-1044
Tel 423-283-4677; 423-773-3812
www.tnbuyerbroker.com
info@TNBuyerBroker.com

Tip: If you feel inclined to participate in house auctions but lack the relevant know-how, a suitably experienced EBA may be the ideal solution. First, though, read the next chapter on auctions for a general guide to what goes on. You'll learn about pitfalls, tricks, stooges and bidding strategies, and you'll know better how to protect yourself.

If auctions are not your thing, move ahead to Chapter 14, the first of three chapters on how to save serious money shopping for your home loan. You'll find there ideas and tips I'm pretty certain no one has ever told you.

CHAPTER 13

Buying at Auction

What is wanted is not the will to believe
but the wish to find out, which is the exact opposite.
— Bertrand Russell

You've probably heard stories of auction 'bargains', but all that glistens is not gold. This chapter will give you a basic introduction to auctions and how to participate safely. However, if buying at auction is your goal, you'll need to learn more than you'll find here. Auctions are not suited to inexperienced homebuyers.

In the US, auctions are commonly used to sell distressed and foreclosed properties, though not exclusively so. The way government-regulated foreclosure auctions work is very specialized. Ordinary homebuyers are better advised to steer clear of this field. Unless you possess the required know-how or are prepared to acquire it, leave this to the professional speculators who can afford to take the risks.

Foreclosure regulations vary a lot from state to state, even between nearby jurisdictions. If you are hoping to buy in this way you'll need to learn how this works in your area and be prepared for the challenges attached to foreclosures.

You may also have come across builders' auctions, which can be public or private. These, too, call for a level of expertise and familiarity the average homebuyer does not possess. When they are private affairs, buyers can be required to register beforehand, even to demonstrate their genuineness by placing a deposit with the auctioneer before entering or bidding at the auction.

If you are determined to participate in builders' auctions or foreclosure auctions, the best advice I can give you is to discuss the matter with knowledgeable professionals. A suitably experienced Exclusive Buyer Agent or local auctioneer is a good starting point. Also, read as much as you can on the subject and attend as many auctions as is necessary to gain the required confidence and know-how.

A third type of auction, which we'll look at here, is the conventional house auction, which is open to the public. These are not popular everywhere and in some areas feature only higher priced homes. However, these are the auctions that are most relevant to the non-professional homebuyer.

Now that you are aware that I advise caution, I'll assume that if you are attracted by the idea of buying at auction you appreciate the importance of becoming thoroughly familiar with how the process works. Though my remarks here relate to conventional public auctions, many of the tips and techniques are relevant in any auction situation, be it real estate, art, antiques or anything else.

Know the Property Before You Bid

Know-how is obviously imperative. But it means more than just knowing the location and condition of the home. You'll need a reliable estimate of value, with the emphasis on reliable. If your own knowledge is insufficient, consult with an Exclusive Buyer Agent or local real estate agency, and perhaps a few neighbors close to the property. Ask about recent nearby sales and selling prices.

You can also contact the auctioneer's agent and ask if a recent appraisal (valuation) has been done on the home. If so, was it by the agent's company or an independent appraiser, and how recently? If an independent appraiser, get the appraiser's contact details, tell them you are interested in the home and ask if the appraised value is still valid.

When no recent independent appraisal is available you'll need to rely on your research and knowledge of the market. Or hire a professional appraiser. Unfortunately, this can be difficult or impossible to arrange with certain types of auction. Ask the agent about this.

If you have a lawyer who understands real estate, get guidance on your situation; you need to understand your legal rights and obligations before you commit. Then, contact the selling agent and get copies of relevant documents and *as much information* as you can. Ask also about the bidding. What can the salesperson tell you? What's the reserve price (the price below which the property will *not* be sold)? The salesperson may or may not know this figure before the day of the auction. Or they may know it and not tell you. If the salesperson seems to be hedging, push for an estimate of the selling price based on his or her 'professional experience'. You'll be surprised at how a question phrased like this can get you the needed details (the Massage-the-Ego tactic).

Buying at auction requires special care for a number of other reasons. You'll be buying without some of the safeguards you get with a conventional purchase. Auction contracts are usually drawn up by the selling agent and must be signed immediately the sale is made. The right of the buyer to impose conditions on the agreement is either severely limited or entirely prohibited. This can mean no escape clauses and no opportunity to make the purchase subject to your partner's or attorney's approval, or even to make the deal conditional upon a satisfactory professional home inspection.

Nor can you typically buy the home subject to obtaining financing. You are expected to have the money sorted out ahead of time. Also, well before the auction get assurance from the agent that the title to the property is clear and guaranteed. If this is not forthcoming, for whatever reason, you could consider having a title search conducted, if time permits; but discuss this first with your attorney.

Before we move on to auction tactics and bidding, I'll assume you have carried out all the necessary research and checking and that everything meets with your approval. You are now in place as the auction begins and you know the value of the home to be sold. If you haven't done so, set the limit to which you are prepared to bid, the point at which you will stop bidding and leave the property to another buyer. Remind yourself that you will *not* increase your limit in the heat of bidding (a common mistake buyers make).

On the Day of the Auction

After calling the auction to order, the auctioneer is likely to present an exaggerated description of the merits of the home, and then invite someone to start the bidding. At this stage a smart buyer will make only one type of response — total silence. Let those who are less astute bid (they will!). Your aim is to do nothing to advance the momentum of the bidding.

For you, the slower things move, the better. Most naive buyers are too anxious to get in the action and to throw out early bids. They are doing their cause a disservice. Of course, the auctioneer would like everyone to think the opposite. One common phrase you'll hear is: *It doesn't matter where we start; it's where we finish that counts.* Remarks like this are used to fire up the bidding. Ignore them.

Even more dangerous in the early stages of an auction is the temptation to outbid another buyer. Buyer competition plays into the hands of the auctioneer and drives up the eventual price. The aim of the auctioneer — to get the highest price possible— is the opposite of yours. The auctioneer is your competitor, despite the congenial image usually projected.

So, should you restrict yourself to just one or two late bids? Not necessarily. When to start bidding will be dictated by how the auction progresses, how the price builds, how many buyers are active, and whether the auctioneer will actually sell when the bidding slows up or stops.

If a reserve price has been set but not reached, the auctioneer can there and then request the seller to lower the figure, in which case it might become clear the home *is* going to sell. If the reserve is not reached, the auctioneer can terminate the auction without accepting the highest bid, then, sometimes, list the home for conventional sale.

When you don't know the auctioneer's style, it can be difficult to know when he is going to bring down the hammer. Most good auctioneers use calculated dramatics to convince interested buyers the property is about to sell to the then-highest bidder. This 'threat to sell' is a ruse, until the final 'going, going, gone'. The aim is to scare buyers into bidding, and to lure in buyers who haven't yet entered the fray. Knowing the auctioneer's style gives you an advantage here; you'll be aware of the signs to watch for. However, before the auction, a colleague of the auctioneer might be willing to give you some pointers on this, particularly if you present yourself as a potential future client.

Staying out of the bidding until a sale seems imminent won't endear you to the auctioneer. But if it upsets him, let it be *his* problem, not yours. I've watched auctioneers try to intimidate low-profile buyers into playing the game *their* way. The best defense is to totally ignore them, in the knowledge that the auctioneer deprived of a response will soon look foolish. By sticking to your game plan you'll avoid the risk of being embarrassed into making decisions you might later regret. It's called putting the pressure back on the auctioneer. That's exactly what your non-reaction will achieve.

The keys are to know the rules of the game and to make your own decisions. How the auctioneer feels toward you is *completely irrelevant* to your goal to buy at the lowest price possible. Keep that thought firmly in mind.

How to Bid Wisely

Let's build a hypothetical scenario to illustrate key points about how to bid wisely. Suppose the auction has been rolling along with buyers bidding up the price in $10,000 bids, and now $5,000 bids. But at $245,000 no one seems willing to go further, and you haven't yet bid. Your pre-set limit, the most you are prepared to pay, is $285,000. What do you do next?

Do you raise the bidding by another $5,000 and make your offer $250,000? You could. But let's examine the situation more closely and see if you should.

The auctioneer wants nothing more than to sell the home. Perhaps he has told the owner that a sale is all but certain. But now excitement seems to have faded. This suggests a resistance point has been reached. It's possibly a natural stall. Or they may be at or close to the maximum price attainable on the day. Expect the auctioneer to put on a show of disbelief. Behind that, however, his fear is that further bids won't come easily. In fact, it might be hard to get any.

Now, in light of this, do you believe it would be a good idea to bid another $5,000?

I'd suggest offering $246,000, an increase of just $1,000. Because the size of the bid is being changed (from $5,000 to $1,000), the new bid would have to be spoken very clearly 'Two-forty-six'. A nod or hand gesture alone could be taken as a $5,000 bid and result in a situation where you are forced to explain your intention.

It is possible also that the auctioneer will act like he is rejecting your $1,000 bid, pressuring you to bring the price to $250,000. He might say he hasn't got authority to accept bids lower than $5,000. I've often seen this; it's always bluster. By focusing attention on you, the auctioneer hopes you'll be sufficiently bugged to give in to him. Answer such tactics with stoic silence. He will accept your bid unless another buyer offers more. A second option, often as good, is to repeat your bid 'Two-forty-six' and nothing else.

Do not to be drawn into an open exchange with the auctioneer. That is *his* game. It's not a polite conversation, leave your best manners at home. I'm not suggesting be rude, but you are engaged here in a battle of wits. Silence and persistence are the effective tools at your command.

Any time the bidding stalls, the auctioneer is likely to lapse into a repeat of the virtues of the property and the value-for-money opportunity it represents. This is called 'talking-up the price' and it can go on. Don't let it affect your resolve. Your bid is *still* $246,000, whether accepted or not. If there are no further bids it would be unheard of to sell to the underbidder ($245,000). That won't happen.

Sometimes you'll find yourself tempted to jump in with an increased bid, hoping to drop the other bidders. This is risky but can sometimes work; let your research, knowledge of the property, and what you know about auctions guide you (more on this in a moment). But, *inactive bidding* will almost always serve you better: Bid only when you have to, when it looks like the auctioneer is about to sell to another buyer, and dictate the size of your bid — until you reach your spending limit. Then stop! Inactive bidding tends to slow the auction's momentum and keep down the price; leave the competing to other buyers, especially in the early stages.

But what if you are apparently the only interested buyer? You will be forced to open the bidding (after letting the auctioneer plead). Here, your opening bid may be all you need to buy the property. Of course, this isn't a common occurrence, but it certainly does happen because some properties *must* sell at auction. Keep your opening bid extremely low, and if other bids follow, stay out until the business end of the bidding.

Understanding the Blast Bid

This is a tactic you should be aware of, not necessarily to use it, but to recognize when it is being used by a competing buyer. It's certainly not as safe a tactic as inactive bidding; however, when used intelligently it can work well.

You might hear the blast bid referred to as *shut-out bidding* or *power bidding*. The objective is always the same, to make a large bid that frightens off other buyers.

Let's return to our example to illustrate this. You've decided you'll pay a maximum of $285,000 for the home. You have satisfied yourself it is worth that. The bidding had been creeping up in $5,000 bids and has temporarily stalled at $210,000. You know that two or three buyers are interested. Here, a blast bid might win the property. You decide to bid $245,000 (an increase of $35,000) in the hope of killing off interest from other buyers.

Perhaps a blast bid of $245,000 would not accomplish that. Maybe it would need to be as high as $255,000 or $260,000. You just don't know, which is why this is a risky strategy. The message you're sending is 'power', that you want the home enough to out-muscle all those offering small bids, and that anything they might offer, you'll beat.

You can see the risk. If your blast bid buys the home at, say, $245,000, you won't know if you might have got it for less. Maybe the inactive bidding tactic would have saved you money. Or cost you more. Or maybe a smaller blast bid would have been sufficient. For all these reasons, I don't recommend blast bidding unless the buyer is experienced in buying at auction and confident about the property's value. Knowing the reserve price (if there is one) and how firm it is would also be beneficial.

This is where solid research and auction experience come in. You need to be certain you can rely on the information your strategy is based on, and have an accurate assessment of the value and condition of the home.

Case Study: When Things Go Terribly Wrong

Here is an account of an auction incident I witnessed personally in an average suburban neighborhood.

As a favor, I investigated a period-style home on behalf of an associate but recommended against it after my first inspection. That recommendation was accepted. The home was interesting and perfectly salable but suited to a different type of buyer.

The salesperson handling the auction confirmed my estimate of value; he expected it to sell at around $180,000 or a little higher on the day.

Out of curiosity I attended the auction on a Saturday morning. I expected the auctioneer would ask for an opening bid of around $120,000 to get the interested buyers involved. If two or more keen buyers had come to bid, I felt the selling price might be pushed to $190,000 or $200,000. (Incidentally, many auction buyers know nothing about smart buying or the wisdom of inactive bidding.)

After going through a lengthy description of the home and its attributes, the auctioneer asked for an opening bid. He had no sooner uttered those words (he hadn't even yet asked for a specific figure) when a man at the back of the audience shouted '$280,000'. Everyone gasped. The auctioneer froze, then enquired: 'Could you repeat the bid please, sir?' The man said again, '$280,000', this time more strongly.

No need to tell you, that was the only bid — a disastrous use of the blast bid. And it bought the home. The unfortunate buyer had either been very badly informed, or was just foolish, or both. He paid $100,000 more than the property was worth! It was painful to watch. I wanted to advise him but the hammer had come down.

The salesperson told me later that the buyer discovered the magnitude of his mistake soon after but ultimately went through with the purchase.

I don't want you to take from this that the blast bid has no validity. Like any tactic, it can be used wisely or unwisely. Had the buyer followed the steps in this section, he could have bought the home with $100,000 left in his pocket.

It was this buyer mistake, more than any other single incident, that pushed me to write this book.

Recognizing When the Auctioneer Is Going to Sell

You need to be able to predict when the auctioneer is about to sell. This will dictate the timing and size of your bid. The problem is that most auctioneers bluff continually that they are on the verge of bringing down the hammer. This is designed to draw higher bids and ferret out previously undisclosed interest.

Without experience of auctions, and of a particular auctioneer, it isn't easy to be sure when a bluff is taking place. Some auctioneers use specific phrases only when they are actually about to sell. Some examples: 'I'm going to sell' or 'the property is now on the market'. And of course, 'going once, going twice…' When the hammer hits, the buyer holding the highest bid has bought the home.

But a bid can be made right up to the moment before 'Sold' is called. Making a very late bid can lead to a number of advantages. The biggest is usually when the buyer holding the previous highest bid is prematurely confident. Your deliberately timed late bid can cause that bidder to drop out.

It isn't necessary to cut it so fine that you wait until the hammer is on its way down. It's more important to ensure you get your bid in, even if it's earlier than you preferred. A less than fully observant auctioneer can fail to notice a last-second bid. Take advantage of late bidding but don't risk being missed. If you can spot when the auctioneer is bluffing you'll time your late bids better.

Shills, Stooges and Conspirators

Shills and stooges are individuals who work secretly with an auctioneer but pose as legitimate buyers. I'm sometimes asked if they are still used today. It may be that only a small percentage of auction companies do this. It's a figure that's impossible to determine accurately, for obvious reasons. But it does happen.

These conspirators force up bidding by offering fake bids, particularly when several genuine buyers are competing for the property. They are also employed when bidding is sluggish, to get or keep things moving.

Here's how it works: To get the stooge to bid, the auctioneer uses a set of pre-planned signals, usually certain phrases or hand gestures. Even the size of the bid the auctioneer wants can be communicated in this way.

One big problem for genuine buyers is that stooges are difficult to spot, unless you've been around auctions for a while. Even then, there's no guarantee. The most even an experienced buyer can hope for is to be able to pick out potential conspirators and observe them during the auction. Sometimes the same person can be seen bidding at a number of a particular company's auctions, but never buying. This could be a stooge. But maybe not. Some people, for whatever reason, just like the 'fun' of bidding (as I said a few times before, we are psychologically complex beings). In either case, there isn't a lot you can do except stop bidding, which is far from an ideal solution. Even when you feel convinced the bidder is a shill or stooge, open challenge may not be the best remedy.

One response is to reduce dramatically the size of your bids. For example, from $5,000 to $500 while fixing a stare on the suspect. You might also ask the auctioneer to point out the bidder, bringing general attention to the situation. In either case the auctioneer is likely to signal the stooge to back off. Protecting the company's reputation is more important than the outcome of any single auction.

In some situations you may be entitled to ask, before the auction begins, for evidence of the genuineness of prospective bidders (who may be on a register). However, this involves privacy laws and legal rights and is outside the scope of this book, not least because legal rights vary from place to place. A real estate attorney is a good source of advice in this regard. Working with an Exclusive Buyer Agent familiar with auctions is also worth considering.

As I said, auction buying is not for the unknowledgeable, inexperienced home-buyer. If you decide to participate, attend as many auctions as necessary to learn how things work in your area, but only as an observer. Also, talk to real estate auction professionals. Ask a lot of questions and learn the ground rules: How do you get the most complete, factual description of the home before you bid? What is specifically included and excluded in the sale? What do you need to know about the method of payment required? Is settlement fixed or flexible within limits to suit the buyer? What reserve has been set? And so on. These questions and others help reduce the risk of unpleasant surprises.

When you are sure of what you are doing, you can expect to find bargains from time to time in the auction arena.

No Time to Let Your Guard Down

In one way, there is no difference between buying at auction and buying in the conventional way. The auctioneer is just as much your competitor as the real estate agent or salesperson. Their objective is clear and unambiguous — to get you to pay the highest price possible for the home!

In both cases you must keep your guard up. All the protective moves I advised in earlier chapters are just as necessary when buying at auction, even more so. Keep your cards close to your chest; never reveal how much interest you have in a property, nor how much you are prepared to pay; and never tell the size of your budget nor details of your personal circumstances that might stop you achieving your goal of buying the home safely and on the best price and terms possible.

Caution: When you set out to buy a home in the traditional way, or at auction, you will be up against a system that is designed to *stop* you achieving your goal. Nobody out there (except an Exclusive Buyer Agent or a 'true' or 'single' agent) is working to protect your present and future wealth, your peace of mind, and help you get the best deal all around.

The difference between homebuyers who get the best deals and those who don't is the know-how in this book — that means knowing how the game of real estate is played and using basic negotiation skills to turn the odds in *your* favor.

We are moving next to mortgages and financing, a critical part of your home buying journey. The next three chapters will simplify things, spell out what you need to do to get the best home loan, and tell you how to save thousands of dollars with, literally, *zero* risk to you!

PART FIVE

HOW TO SAVE BIG ON FINANCING YOUR HOME

CHAPTER 14

What You Need to Know About Mortgages

Almost any man knows how to earn money
. . . not one in a million knows how to spend it.

— Henry David Thoreau

Being a smart buyer means more than negotiating confidently with real estate agents and sellers.

When it comes to shopping for a mortgage, homebuyers frequently feel intimidated and out of their depth. Confused by jargon and industry posturing, many turn compliant and unquestioning. No doubt, borrower anxiety, naivety and lack of know-how are to blame, but so are those mortgage professionals who favor holding on to their haughty image. Be that as it may, shopping for a home loan is far too risky an undertaking for consumers to be passive about.

As with shopping for the best home deal, getting the best mortgage requires at least basic know-how. It's no exaggeration to say that the reward can be tens of thousands of dollars and priceless peace of mind, because getting the right loan can sometimes save you more than you negotiate off the asking price of the home. And the wrong mortgage can go on costing you money unnecessarily for as long as you hold it, in some cases thirty years.

It doesn't have to be that way!

Understanding mortgages is not so difficult — when it is taught well. In this chapter I'll set you on a safe path. So, even if it still feels challenging, stick with it, at least for now. You'll definitely grasp the basics of mortgages and mortgage shopping. You won't learn everything there is to know, nor should you, but you'll get enough know-how to protect your money and get top service from lenders. And I'll tell you about additional sources of help you can rely on.

The first point to keep in mind is that lenders need your business. The industry is extremely competitive. Gone are the days when homebuyers had to plead for a loan from their local bank. Today, nearly all homebuyers can expect to get a loan, even borrowers who have had financial problems, erratic employment histories, and delinquent debts. Borrowers in this latter group can usually be matched with loans and programs designed specifically for them.

Before we explore your options as a borrower, I want to re-emphasize two of the best moves I believe you can make.

First, use the resources of an Exclusive Buyer Agent. This agent (who is always 100% on your side) is a source of invaluable information and can frequently advise on particular loans and lenders, and save you considerable time and effort.

Second, engage the services of an attorney who specializes in real estate, one who demonstrates personal commitment to protecting your interests. Do this as soon as you decide to buy.

For many buyers, an Exclusive Buyer Agent won't be hard to find (more information on this later). Finding the right attorney might require more work. But once again, an Exclusive Buyer Agent will be able to give you at least a couple of referrals. Alternatively, have a short initial chat with two or three attorneys; most won't charge for this (but check). In each case, make sure to confirm fees and charges you'll incur if you go ahead. We live in a commercial world; attorneys want your dollars just as much as anyone. Many are willing to be flexible, especially if you offer to take care of some of the simpler information gathering tasks yourself. Enquire.

It is imperative to have an attorney *before* you sign any documents or make any binding commitments. Not after! Get a legal opinion on all loan agreement forms and home purchase contracts, and confirm that all settlement requirements and procedures will be taken care of. Between your offer being accepted and date of settlement (closing) an Exclusive Buyer Agent will usually orchestrate and monitor all the complex events that must take place — an enormous relief to you.

Your Mortgage Loan: Know What's at Stake!

As a smart buyer, your first and most critical goal is to understand clearly what you stand to win, or lose. Almost certainly, that's more dollars than you have stopped to think about. It will probably shock you to discover (below) just how costly going with the wrong loan can be. I'll show you clearly why you need to keep your wits about you.

When it's time to start your loan search your goal will be to identify the best mortgage deals available to you (rates and fees). This means information gathering, perhaps initially just reading lenders' ads and websites and maybe a half-dozen phone calls. And as I said earlier, discuss your plans with your Exclusive Buyer Agent, if you have one.

As this third edition is being written, typical home loan rates range from 4%-4.6%, but rates might be lower or higher as you read this.

First, using a few simple examples let's illustrate just how much money can be at stake. I'll use a range of interest rates so you can appreciate their effect on your repayments (figures are rounded slightly). Pay attention to the *huge* amount of interest paid in each case. And keep in mind that rates fluctuate, but the principles explained here always hold true. Remember too that these examples show only Principal (the loan amount) plus Interest (the cost of the loan) — usually abbreviated P+I. Your monthly repayment will usually also include other charges such as: property taxes, homeowner's insurance and Private Mortgage Insurance (PMI is generally required if your down payment is less than 20%).

Example 1:
Suppose you take a $100,000 mortgage at 7% interest for 30 years. If you keep the loan for the full term (30 years) you'll pay back in total: $239,500. That's your $100,000 loan (the principal) plus interest of *$139,500!*

Example 2:
Let's take that same loan of $100,000 over 30 years, but this time at just 5% interest. Over the full term you'll pay back in total: $193,250. That's your $100,000 loan, plus interest of *$93,250!*

Now let's see what shaving just one half point off that 5% rate will save you.

Example 3:
Loan: $100,000 over 30 years at 4.5% means you'll pay back in total: $182,400. That's your $100,000 loan, plus interest of *$82,400!*

So, cutting that half point off the interest rate saved you $10,850 over the 30-year life of the loan: ($93,250 minus $82,400).

Notice, however, that even the 4.5% loan required you to pay back almost twice the amount you borrowed: You borrowed $100,000 and paid back $182,407! It doesn't seem like a mere 4.5% interest rate would whack you that hard, does it?

Interest on the 7% loan hits a lot harder. You pay back nearly two and half times the loan amount. You borrowed $100,000 and paid back $239,500.

Total payback figures like these are far too seldom spelled out for borrowers. When they are, they usually come as a shock.

Now let's see what each of these loans would cost you in monthly repayments (P+I):

Example 1:
$100,000 loan at 7% for 30 years: $665 per month

Example 2:
$100,000 loan at 5% for 30 years: $535 per month

Example 3:
$100,000 loan at 4.5% for 30 years: $505 per month

Notice that the difference between the 5% and 4.5% loans is $30 every month.

Cutting that half point off your interest rate, on this $100,000 loan, saves you $360 every year ($30 x 12).

Now let's widen the comparison.

What if an unwary homebuyer pays 5.5% when a similar loan might be available from another lender at 4%? This is not typical but it certainly does happen. Here's the outcome:

Loan A:
- $100,000 at 5.5% for 30 years. Total you'll pay back over full term: $204,400.
  You pay back the $100,000 loan plus $104,400 interest.

Loan B:
- $100,000 at 4% for 30 years. Total you'll pay back over full term: $171,870.
  You pay back the $100,000 loan plus $71,870 interest.

By going with Loan B you save $32,530 ($204,400 minus $171,870).

Remember, these are total P+I payback figures based on the loan running 30 years. Now let's see what will be the difference in monthly repayments between Loan A and Loan B:

Loan A:
- $100,000 loan at 5.5% for 30 years: $568 per month.

Loan B:
- $100,000 loan at 4% for 30 years: $477 per month.

As you can see, Loan B (4%) saves you $91 every month ($568 minus $477). That's $1,092 saved per year. Over 10 years you save $10,920. And as we saw above, over 30 years you save $32,530! (figures are rounded to nearest dollar).

With these fixed-interest-rate loans your P+I repayment will be the same every month for as long as you hold the loan (unless you decide to change them; more on this later).

As these examples show, it is critical to find the best loan for your circumstances. Your money is always at stake, sometimes tens of thousands of dollars, as we've seen.

Note: Before we move on I'll clarify two terms that confuse homebuyers.

The first, Mortgage Protection Insurance or 'MPI', is also called Mortgage Payment Protection Insurance or 'MPPI'. This is an *optional* life insurance policy that will pay off your mortgage if you die. It is *not* legally required. Some of these policies also cover disability resulting from injury, job loss, etc.

Buying a home is one of those life events that should trigger your meeting with a financial planner to look at your life insurance needs and explore your options. MPI and MPPI are the most expensive life and/or disability covers you can buy, and are extremely profitable for banks and insurance companies.

A better starting point is to review your *overall* financial situation and try to find a life and disability plan that covers *not only* your mortgage but also ongoing expenses for survivors, etc. You should be doing this anyway but most people neglect it. So, let your home purchase be a reminder to review your situation with a financial planner as soon as possible. Financing a home means taking on a major debt. Unless you put down a big down payment the price you'll get by selling the home within five years or so will usually *not* cover the loan outstanding plus your selling costs.

The second type of insurance is Private Mortgage Insurance or 'PMI'. This is the second 'I' of PITI (Principal, Interest, Taxes and Insurance) and is part of your monthly repayment. It has nothing to do with illness or disability benefit or you dying unexpectedly. It exists simply to pay the lender if for any reason you stop paying your mortgage and the home goes into foreclosure. As noted earlier, you are generally required to take out PMI when your down payment is less than 20% of the purchase price. However, this is not so in every case. With some loan programs, lenders will waive PMI even though the down payment is less than 20%. Be sure to ask your lender if you qualify for one of these loans.

But interest rates are not the only feature you'll need to watch out for when comparing loans. You'll also encounter: points, fees, special conditions and loan terms, and lock-ins. We'll look at each of these as we move forward.

First, it's best to get a basic understanding of the types of loans available and how you might choose what's best for you. We'll then move on to explore the loan application process and ways to keep your out-of-pocket expenses to a minimum.

And, like it or not, mortgages mean math. I'll show you — simply — how the figures work. Even if you're a math hater, stick with it. All the figures are worked out for you, and clearly explained; it really isn't as confusing as you might have imagined.

Understanding Fixed-Rate Mortgages (FRMs)

You are probably aware of what is often referred to as a conventional home loan, the *30-year fixed-rate mortgage* (usually abbreviated: '30-year FRM' or similar). What it means is this: The amount borrowed is paid back in same-size monthly payments over 30 years (the *term* of the loan) at a specific (fixed) rate of interest that is set at the outset.

Simple, yes, but you need to be discerning. Because one lender's FRM might carry a rate of 4.5%, while another lender's FRM could be 4%, or even 5%. You want the least expensive loan, naturally, so pay attention first to the different interest rates lenders are charging on their loans.

Another option is the 15-year FRM, which you'll pay off in half the time. These are less common, but FRMs can be for any length: 10 years, 20 years, etc. Occasionally, even 40-year FRMs have been offered, but I don't recommend these for two reasons: 1) the monthly payment is only marginally lower than the 30-year

FRM, and 2) your total payback amount is extremely high.

Remember: All FRMs, short or long, require you to make equal monthly P+I payments over the life of the loan. This applies whether you hold the loan for the full term or sell the home and pay off the loan early.

Risk and Interest Rate Variation

Here's something else to bear in mind. Mortgage lenders deal in risk, and they price their loans accordingly. Their two big fears are that you'll fall behind in your repayments, and that you'll stop paying altogether. These are their risks. The risk is higher, they believe, on longer loans. For that reason they usually charge a slightly higher interest rate on a 30-year loan than on a 15-year loan. As I write, the following rates are being offered:

- 30-year FRMs up to a loan limit of $240,000 available at 4.25% to 4.75%.
- 15-year FRMs up to a loan limit of $240,000 available at 3.75% to 4.25%.

At such historically low interest rates, FRMs are a good choice, and are by far the most popular types of home loans.

But FRMs are not your only option, nor are they the right choice for all borrowers. Since you may be in the latter category, or be reading this at a time when those low FRM rates have passed, I will shortly explain some alternative loan types that are worth your consideration. Before doing that, however, let's clarify some fundamental facts of loans in general.

How Does the Length of the Loan Affect Your Repayments?

As you saw above, the longer the term the smaller the monthly repayments on the amount you borrow (even though the longer loan's interest rate is usually slightly higher). And, although your income will determine how big a loan you can get, the term of the loan will determine the size of your monthly repayment. A longer-term loan keeps your monthly repayment lower but you have a greater number of payments, and you pay back more in interest (take a look back at the previous examples).

But sometimes you won't have a choice. Based on the lender's qualifying criteria, the monthly repayment on a 30-year mortgage might be within your ability to repay, whereas the repayments on a 15-year loan might be considered too high by the lender.

Neither of these loans is inherently better; any loan must be matched to your financial circumstances and your personal feelings about debt. For that reason, you'll benefit from knowing a little more before deciding which loan is right for you.

Let's compare two FRMs side-by-side, with only the term being different. I'll once again use $100,000 as the loan amount, but note that the effect of longer and shorter terms applies to any amount you borrow. (*Reminder:* P+I stands for

Principal plus Interest):

Loan A:
- $100,000 borrowed at 5% over 30 years. Monthly P+I repayment: $537.

Loan B:
- $100,000 borrowed at 5% over 15 years. Monthly P+I repayment: $791.

In reality, the 15-year loan will carry a slightly lower interest rate. So let's re-do those figures:

Loan A:
- $100,000 borrowed at 5% over 30 years. Monthly P+I repayment: $537.

Loan B:
- $100,000 borrowed at 4.5% over 15 years. Monthly P+I repayment: $765.

At 4.5% this 15-year loan will cost you an extra $228 per month (up from $537 to $765). And it might be perfectly suited to your circumstances. The big benefit, and it is *big*, is that your total payback amount on a 15-year loan will be *significantly less* than on a 30-year loan. More detailed examples follow soon.

For now, we'll explore another type of loan you might want to consider, the ARM.

Understanding Adjustable-Rate Mortgages (ARMs)

How do you tell an ARM from a FRM? You'll see ARM loans written like this: 1/30 ARM, 5/1 ARM, 3/3 ARM.

ARMs are different from FRMs in a number of ways. The biggest difference, as the name implies, is that the interest rate on the loan is *not* fixed; it's adjustable and can move up or down. This means your monthly repayments *will* change. How frequently they can change is set by the type of ARM you decide on. ARMs can be any length: 30 years, 15 years, 5 years, etc.

Let's look at the details:

A '1/30 ARM' means this: 1) the loan is for 30 years, and 2) the interest rate can be adjusted up or down by the lender once per year (that's what the '1' means).

The ARM's interest rate is hooked to an index used by the lender, and as the index goes so goes your repayments. An 'index' is just a fluctuating scale reflecting the cost of money to lending institutions; you don't need to know any more about this. These 1/30 ARMs come into and go out of fashion; they're not as common as I write as they once were.

Instead, a slightly different type of ARM is currently popular. It's written like this: 3/1 ARM, or 5/1 ARM, or 7/1 ARM.

Let's break down the '3/1 ARM': 1) the '3' means that the initial interest rate remains unchanged for the *first three years* of the loan, and 2) the '1' means that after that initial 3-year period the rate can be adjusted once per year. It's the same idea with a 5/1 or 7/1 ARM.

We'll take a closer look now at how these loans work.

Important Features of ARMs

Every ARM has the following features:
1. Initial interest rate
2. Interval (period) for changes in interest rate
3. An index to which the loan is pegged or hooked
4. A 'margin' (the lender's profit) added by the lender to the index rate
5. Periodic cap, a limit on how much your loan can be adjusted in each period
6. Lifetime cap, a limit over which your loan's interest rate cannot be raised during its life.

Time to de-jargonize. Here's what all that means.

1. Initial Interest Rate

This is the rate the ARM starts out at. It's always lower than comparable FRMs. For example, a 30-year FRM might carry a fixed interest rate of 5%, while a 30-year ARM might start out at 3.5% (of course, it will not stay at 3.5%). In this case, the 3.5% is the rate on which your repayments will be based for the initial period of the loan (three years on a 3/1).

After this period, the adjustment phase begins (usually on the anniversary of the loan being issued); then the lender may, and typically does, change the rate yearly. So, on the first adjustment date your initial 3.5% ARM might be raised to 4%, 4.5%, or possibly lowered to 3%.

If interest rates are rising, your loan will be adjusted accordingly and your monthly repayments will increase. If rates are trending lower your payment may reduce. No one can be certain where interest rates are going a year into the future. However, general interest rate trends are sometimes predictable. If you are considering an ARM, talk with financially savvy people whose views you trust. Your view on interest rate direction will be one consideration when choosing a loan.

One advantage of ARMs is that they can sometimes be a little easier to qualify for. And the lower payments starting out are kinder on your pocket. Also, ARMs can be a good choice if you plan to remain in the house for between three and seven years, while the initial interest rate remains low. Of course, a lot depends on the difference between the ARM and FRM interest rates when you take out the loan, and on how the ARM rate might change if you hold it beyond its initial fixed-rate period.

So, are ARMs a gamble? Yes! But not until you move beyond the initial fixed-rate period. Over shorter periods, going with an ARM often pays off. Along with that, there are borrower safeguards on all ARMs, which we'll come to.

For now, to get an even better grasp of all this, let's apply it to a realistic situation. Assume you can qualify for a $100,000 FRM (which of course carries a higher interest rate than an ARM's initial rate). Your loan options might look like this:

Option 1:

- $100,000 FRM 5%, 30-years. Monthly payment (won't change): $537.

Option 2:

- $100,000 1/30 ARM 3.5%, 30-years. Initial monthly payment (will change): $449.

As you can see, this ARM will save you $88 per month in the first year ($537 less $449). After twelve months you'll be ahead by $1,056 ($88 x 12) over what the FRM would have cost.

Clear enough, I hope. Now let's see where you might stand when the 1/30 ARM's interest rate fluctuates moderately over the first four years. Here's how your: 1) monthly P+I repayments, 2) annual P+I costs, and 3) total P+I payback amounts will differ between the two loans over the first four years:

Year 1: FRM 5%: $537 x 12 = $6444   ARM 3.5%: $449 x 12 = $5,388
Year 2: FRM 5%: $537 x 12 = $6444   ARM 4.5%: $507 x 12 = $6,084
Year 3: FRM 5%: $537 x 12 = $6444   ARM 5.0%: $537 x 12 = $6,444
Year 4: FRM 5%: $537 x 12 = $6444   ARM 4.5%: $507 x 12 = $6,084
TOTAL PAID   **$25,776**   **$24,000**

In this realistic comparison, after four years the ARM will have saved you $1,776 ($25,776 less $24,000). Because the average interest rate you paid on the ARM added up to just 4.375%, as against the FRM's 5%. Correspondingly, your monthly repayments were lower in three of these four years.

Let's now consider years 5, 6, 7 and 8, and how the ARM interest rate might fluctuate; we'll then review where you stand at the end of the Year 8.

Year 5: FRM 5%: $537 x 12 = $6444   ARM 5.5%: $568 x 12 = $6,816
Year 6: FRM 5%: $537 x 12 = $6444   ARM 6.0%: $600 x 12 = $7,200
Year 7: FRM 5%: $537 x 12 = $6444   ARM 7.0%: $665 x 12 = $7,980
Year 8: FRM 5%: $537 x 12 = $6444   ARM 6.5%: $632 x 12 = $7,584
TOTAL PAID   **$25,776**   **$29,580**

You can now see that after Year 8 the ARM's earlier advantage has been wiped out because of interest rate fluctuation. It's possible of course that rates might have fallen, or remained static (less likely). Or they could have risen more steeply than shown. I am speculating here to make the point clear.

In our example, at the end of Year 8 the FRM has cost you $2,028 less than the ARM:

Cost of FRM up to end of Year 8: $537 x 12 months x 8 years = $51,552
Cost of ARM up to end of Year 8: $24,000 + $29,580 = $53,580

DIFFERENCE in cost of loans: = **$ 2,028**

If you dissect the math you'll see that you are saving money with the ARM all the way up to Year 7. It's only then that the FRM becomes less expensive overall. Bear in mind, again, that this is a hypothetical example. Nonetheless, it illustrates why ARMs are often a better choice if you plan to hold the loan for between three and seven years.

This argument also assumes you'll be able to get a 1%-2% lower initial interest rate on the ARM, which has typically been available. It assumes that interest rates do not suddenly shoot up, spiking up your ARM rate. However, as I alluded to earlier, the borrower has a safeguard here because ARM interest rates are limited or 'capped' at a certain level, meaning they can go so high and no higher (you'll see examples of this shortly).

When home loan interest rates are low, the difference between initial ARM rates and FRM rates shrinks, making fixed-rate mortgages more popular. But as rates increase, the difference between ARM and FRM rates also increases, often creating a gap of 2% or more between them, making ARMs more attractive.

If you tend to be overly anxious about risk, an ARM might cause you more worry than it's worth. Peace of mind should figure strongly in your decision. Many borrowers are more comfortable with the predictable repayments of a FRM even when ARM interest rates are attractive.

Before we move on, here's something to keep in mind before you apply for a loan: With one-year ARMs (1/30, 1/15, for example), lenders do *not* use the ARM's initial lower interest rate when assessing your ability to meet the required repayments. They use instead a higher rate, for extra security (for them).

For example, on a 3.5% ARM many lenders will expect you to qualify as if the loan was at 5.5% (3.5% plus 2%). Their rationale is that you might be able to handle the initial Year 1 low monthly repayment of a 3.5% loan rate, but could struggle with higher repayments in subsequent years, when the ARM's interest rate might rise to 5.5%. However, this stricter qualifying method is usually *not* applied to multi-year ARMs: 3/1, 5/1, or 7/1 ARMs, for example, just to 1-year ARMs.

As I mentioned earlier, for most borrowers planning to hold a home loan *longer* than six or seven years, a low-interest-rate FRM will often be a better choice. The problem of course is that new homebuyers can rarely predict how long they will stay in a home. National surveys report that most homeowners pay off their loans within the first ten years; they pack up and move to a new home. The best advice I can give you here is this: Ask lenders or a mortgage broker to show you comparison payment projections over varying periods of years — for both ARMs and FRMs.

One group of borrower's to whom ARMs are often particularly appealing are those taking very large loans. On loans of $300,000 and up, a borrower can sometimes save money by refinancing when their current ARM's initial lower rate is due to end. Refinancing is not cheap, but the money saved on lower loan repayments (due to the ARMs lower interest rate) might cover the refinancing cost with a tidy sum left over. As always when comparing loans, you must run the numbers side by side and look into the future.

Now, let's continue with our list of the six factors that describe ARMs.

2. Adjustment Period (Interval)

With a 1/30, as we've seen, the adjustment date comes along once each year, typically on the anniversary of the loan's issue date. That's when the applied interest rate (meaning your repayment) can change. Some weeks ahead of the adjustment (if the rate is going to change) you can expect to receive a New Payment notice from your lender.

One-year ARMs can be for 10 years (1/10) or 15 years (1/15), or just about any length of time up to 1/30. What's common to each is the single annual adjustment.

3. The Index

This is the underlying scale or financial measure of interest rates that a lender uses to determine the rate to charge on a particular ARM. For example, a one-year ARM will usually be pegged to the One-Year Treasury Securities Index. Whatever happens with that index will be transferred to your loan's interest rate. There are at least a half-dozen indexes used to set interest rates on different length ARMs. Once again, you don't need to burden yourself with trying to understand how indexes work.

4. The Margin

The margin is a percentage the lender adds to the index rate to create the market rate (the rate you pay). If the index to which your loan is pegged has a rate of 1%, the lender might add a margin of 2.75%, making the market rate on your ARM 3.75%. This add-on is the lender's profit. If you can find a lender that imposes a lower margin you might be able to save money.

5. Periodic Cap

If interest rates were to jump 3-4% in a short time span (this would be a steep increase), the lender *cannot* add this percentage increase onto your ARM when your loan's adjustment date comes around, because all ARMs come with safeguards called *caps*. If your 1/30 ARM's *periodic cap* is 2% (quite common), the interest rate you pay can never be increased (or decreased) by more than 2% in any one year.

Let's say your initial ARM interest rate is 3.5% and has a 2% periodic cap (as in the example above). If interest rates jump 2.5% in the year after you take your loan, that 2.5% cannot be added to your ARM rate on your loan's next annual adjustment date. The lender can increase your rate by no more than the 2% periodic cap, making your new rate 5.5%.

This provides you with some comfort but not as much as you might think.

Because let's say your 30-year ARM has a 3.5% initial rate on a loan of $100,000, your first year's P+I repayment will be $449 monthly. However, if your loan rate rises to 5.5% (3.5% plus the 2% increase) your monthly payment in the second year goes up to $568, a jump of $119.

Note: In the above example, your outstanding loan balance at end of Year 1 will have gone down (you'll then owe a little less than $100,000); so your new payment at 5.5% interest will be based on this lower *principal outstanding* figure. Plus, the term then remaining on your loan will be down to 29 years rather than thirty; which also affects what your new payment amount will be.

6. Lifetime Cap (Life Cap)

We've just seen that on a 1/30 ARM with a 2% periodic cap the lender is restricted in how high they can increase your interest rate in a single year (for an ARM with a one-year adjustment period). The *lifetime Cap* is yet another safeguard that works in the same way, except that it sets the highest level to which your interest rate can *ever* be increased above its initial rate.

For example: On a 3.5% 1/30 ARM with a 2% periodic cap and a 6% lifetime cap, the maximum annual interest rate you could *ever* be charged is 9.5% — your initial rate of 3.5% plus the 6% lifetime cap. So, even if mortgage rates soared to 13% (which has happened), you won't ever pay more than 9.5% on that particular loan. Naturally, you would not welcome your rate climbing to 9.5%, but the lifetime cap helps you envision a worst-case scenario. Consider this carefully when comparing loans.

Other Types of ARMs

Arms can vary quite a lot, and new features are introduced all the time. In the two variations below you'll recognize common characteristics we've already explored.

Hybrid ARMs

These loans, introduced earlier, have become popular for reasons we've already seen. First, they typically carry a lower initial rate than FRMs. And second, they do so for more than one year. A 5/1 ARM or a 7/1 ARM means that these loans hold their initial interest rate for five years and seven years respectively (other options are 3/1 and 10/1).

Sometimes called *multi-year ARMs,* these loans do not generally carry as low a rate as the 1/30 or 1/15 type, simply because the lender cannot adjust the rate as frequently.

If you see yourself moving within the loan's initial lower-rate period (five years or seven years, for example) these loans are worth considering because, as we saw, they can work out cheaper than FRMs, and they offer stable payments for an extended period (unlike 1/30 or 1/15 ARMs, whose rates can change every year from year one).

With Hybrid ARMs, after the initial period (three years, five years, seven years, etc) the loan turns into a one-year ARM for the rest of its life, meaning the interest rate can then adjust annually, just like a 1/30 or 1/15 ARM.

Caution: Ask your lender (then confirm with your attorney) if there's an early payoff penalty clause with any loan of this type, and what it could mean for you.

Convertible ARMs

As the name implies, this loan allows the borrower the *option* of converting to a FRM at some future point. The fee for converting can range from $250 to $600, but that certainly beats the thousands of dollars refinancing to a new loan would cost.

A Convertible ARM's initial rate is always lower than the conventional FRM. And the timeframe in which the borrower can switch over to a FRM is always specified in the terms and conditions. Often, the switch cannot be made within the first year, nor after the fifth year, though this can vary. Be sure to confirm such details.

Why would converting make sense? Typically because a less-costly loan is available. During the Convertible ARM's allowed period you might decide to switch to a lower-interest FRM and thus reduce your monthly repayments. Naturally, if interest rates on alternative loans are higher or the same you'd stay with your ARM. In practice, Convertible ARMs do not typically convert to the current FRM rate, but to a rate about 0.25% (one quarter point) higher, which might still be a good deal. If you are contemplating converting, be sure to discuss your options with a competent professional.

Comparing ARM Features

Here's a key question: What are the most important features to evaluate when shopping for an ARM?

Mortgage experts sometimes advise that you watch the indexes, and choose your loan according to how interest rates are headed (remember, the interest on your ARM is pegged to one particular index).

However, my own view differs: As long as you can get good advice you don't need to track financial indexes. If learning a little more about indexes isn't for you, skip ahead to *Points, Fees, and Closing Costs,* below

There are two main types of index, a leading index (leads the interest rate trend up or down) and a lagging index (stays behind the trend). If interest rates are falling, the leading index will take your loan rate down more quickly (to lower repayments), and the opposite if rates are on the up.

When rates are rising, a lagging index is slower to rise; it won't take your loan rate there so quickly (to higher payments). One popular leading index is the One-Year Treasury Bill Index, and a popular lagging index is 11th District Cost of Funds Index.

How do you find out what direction the indexes are moving in? Ask lenders or mortgage brokers. And ask which indexes their loans are pegged to.

Another important feature to know about is the lender's margin. As we saw earlier, this is the part (profit) added to the index by the lender to arrive at the rate you'll pay. When you know the index rate, you can add on the margin to get the loan's *market rate* (the lender has already done this). Remember, your initial ARM rate will typically be a few percentage points below the market rate, a move designed to win your business, often called a *teaser rate*. But you need to be cautious here too, because a low initial ARM rate, can rise steeply in the course of a few years, as we noted earlier.

The third feature you'll need to compare and understand is the initial interest rate being charged on the ARM, and what this might mean for you in the short term and long term. We saw earlier that typically there has been a 1%-2% difference between initial ARM rates and conventional FRM rates.

Recap: Three important questions to ask are: How often can the loan be adjusted? By how much can it be adjusted periodically? What is the lifetime cap on the loan?

Points, Fees and Closing Costs

When you go for any type of loan you are presented with a litany of fees. Some are hard to understand but are small enough not to cause you too much worry. However, one fee that can be costly, that you'll see again and again as you compare mortgages, is *points*.

In fact, there are two different fees referred to as points, and you need to be able to distinguish them. First, 'one point' always means 1% of the loan amount. On a loan of $100,000, one point is equal to $1,000; on a $250,000 loan, it's $2,500.

Some lenders charge an *origination fee,* which they refer to as a 'points'. This fee is often one point (1%) but can be two points or more. It's simply a charge you pay to the lender for processing your loan, usually at closing (settlement). Sometimes it's negotiable — well worth trying!

The second kind of point, and better known, is called *discount points.* But this is a misnomer; it isn't strictly a discount. The term was created by lenders, who see charging the borrower this fee as a way to keep the interest rate lower than it might otherwise be. You'll usually see this figure quoted along with the loan rate. When a lender advertises an FRM at '4%/30 1+2' you are being offered a fixed-rate mortgage at 4% interest rate over 30 years, plus one point (1% of the amount you borrow) as an origination fee, plus two discount points (another 2%) paid to the lender.

Let's see how this works out:

You borrow $100,000: You'll pay $1,000 to the lender as a 1% origination fee. You'll pay an additional $2,000 to the lender (2%) in discount points. Total: three points ($3,000). Some lenders combine these two fees and state simply: '3 Points'.

Remember, points and lender fees are *not* carved in stone. With mortgage brokers and bankers these charges are almost always negotiable to some degree. A broker or lender might well decide to give up part of their profit in order to get your business, particularly when you make it known that you can get as good a loan, or better, elsewhere. Expect some loan professionals to be tough; others will make concessions more easily, even on interest rates. In either case, *only* borrowers who negotiate for concessions will get them.

What's more, you might be offered the option of paying extra points in return for a lower interest rate. On the $100,000 loan we looked at earlier the lender might offer to reduce the 4% interest rate to 3.75% or 3.50% provided you pay one extra point (an additional fee of $1,000). This is called *buying down* the rate; you 'buy' the reduction. Ask about such options if it seems appropriate. But don't fail to ask the lender to reduce the lender fees as an incentive to get your business.

Finally, the number of points charged varies from lender to lender and from loan to loan. This is a significant charge to keep in mind when comparing loans. And don't be dissuaded from questioning lenders or mortgage brokers until you are certain you understand all the fees you'll incur.

Since 2015 it has been easier for the borrower to gain this full awareness of loan terms, conditions and costs. All lenders are now obligated to give you a 'Loan Estimate' within three business days of receiving your mortgage application. This official 3-page document spells out important details relating to the loan you have requested, and makes it simpler for you to compare costs and other details between different loans and loan providers.

The Loan Estimate requirement came into effect as part of regulations overseen by the Consumer Financial Protection Bureau (www.cfpb.gov). The document you'll be given includes estimated interest rate, monthly payment, and total closing costs for the loan, and other information. It also provides details on the estimated costs of taxes and insurance, and how the interest rate and repayments may change in the future. Even better, it's written in clear language and is designed to help you better understand the terms of the mortgage loan. Be sure you get it, and read it.

Note: See additional important advice later on on how to save money on points and lower your loan rate under *How You can Benefit from Understanding Lenders' Loan Pricing Adjustment Chart* in the chapter *Shopping for Your Loan: Where and How.*

More About Closing Costs

These costs are many and varied. That's why you should expect to spend an additional 5%-7% over the loan amount. Closing costs are generally considered to include the fees paid to the lender and the lender's attorney, but include also fees that are unrelated to the lender, such as title insurance and homeowner's insurance fees.

When making your application, I advise that you question the necessity of each individual fee, and ask for a waiver on each as you go down the list. Some cannot be waived, of course, but others can and often are, for borrowers willing to negotiate. When faced with the risk of losing a confident, pre-qualified borrower hardly any lender would be so foolish as to reject all your requests.

The following list gives you approximations of fees you are likely to be asked to pay:

- Loan application, sometimes negotiable: $0-400;
- Origination fee, negotiable, usually 1% of loan amount, some lenders don't charge this as a separate fee;
- Home Appraisal: $350-400;
- Credit check: $50-75;
- Lender's attorney: $300-500, ask for this to be waived entirely;
- Title insurance: $550-700;
- Survey: $500-700;
- Homeowner's insurance: $500-1,000;
- Recording: $75;
- Tax service: $75;
- State transfer tax: $0-750;
- Discount points, negotiable: $0-4,000;
- Homebuyer's attorney, negotiable; $400-1,250.

Please understand that these are general approximations. The fees you'll pay may vary quite a bit depending on the lender, the location, and the home. Again, a local Exclusive Buyer Agent, or your lender of choice, will give you the details that apply to you.

Loan Lock-ins

'Locking in' (a *lock-in*), also referred to as a *rate lock*, means getting a guarantee from the lender that the interest rate, terms, and the costs you've been quoted will be honored for a certain period of time. Ask for this guarantee in writing. The reason you would want to lock in is because you don't want surprises later, especially if you suspect interest rates are headed up or you are suspicious about the lender following through.

Lenders' policies on lock-ins differ; be sure to get a clear explanation. Importantly, keep in mind that rates and terms quoted to you verbally at application (including points) may *not* be the ones you get when you go to settlement — unless you lock-in.

Lock-ins, as you would expect, have a life; they expire typically after 30, 45 or 60 days, though some lenders offer a ridiculously low 10-day lock-in (which you should protest). A 45-day lock-in period should give you and the seller sufficient time to settle. But 60 days is better, and 90 is better again.

On the other hand, if interest rates are clearly falling you may not want to lock in until you are ready to go to settlement, especially if you think rates might be one half-point lower. To judge such things, seek out good advice and stay informed about conditions in the market.

On your first contact with a lender it's a good idea to ask for a blank copy of the lender's lock-in form. Show it to your attorney, because some of these forms are worthless; they contain escape clauses that allow the lender to get out of the obligation if certain market changes occur. Your attorney will spot these clauses. This is another important reason to engage a good real estate attorney; smart buyers make use of their attorney's specialized knowledge, usually at no extra cost. Buyers who fail to do this waste a good resource, and take unnecessary risks!

Finally, lock-ins aren't always free, unfortunately. Many lenders will charge a flat fee or a percentage of the loan amount. Whether or not you have to pay (argue the point!), ask the lender to agree to honor a drop in interest rates. This means that if rates go down before settlement, the lender will allow your loan rate to *float down*. Some will do this, some won't. None will unless *you* request it!

Next, applying and qualifying for a home loan.

CHAPTER 15

Applying and Qualifying for a Mortgage

Great things are not done by impulse,
but by a series of small things brought together.

— Vincent van Gogh

There is little point in shopping seriously for a home until you are at least pre-qualified by a lender, or you are confident you have provisionally pre-qualified yourself.

Most lenders do not charge for pre-qualifying. This is not a loan application and not pre-approval; it is simply the process in which a lender (any lender or mortgage broker will do this) considers your financial situation and tells you how large a mortgage you are likely to get. It typically takes less than half an hour and little if any documentation is required.

Do not inflate your income or understate your debts and expenses as this will skew the process and could cause you to be turned down later for the loan you require. Knowing the size of loan you can get will tell you how much you can pay for a home.

I recommend you get loan pre-qualification as soon as you decide you want to buy a home, before you start your search. Remember though, pre-qualification is nothing more than a preliminary guide. On the other hand, 'pre-approval' tells you the size of loan the lender is willing to offer you, and other details. Don't confuse the two (more details on this coming up).

If you find a home prematurely, before getting loan pre-approval, you're likely to endure some anxious days or weeks as the lender processes your application. If this happens, you can speed things up somewhat by knowing ahead of time what documentation is required, then bringing everything with you on the day you apply. All mortgage lenders require specific standard information about you in order to assess the risk you present.

Let's see what that documentation can include:

What Lenders Want to Know About You, and How To Understand Your Credit Score

The three main questions lenders want answered are:

1. Is your income stable, and sufficient to pay back the loan you are seeking?
2. Is the home you are hoping to buy adequate collateral for the loan?
3. Is your credit history that of a person who pays bills on time?

If your income has been fairly stable over the past few years, despite several changes of jobs, you are likely to get approval for a loan amount the lender considers safe. A consistent saving record can make up for some minor lapses in employment. Also, job switching is more common today and, fortunately, is considered less an indicator of credit risk than it once was.

The second of the three questions above relates to the home you want to buy, whether it provides adequate value to protect the lender's investment. But this is outside your control. The lender will organize an appraisal of the home (for which you pay). If you managed to negotiate a good purchase price, and presuming the home was not grossly overvalued by the seller or salesperson (unlikely but possible), this will present no problem.

The third question deals with your credit history and 'credit score', a topic that is so important to the homebuyer it's the focus of the next section.

Credit Reports & Credit Scores:
What you Need to Know

Get your credit report and check it — early! This is one of the most important pieces of advice you can take from this book. If your credit report is inaccurate (don't be surprised) or not as healthy as you require, get to work immediately and sort it out. Your home buying success may depend on it.

Too many buyers wait until they have a home under contract or a mortgage application submitted before obtaining and checking their credit report. This is a serious mistake.

Credit reports commonly contain errors (see survey later). If you discover errors or problems late in the home buying process, expect a hugely stressful crisis, and potentially the loss of the purchase. It can take three months and longer to get inaccurate information removed from your credit reports, and longer again to get your credit scores to rise to where you can qualify for the mortgage you need, or qualify for a reduced interest rate. Most sellers won't wait, period. And you may already have spent considerable money on inspections and other home related services. Then you just end up poorer and back to square one.

Let's do an overview of this whole area of credit and credit reports, and how you can ensure you don't get caught out. We'll look at a few terms you'll need to grasp and one or two techniques that will enable you to steer clear of nasty surprises.

What is your Credit Score and Why is it Critical?

The term 'Credit Score' usually refers to your FICO score, a number based on a formula developed by the Fair Isaac Corporation, which looks at a summary of all your credit accounts and payment history. As noted above, getting a copy of your credit reports and credit scores early in the process is an absolute must.

Your FICO score determines your access to — and cost of — the credit you'll need. Most lenders use it as the basis for loan or credit approvals, so the higher your score the better; a low score will bring you more problems than you realize. FICO credit scores range from 300-850. Fair Isaac Corp calculates them for each of the three big credit-reporting agencies: Trans Union, Equifax, and Experian. You can get more information on this at: www.myfico.com.

How your FICO Credit Score is Compiled

Thirty-five percent (35%) of your numerical score is determined by your payment history. Do you regularly pay your bills on time to creditors that submit information to the credit bureaus? Overdue medical bills, utility bills and other bills may negatively affect your score.

Thirty percent (30%) is based on the amounts you owe to each of your creditors, and how that compares with the total credit available to you, or to the total loan amount you took out (debt to equity ratio). Also, if you're maxing out your credit cards, your score may suffer. It appears that it is best to keep your outstanding balances below 30% of your maximum credit available (for example, maximum of $6,000 if your credit limit is $20,000, though this is the ideal, not a requirement).

Fifteen percent (15%) is based on the length of your credit history, how long you've had each account and how long it's been since you had any activity on those accounts. Usually, the fewer and older the accounts, the better.

Ten percent (10%) of your score is based on how many accounts you've opened recently compared with the total number of accounts you hold, and also on the number of recent inquiries on your report made by lenders to whom you've applied for credit. Your score can drop if it looks like you are seeking several new sources of credit, which is interpreted as a sign that you may be in financial trouble. However, when a lender initiates an enquiry about your credit report without your knowledge (such as when making credit offers to you), it should not affect your score. Making applications with different mortgage lenders shouldn't hurt either, but try to keep this within a six week period, if possible. Also, every enquiry you trigger when you apply for a credit card can negatively impact your score, so be selective.

The types of credit you make use of determine the final ten percent (10%). Having installment debt, like a mortgage on which you pay a fixed monthly amount, demonstrates that you can manage a large loan. But how you handle revolving debt, like credit cards, tends to carry more weight; it is seen as more predictive of your future behavior. For example, do you pay off the balance each month or just the minimum? Do you charge to the limit of your cards or rarely use them? These are the kinds of activities that are looked at in determining your credit score.

Most important: Do NOT take on new credit or apply for credit in the months leading up to buying a home, and certainly never when you have a home under contract. Oddly, prospective homebuyers make another big mistake: they finance the purchase of a new car while their mortgage application is being processed. When the mortgage company discovers that a new loan is being taken on, it will often refuse to qualify the buyer for the mortgage, and the buyer can then lose the purchase.

What is Not in Your FICO Credit Score?

Contrary to popular belief, your age, your employment history, and where you live are not used in determining your credit score. This is not to say lenders won't consider this information — they will — but these are not computed into calculating your FICO score.

Why do Mortgage Lenders Pay so Much Attention to Credit Scores?

Statistics indicate that one in every eight borrowers with a FICO score below 600 will be severely delinquent or will default on their loan. However, only one borrower in thirteen hundred with a score above 800 will have such problems. That's why lenders rely so heavily on the scores.

What Can You do to Get and Keep a Higher Credit Score?

1) Don't have late payments! 2) Avoid sudden surges of credit activity and credit enquiries, and 3) Don't tap-out your credit. Using more than thirty percent of your credit line can negatively impact your credit score, as we've just seen.

Where Can you Get Your Credit Reports and Credit Scores?

As part of a mortgage pre-qualification and pre-approval, your mortgage lender will pull a 'tri-merge credit report' showing your FICO credit scores as well as your credit reports from all three major credit reporting agencies in the US: Equifax, Experian, and TransUnion.

Tip: Some lenders and mortgage brokers may want to pull your credit report and credit score from *only one* credit reporting agency for your pre-qualification. But, you should insist they pull reports from *all three* agencies (tri-merge), thereby obtaining credit scores they'll actually use in processing your full loan application later. Pulling from just one agency can be damaging to you because a single report might show your *highest* credit score, while either or both of the other two could show a lower score and additional issues you'll need to deal with immediately. In this way, a lender or mortgage broker could pre-qualify you successfully based on a *single* report, then disqualify you later based on the second or third report. Keep this in mind.

You will later pay just a small fee for this tri-merge report (typically at closing) but your lender should be able to pull it initially and review it with you, and even provide you with a copy (be sure to request one). They will also be able to make suggestions on how to improve your credit and credit score. Working with the lender in this way is the least expensive method for obtaining your tri-merge credit report plus official FICO credit scores. It's also the most timely and most reliable way to evaluate what's there and receive help, if required.

If you wish to obtain your credit reports *before* meeting with a lender or mortgage broker you have an ally. A federal law, the Fair and Accurate Credit Transactions Act (the FACT Act of 2003), requires the credit reporting agencies to provide you with one free credit report every twelve months. The official website is www.annualcreditreport.com.

You can obtain additional credit information from the Federal Trade Commission at www.ftc.gov, just click the 'Get Your Free Credit Report' button. You'll see an introduction on how to use the above website on www.annualcreditreport.com, and a direct link to it.

However, while these are easy and worthwhile ways to check your credit — rather than buying your credit report and credit score from each of the big credit agencies — they do *not* include your FICO credit score. Each credit bureau charges you for that (this is why it's better and cheaper to do it through your lender or mortgage broker). And here's another caution to bear in mind: The 'credit scores' given to you by the big credit bureaus and others are called 'consumer scores'; they are *not* the same FICO credit scores they give to lenders qualifying you.

These and other 'inconsistencies' (that's putting it nicely) led to the Consumer Financial Protection Bureau (CFPB) taking an action against one of the main credit reporting agencies and its subsidiaries for deceiving consumers about the 'use' of the credit scores it sold them. The agency in question claimed these credit scores were used by lenders to make credit decisions, but lenders *did not*, in fact, use these particular scores to make such decisions.

And things get even curiouser: When you apply for a car loan, *that* credit 'score' is different again from the FICO 'score' used when you are applying for a mortgage, and both are different from the 'consumer scores' I mentioned above, which agencies send directly to homebuyers. Each 'score' is compiled using a different method to arrive at a particular three digit number. Potentially very misleading. Stay alert, and informed.

Typically, mortgage lenders use FICO scores from Equifax. At www.myfico.com you can get all three credit reports (details below), along with your three FICO scores. For this they'll charge you a one-time fee of around sixty dollars.

The three Major Credit Bureaus are:

- EQUIFAX: equifax.com 800-685-1111
- EXPERIAN (Formerly TRW): experian.com 888-397-3742
- TRANSUNION: transunion.com 800-888-4213

As I mentioned above, mortgage lenders get credit information from all three big credit reporting agencies when processing your mortgage application. You should do the same. If you are married, get individual reports rather than joint reports; this makes it easier to deal with errors and inaccurate information for each partner.

Note that it's also easier to challenge information on reports obtained from individual credit reporting agencies, rather than on reports that combine information from two or all three agencies. The three credit reports you'll get through www.annualcreditreport.com are separate, and thus are easier to review and challenge.

How To Correct Errors and Inaccuracies on Your Credit Report

Here's a tip that might well save you untold heartache. When you receive your reports go over them carefully. Note errors and inaccurate or unknown information, then contact the respective credit reporting agency in writing and ask them to 'validate' the inaccurate items.

Most people ask the agency simply to 'verify' rather than 'validate' the inaccurate information. Don't do this. It is easier for the agencies to meet the legal threshold of 'verify' than it is the threshold of 'validate'. The law requires the agency to 'validate', when asked. Let them know you know this, and that this is what you require.

Simply circle the incorrect or inaccurate item and mark it 'inaccurate' or 'incorrect' or 'not mine' or 'unknown', as the case may be. Make a copy for yourself and mail the original to the credit bureau you got the report from. Send it via Priority Mail so that you have a mailing receipt. Then go online and print out a copy of the USPS confirmation of delivery. Keep these for future reference. The credit bureaus are required to respond to you within 30 days of receipt of your enquiry. However, you might find that several attempts are needed to get a corrected report from each agency. They are good at using delaying tactics. Be persistent. Stick to your guns; let them know you know the law.

Although getting inaccurate information removed from your credit reports may take time and patience, you don't need to engage a 'credit repair company' to do this for you. They're expensive and often not worth the cost. Besides that, they do the same work and follow the same procedures you can do on your own. But do ask your lender or Exclusive Buyer Agent to help. Both will have experience of such matters and should be able to advise and assist you.

And keep in mind too that some lenders have an expedited method of dealing with the credit bureaus to speed up the process when there are obvious errors in your reports. Don't hesitate to ask the lender for this assistance.

Dealing with Negative Information such as Bankruptcy, Judgments, and Collections

Bankruptcies *must* be removed from your credit report after ten years. Judgments, collections and other negative items after seven years. For this reason, you might assume that if you have a bankruptcy or other negative item on your record that you are in 'credit prison' for seven or ten years.

But maybe not. Keep this in mind: Nothing in the law requires any negative item to remain for a 'minimum' length of time on your report. In actuality, if 'inaccurate information' is being reported *within an item* that otherwise is accurate, you can legally challenge it, and if the agency cannot *validate* the item and correct the inaccuracy, they *must* remove it from your credit report. Ask you attorney for guidance.

Why You Need to be Vigilant

Not long ago a survey reported by the US Public Interest Research Group (US PIRG) found that:

> *'One in four credit reports contains errors serious enough to cause consumers to be denied credit, a loan, an apartment or home loan, or even a job. The big credit bureaus and big business tolerate big mistakes in credit reports, but those mistakes ruin the financial reputations of hardworking Americans.'*
>
> — *Ed Mierzwinski, US PIRG Consumer Program Director*

PIRG and other consumer organizations have issued numerous reports showing that sloppy credit bureau practices are at fault for errors in consumer credit reports. US PIRG collected two hundred surveys in thirty states from adults who reviewed their credit reports for accuracy. Key findings include:

- Twenty-five percent (25%) of the credit reports contained errors serious enough to result in the denial of credit,
- Seventy-nine percent (79%) of the credit reports contained mistakes of some kind,
- Fifty-four percent (54%) of the credit reports contained personal demographic identifying information that was misspelled, long-outdated, belonged to a stranger, or was otherwise incorrect,
- Thirty percent (30%) of the credit reports contained credit accounts that had been closed by the consumer but incorrectly remained listed as open.

Enough said, with 79% of credit reports containing mistakes? As a smart buyer you'll obtain and check your credit report as soon as you make the decision to buy a home!

Help From the Consumer Financial Protection Bureau

Finally, another excellent source of information about credit and home buying is the CFPB, Consumer Financial Protection Bureau. CFPB is a US government agency that makes sure banks, lenders and other financial companies treat you fairly. Log on to www.consumerfinance.gov and click 'Consumer Tools' for more information on a number of finance related subjects.

Let's look now at going shopping for a mortgage.

CHAPTER 16

Shopping for Your Home Loan: Where and How

Doubting everything and believing everything are two equally convenient solutions that guard us from having to think.

— Henri Poincaré

As in other areas of home buying, I believe the consumer is too often badly served when shopping for the best loan.

Potentially misleading lender promotions are common. Even worse, there are people in the mortgage industry whose training does not qualify them to expertly advise the borrower, yet they presume to do so. Some don't recognize when the loan they are offering is unsuited to the borrower's needs.

Your best recourse is to find a trustworthy advocate, a professional whose integrity and knowledge you can rely on. But how do you find such an ally? Well, first, let me suggest here an idea backed up by long experience: Using a local mortgage lender or broker is usually the best approach.

Shopping at Banks, S&Ls & Mortgage Companies

When shopping for a mortgage your goal should be to find a loan professional who possesses competence and integrity. That person may be working at your local bank or S&L, or could be a mortgage broker or mortgage company representative.

I don't recommend that you walk into your local bank or S&L and accept the first loan you are offered. Your responsibility to yourself is to be discerning, assess and compare different loans and different lenders. To do that well you'll need to make use of your notebook, to record names and contact numbers and clear details of loans well before you start your search for a home.

If you choose to review loans offered by local banks, stay clear of the least experienced loan officer or clerk, which will often be the person staffing the loan desk. A talk with the manager might save you from the wrong loan or unjustified disapproval of your application. Better yet, ask to deal with an experienced mortgage loan officer. And when you meet this person weigh up the level of synergy between you. If it's not positive and congruent, go elsewhere; this relationship is critical.

Also, while many banks do not charge a loan origination fee (unlike most mortgage brokers and mortgage companies), the typical 1% fee you might save can quickly be given back through an inept advisor selling you the wrong loan. (The origination fee is usually 1% of the amount you borrow.) But note, inept salespeople are not found only in banks; mortgage companies have their share. Stay alert.

On the other hand, a good mortgage broker can save you a lot of shopping-around time, and often a chunk of money. Again, look for competence and integrity. Most brokers will do their best to get you the loan that is right for your circumstances, but it is always smart to question the product you are being offered. Commissions are higher on some loans than on others, which creates a temptation for salespeople to push these loans even when they might not be ideal for a particular buyer, or might not be the least expensive loans available.

When interviewing mortgage brokers, ask questions like these:

- How many loans have you placed in the past year?
- What percentage of your loans are approved (look for 90% or more)?
- What types of loans do you specialize in?
- How are you paid? Is commission taken from my fees at closing, is the fee paid by the lender the loan is placed with, or through a separate fee paid by me?
- What recent loans have you placed for clients whose situations resemble mine?
- Are there recent clients I can talk with for references?

A knowledgeable, honest, hard-working mortgage broker is a blessing. This is especially so when your employment record, credit history, or current financial situation make getting a loan harder. Good mortgage brokers provide quality advice and can solve problems your bank or mortgage company may not be able or willing to tackle.

Obtaining a loan from the bigger banks requires extra caution. They often have their own subsidiary mortgage companies where you are likely to find yourself dealing with commissioned reps. You'll need to ask the kind of interview questions listed above, and others. For example, does the rep make a higher commission on certain types of loans (maybe a type not right for you)? Is the rep's personal commission higher on loans made *above* a certain interest rate? In other words, are there salary incentives for the rep to get the most out of you — a conflict of interest? You need to know.

You are searching for someone who will place *your* best interests first, a professional who will get you the best loan possible.

By the time you are ready to get down to the serious business of making a formal loan application you should have talked with a number of lenders or brokers.

You'll then have a good idea of the loans and rates being offered in the market. This preparation is invaluable, and it doesn't all have to be done out on the street. You can monitor rates online, but I *do not* recommend 'signing up' or providing your personal details to online sites. In doing so you often unknowingly give these sites permission to pass on details and personal information about you to various other service providers who'll use your information in ways you may not be aware of and might later regard as inappropriate.

Finally, you'll also do well to look with skepticism at 'online pre-qualification' and 'online pre-approval'. Some websites claim to offer such services but almost invariably they lead to problems that can derail your home search and cause you grief. Some consumer advocates say about these online services: 'They aren't worth the paper they're written on'. Stick with the local, face-to-face approach to getting pre-qualification and pre-approval. An Exclusive Buyer Agent will always be able to direct you to quality, trustworthy service providers, which is an excellent starting point.

I'll say more about pre-qualification and pre-approval shortly.

Pre-Paying Your Mortgage, Pre-Payment Clauses & What You Need to Know

Lenders sometimes impose penalties on borrowers who pay off their loans ahead of schedule — 95% of buyers do this. Certain lenders have always imposed these penalties on ARMs paid off in the early years, but now banks and mortgage companies frequently insert these 'pre-payment penalty' clauses into fixed-rate mortgage (FRM) contracts.

The sting is this: Pre-paying your mortgage may mean you have to hand over an additional 1%-2% of the original loan amount, in some cases after being in the house for five or ten or more years.

So, what can you do?

Before agreeing to a loan offer, make sure the mortgage does *not* contain such a clause (unless of course you are willing to accept it). If you find such a clause, ask the lender to remove it. If the answer is no, you may be well advised to refuse the loan, at least while you explore what other lenders can offer. The last thing you need is having to hand your lender another chunk of money when it comes time to sell.

Recap: This type of pre-payment penalty hits homeowners who pay off a mortgage when they move to another home, as homeowners do on average within ten years.

Soon we'll look at a totally different type of pre-paying — systematically paying off your mortgage ahead of schedule and saving many thousands of dollars by doing so. First, though, let's clarify a few terms you'll encounter.

APR: What Is It?

No doubt you have seen the term 'APR' in lenders' ads and promotions. Something like: *'Interest Rate 4.25%, APR 4.38%'*.

APR means Annual Percentage Rate. Lenders are required to disclose and display this rate for every loan, ARMs and FRMs. This is to help borrowers compare loans having different rates, points, and fees, and arrive at a 'true rate' for each. On the surface it appears to achieve that goal, but underneath it is often a misleading and inadequate measure.

APR is always a higher figure than the loan's quoted interest rate because it takes into consideration the quoted interest rate *plus* additional fees you will have to pay (including points). Naturally, these extra fees make the loan more expensive than the quoted rate alone would have you believe, a discrepancy that APR is *supposed* to make clear.

However, it does and it doesn't. In my view, the major shortcoming of APR is this: It is calculated on the assumption that the borrower will hold the loan for its full term. So, if you take out a 30-year loan, the APR figure is accurate *only* if you hold the loan for that period. Only about 5% of home loans run their full term. For the other 95%, APR is not an accurate measure of anything.

Nonetheless, my advice is to pay heed to APR when you are scanning lenders' offerings; this will give you one broad criterion of comparison. But when you find loans that could interest you, dig deeper. Compare their interest rates, first; then add in or estimate all additional fees payable on each loan. With the help of the lender, mortgage broker, attorney or Exclusive Buyer Agent, work out total costs for each loan over different periods of time that interest you (5, 10, 15, 20 years).

This is even more important the shorter the time you believe you might hold the loan. Tell the lender that you'd like to see comparison figures that enable you to make accurate side-by-side evaluations. If your lender balks, move on; there are lenders out there who'll do this for you.

Understanding Mortgage Pre-Qualification and Pre-Approval

I said we'd return to this critical issue, in part because homebuyers frequently confuse loan pre-qualification and loan pre-approval. And because these terms have been made less useful by federal regulations that came into effect in the US in 2015.

First, why is mortgage loan pre-approval so important? When you get pre-approval from a lender, that lender is confirming they will give you a mortgage of a particular size, provided certain conditions are met.

Therefore, lender pre-approval makes you a preferred buyer in the eyes of the seller, which gives you greater leverage in negotiating the best price and terms. It's almost the same as being a cash buyer; you go confidently after the home you want knowing you have the financing you require.

What is the Difference Between Pre-qualification and Pre-approval?

Traditionally, mortgage *pre-qualification* meant merely a personal opinion (not a guarantee) by a lender as to your *potential* ability to get a mortgage loan amount. This opinion was based on unverified information you provided; for example, your gross monthly income, an estimate of your monthly debt payments, your social security number and date of birth. Usually, the lender then ordered a credit report and credit score, as we saw earlier, from just *one* of the three major credit bureaus. From this data an estimate of how much you 'qualify' for was created. Pre-qualification on its own still carries no commitment from a lender.

Pre-approval, then and now, is a more involved process that requires you to submit lots of documentation. When successful, the lender *commits* to giving you a specific maximum loan amount (also referred to as a 'loan commitment') subject to you getting a home under contract and the home appraising for at least the purchase price you plan to pay. The lender reviews your credit data from *all three* credit agencies (called a 'tri-merge credit report'), examines your bank statements and sources of funds, W2s, pay stubs, relevant assets, and verifies employment and other information about you.

The reason these terms — pre-qualification and pre-approval — got even muddier in 2015 is this: In a well-meaning move, The US Consumer Financial Protection Bureau acted to eliminate misleading lender practices and homebuyer confusion — buyers often believed they had a loan commitment when all they had was a cursory personal *opinion* from a staff member in a lending company or brokerage or online operation. However, the new regulations caused some lenders to believe they are prohibited from using terms like 'pre-approval' or 'loan pre-approval' and they are now reluctant to do so.

So where does that leave us?

Here's a common-sense solution: It doesn't matter which term is used as long as you can show the seller an appropriately worded qualifying letter from your lender. This letter will need to state that the lender has qualified you as a borrower and is willing to lend you a specific mortgage amount, and that their decision is based on having reviewed all your necessary financial and other documents. The lender's wording should read something like this:

> *This home loan commitment* (or mortgage pre-qualification, pre-approval or similar) *is based on our review of John and Mary Brown's tri-merge credit reports and FICO scores, verification of employment and income, and verification of other relevant assets based on bank statements and other documentation, etc.*

This is what 'pre-approval' always meant when that term was used correctly. But as I said, today, regardless of how you refer to it, all you need do is present your qualifying letter containing wording similar to above.

The big benefit, of course, is that sellers see that you have the financial ability to buy their home, which sets you up to negotiate strongly and get a quicker purchase. Your advantage over buyers without this type of qualifying letter is persuasive, even when your offer is lower. To the seller, it's the old adage: a bird in the hand is worth two in the bush.

Don't ask for this letter from lenders when doing your initial lender search. Instead, ask each one you speak with if they will provide this type of qualifying letter should you decide to use them. Drop any lender that refuses; without a loan commitment — not simply loan 'pre-qualification' — you will be in a weaker position against other buyers. Here, asking an Exclusive Buyer Agent for recommendations to compliant local lenders will save you time and effort.

Here's another smart buyer tip: Start the loan search early, at least three months before you plan to buy. And when you choose a lender don't settle for a 'standard pre-qualification' type letter. Submit all the required paperwork and get a qualifying letter , as above, that shows you have loan pre-approval. Then, go house hunting for the best deal you can negotiate, free of worry about financing.

Loan pre-approval of this kind is even more advantageous if you are a first-time buyer with little money to put down. Make sure sellers know that your financing is pre-approved. Despite the new regulations and other changes, today pre-approval is more easily done; new underwriting technology can tell the lender when items need checking or further explanation.

As I mentioned earlier, if for any reason you don't have a qualifying letter you will be at a disadvantage when negotiating for the best price and terms, even more so when competing with other buyers for the same home.

Keep in mind that what every seller wants to hear is that the prospective buyer has the money required. In fact, it's almost impossible to get a seller to take their home off the market (for 45-60 days typically) while the buyer applies for financing. The seller's life plans are then put on hold and at risk. In such cases, accepting a lower offer from a loan pre-approved buyer is usually preferable.

If a lender claims they don't issue loan pre-approval until you have a house under contract (a few are like this), find another lender! Otherwise, you'll be negotiating from a position of weakness — which is not the way of the smart buyer.

Tip: While your loan pre-approval is being processed, ask the lender to give you an 'initial pre-qualification'. This is simply an estimate of the size of loan you will probably be approved for, and is just for your own guidance.

What Size Loan Can You Afford?

The mortgage industry uses two figures in determining each borrower's loan limit: In general they are 28 and 36 (referred to as 'qualifying ratios'). These ratios are not inflexible. Most lenders, if you are close to the qualifying figure, will try to push your approval through. In fact, certain lenders will use more liberal ratios of 33 and 38, which can enable you to qualify more easily and for a significantly bigger loan.

Note: Although 28 and 36 are 'standard' ratios, they are not the only ones used, as noted above. On FHA loans the ratios are 31 and 43, and can be even higher in particular circumstances. And on VA loans only one ratio is used: 41. Your lender, mortgage broker or Exclusive Buyer Agent will advise you in more detail on your personal circumstances.

Here, let's stay with the more conventional ratios as we explore how they might affect you.

The 28 is the percentage of your *gross* income (before payroll taxes or other usual deductions) lenders consider you'll be able to apply to your monthly mortgage repayment. You can use this figure as a rough guide to 'pre-qualify' yourself, but not in place of formal pre-qualification. In computing income figures, couples are allowed to combine their salaries and other income.

Here's how it might work out. I'll keep the math simple, but realistic.

Example: Applying the 28% Rule

If a couple's combined monthly gross income is $4,500, their mortgage repayment can be a maximum of $1,260 (which is $4,500 x 28%). Bear in mind that by 'mortgage repayment' the lender means: Principal, Interest, Taxes, and Homeowner's Insurance (usually abbreviated to PITI).

Note: When the Private Mortgage Insurance premium (PMI is usually required if your down payment is less than 20%) is paid with the mortgage, this too must be covered in the 28% monthly expense qualifying ratio. Generally, all these items are paid in one single bank debit (or by check). However, whether PMI is payable or not, we'll refer here to this combined monthly repayment as PITI.

Back to our example: That $1,260 the couple are pre-qualified to spend each month will need to cover all components of PITI. To add up these components they'll need to know or estimate property taxes, homeowner's insurance and Private Mortgage Insurance (PMI) costs. When doing this yourself, the easiest solution is to call a local real estate office and ask for assistance with the figures. All offices have this information. If the salesperson presses you to come into the office and learn more about their services, decline; it's too early for that.

Generally, I do not favor buyers being pre-qualified by real estate brokers' in-house mortgage services, because it can lead to a conflict of interest (do you really want the salesperson who might try to sell you a home to know so much about you and your finances?). If you decide not to use a mortgage broker, you should do your own initial research then 'shop the market' for loans. And when you are ready, talk with at least three lenders (more on this later).

So, here's how the PITI figures work out so far:

Combined gross incomes (monthly)	$ 4,500.00
Maximum monthly repayment (PITI)	$ 1,260.00 ($4,500 x 28%)

Monthly property Taxes (T) $165.00
Monthly homeowner's Insurance (I) $50.00

The combined T and I (of PITI) will cost $215 ($165 plus $50). Now take this from the $1260 and what's left ($1,045) can go toward the monthly principal plus interest payment (P+I). Keep in mind that figures are rounded to avoid fractions, this alters computations only slightly.

Naturally, your next question is: *What size loan can $1,045 per month pay for?*

To answer that we'll need to figure in a current interest rate. Let's assume 30-year fixed-rate mortgages (FRMs) are available at 5%.

The question now becomes: *What size loan at 5% can be paid off with a repayment of $1,045 per month?*

If you don't fancy using mortgage payment calculators (lots of options online) or are not mathematically inclined, any lender or broker can quickly provide answers.

Here's what we now learn:

A monthly payment of $1,045 at 5% over 30 years will pay for a loan of $195,000.

Let's continue. We now know the size of loan the buyers can qualify for. Next, consider how much they have for the down payment. We'll assume their savings plus a recent inheritance allows them $24,000 cash. So their *potential spending figure* works out like this:

Loan $195,000 + cash $24,000 = $219,000. On the surface it appears they can safely spend up to $219,000 for a home.

But, we haven't yet allowed for miscellaneous costs. Closing costs (settlement costs) and other fees can run as high as 5%-7% of the loan amount. This will reduce their figure by $10-$15,000. We'll use the higher figure, which makes their new maximum spend $204,000 ($219,000 minus $15,000).

Let's now follow the couple through a hypothetical purchase, and call them the Browns. Just because their budget can stretch to $204,000 does *not* mean they should spend that much. You'll recall I advised in an earlier chapter that you set two budget figures: Your *Comfortable Spending Limit* and your *Upper Spending Limit*. Note, you've set this upper figure at your 'preferred limit'; you may be willing to spend more but only for an exceptional deal.

Anyway, let's suppose the Browns find a home listed at $189,000 and through smart negotiation techniques learned from this book they manage to buy it for $172,000.

Here's what their situation now looks like:

- Cash held in reserve for closing costs (6.5% of $172,000): $11,000
- Cash down payment (7.5% of $172,000): $13,000

That accounts for all the couple's $24,000 in cash.

Price of home: $172,000

- Down payment: $13,000
- Loan required: $159,000
- A 5% 30-year fixed-rate mortgage of $159,000 will cost them $854 per month.

Note: On a conventional loan they'd also have to pay a private mortgage insurance (PMI) fee because their down payment is less than 20%.

Now we can put the four parts of PITI together to arrive at the total monthly payment:

- Monthly P+I payment on $159,000 FRM: $854 (P+I)
- Monthly taxes and Insurance: $215 (T+I)
  TOTAL monthly repayment $1,069 (P+I+T+I)

You'll recall the Browns pre-qualified for a maximum monthly repayment of $1,260. As it turns out they ended up paying just $1,069. Clearly, they didn't over-commit. They could have bought a more expensive home, taken a bigger loan, and had a bigger repayment (up to $1,260). In this example, however, their finances are not stretched.

Example: Applying the 36% Rule

I mentioned earlier that lenders use two standard qualifying ratios in determining how much they will lend you: 28 and 36.

Here's the difference: The 36 is also a percentage, but it is applied to your monthly combined *gross* income *plus* your long-term debts. When the lender uses this ratio your PITI payment plus the monthly payment for your long-term debts cannot exceed 36% of your combined *gross* income.

The Browns had a monthly gross income of $4,500. Here, 36% of $4,500 equals $1,620; this is their maximum monthly outlay allowed. This $1,620 must be sufficient to pay for their mortgage plus all debts which have ten or more months still to run.

Typical examples of long-term debts include car loans, student loans, and other mortgages. However, household utility bills, cell phone bills, etc, generally don't count, nor does modest credit card debt (credit card debt considered excessive can be counted).

Recap: To stay within this 36% ratio, the Browns' PITI and long-term debts *together* cannot exceed $1,620 monthly, which is 36% of their combined gross income.

Remember, that 28% ratio we worked out previously was $1,260. Subtracting this from the 36% ratio of $1,620 leaves $360; this is the amount that will be allowed to cover monthly expenditure on the kind of long-term debt payments we noted above.

If the Browns' long-term debt payments are less than $360 per month the lender will elect to use the $1,260 figure (28% ratio) in approving the mortgage. In this example, the Brown's PITI outlay of $1069 per month for their new home is well under the $1,260 limit, so the 28% ratio will be used by the lender.

However, for additional clarity let's introduce a complication. We'll assume the Browns long-term debt costs them $500 per month. How will this change the amount they can qualify for?

Their 36% qualifying figure of $1,620 must now cover $500 for long-term debt; what's left after that can go for the PITI payment: So, $1,620 minus $500 = $1,120. The Browns now can qualify for a mortgage payment no higher than $1,120 per month.

Lenders compute *both* figures (28 and 36) in qualifying each applicant, then base their decision on the lower figure that results. In our example, the Browns' purchase meant a monthly mortgage of $1,069. This is still under the new lower limit of $1,120, which the 36% ratio produced (directly above) to cover their $500 monthly long-term debt. So their purchase is OK computed against either rate, 28 or 36.

Note: Borrowers are expected to satisfy *both* the 28 and 36 ratios. Fortunately, though lenders don't broadcast the fact, these qualifying ratios contain some flexibility, primarily because lenders are constantly chasing new business. Nonetheless, you should treat them as requirements.

Negotiating for the Best Loan Terms

With every lender you talk to, and with each loan you feel might be right for you, ask the lender to trim the rate, waive some of the fees, and sweeten the terms you are being offered.

If this sounds cheeky, it's not. It's nothing more than being a smart buyer.

The point is that there are other lenders eager for your business, and the industry is extremely competitive. No lender will let you walk away when there is still room to be flexible. Saving even one quarter of one point (.25%) in fees on a $100,000 loan can keep $250 in your wallet at closing.

Negotiating another quarter point (.25%) off your loan's interest rate could save you a minimum of $200 every year. Over ten years that's $2,000, and over 30 years $6,000-plus! On a $200,000 mortgage you can multiply these savings by two. Save an additional quarter point off your interest rate (making it .5%): multiply by two again. So, make sure you emphasize that you'll be shopping hard for the best rate and terms, and you'll settle for nothing less!

Your current bank manager may be especially eager to get your mortgage business. If so, tell her clearly what rate and terms she will have to beat. Mention other lenders by name; they're the bank's competitors. And let it be known that you know that many of the typical closing costs can be reduced or waived entirely. For example, the lender's attorney's fees and document preparation fees can often be quickly eliminated, but only for smart borrowers. Ask!

If you are using a mortgage broker, get his personal assurance that the loan he is offering you is *the best available!* This means the lowest priced and most suitable loan the broker can offer for your particular circumstances, and also that the terms and fees cannot be bettered by the lender concerned, or with another lender the broker knows of. And when you ask that question, or any such question — just stay quiet and wait for the answer. Observe! Then, if you are not fully convinced by the broker's response, sleep on it. In the morning, if you are still not convinced, do more checking elsewhere.

Before you commit to any loan you must be as satisfied as possible that the broker or lender is advising you in your best interest. If you are pressured to sign quickly, don't! Such pressure might be the only warning sign you'll spot. You always have options.

One final tip: If you plan to engage an Exclusive Buyer Agent (a smart idea) do it at the start of your search, and ask for advice and recommendations on mortgage brokers and lenders. If you've already been offered a loan ask how it compares with what the EBA knows is currently available. You'll get either the confirmation you need for your peace of mind, or perhaps a referral to an even better deal.

The principle working for you here is efficiency. Make use of all trustworthy resources available to you.

Reminder: At times, buying a home can seem overwhelming! As you journey through the various stages of finding, financing and buying the right home, know that an Exclusive Buyer Agent is a true ally and a constant source of trustworthy advice and assistance.

In the biggest financial transaction of your life, it makes perfect sense to have a confidant to guide you through. Does it make any sense at all *not* to avail of such a service? I think not. If you are not yet clear on why using an Exclusive Buyer Agent is so rewarding, go to Chapter 2: *When 'Your' Agent is Not Your Agent at All: Who is Really Looking Out for You?*

Making Sense of LTV Ratio, Down Payment & Private Mortgage Insurance

For many homebuyers the hardest challenge is to come up with the cash down payment. Often, however, a buyer can put down as little as 5% of the purchase price and take a loan for 95%. There are even loans that will allow as little as 3% down payment.

Despite this, a larger down payment has advantages you should not ignore. First, it lowers your monthly repayment. Second, you accumulate equity sooner (your percentage of ownership in the property). Third, on most loans when your down payment is 20% or more of the home's value you avoid paying private mortgage insurance (PMI) fees.

Here's how Loan-to-Value Ratio (LTV) works:

When you make a 20% down payment, the lender funds 80% of the home's purchase price. This is referred to as '80% LTV'. It means simply that the lender has funded 80% of the home's value (the 80% mortgage given to you), while you have funded 20% of the home's value (you own 20% equity in the home).

Had you put down 10% and financed 90% the LTV ratio would be 90%. LTV reduces as you pay off your loan — over time what you owe gets smaller, what you own gets bigger.

This concept of LTV is important for one particular reason we noted earlier. When the down payment is less than 20% of the home's value, you generally have to pay Private Mortgage Insurance (PMI). To add insult to this expense, PMI does *not* cover you, the buyer! It protects *only* the lender in case you default on the loan.

What does PMI cost, and how do you pay it? The cost varies from lender to lender. But here's one common example: On a 30-year loan with 10% down (90% LTV), some lenders require an upfront PMI cash payment at closing, typically 0.4% of the loan amount, to cover the first year. On a $100,000 loan, 0.4% will mean $400. In subsequent years the PMI renewal premiums on this loan can run $300-350 annually. Many lenders add PMI into the monthly PITI payment.

Note: When your equity in the home builds to 22% through your repayments plus the home's appreciation in value, these PMI payments should stop. Banks are legally required to eliminate PMI once your equity in the home reaches 22% of the *original* appraised value when you took out the loan.

Although *no* PMI is required when your initial down payment is 20% or more, once you start paying PMI your equity has to reach 22% before it can be stopped. PMI payments are based on the loan's amortization schedule, a copy of which you should be given at closing; this will usually show at which date your equity will be high enough to stop the PMI payment.

However, if you believe at any time that market appreciation or repairs and improvements have increased the value of the home such that your equity has reached 22%, you can request that the lender re-appraise the home. A new appraisal will cost you $350-$500; but you'll recover this cost and more if the appraisal shows your equity at 22% or higher and the PMI payment gets dropped.

Other Important Things You Need to Know About Loans

Here are some other points worth keeping in mind when you consider any mortgage loan. When possible here I will continue to use the Browns' situation to illustrate different points, and occasionally I'll use the FRM example we started with: borrowing $100,000 at 5% over 30 years.

In either case I will spell out simply the principles behind how the various options might work for you in your own personal situation.

Interest Rate Determines the Size of Loan You can Get

The loan's interest rate will determine the maximum amount you can qualify for. All other things being equal, you will qualify to take a bigger loan amount at 4% than you will at 5%.

Going back to our example: Based on the 28% qualifying ratio, the Browns could put $1045 from their combined incomes to their P+I monthly payment. This meant they qualified for a loan of $195,000 with a 5% interest rate over 30 years. Had they found an otherwise similar loan with an interest rate of 4%, they would have qualified to take a mortgage of almost $220,000.

Hard Facts About Shorter-Term and Longer-Term Loans

Another factor determining the maximum loan amount available to you is the term of the loan. A 30-year loan is generally the most affordable fixed-rate mortgage (FRM), and it is right for many buyers.

However, that does *not* mean this loan is the best value for money. It takes a very long time before you'll build up equity (your percentage of ownership in the home). That's because in the early years just a tiny fraction of your monthly payments goes to pay off the principal.

Incredible as it might seem, after ten years paying off a 5% 30-year FRM, the buyer will still owe about 80% of the original amount borrowed (if you borrowed $100,000, after ten years you'll still owe close to $82,000)! Virtually all of the money you paid to that point has gone to pay the lender's interest charge.

For that reason, I'll re-state my advice: Compare different length loans carefully. With shorter loans you build equity in your home faster, and the benefit of that comes back to you no matter when you sell. Shorter-term loans also mean that you will be out of mortgage debt sooner, potentially in half the time. And, you'll own your home free and clear at a younger age. The monthly dollars that once went for mortgage payments will be yours to spend however you wish.

Logically, a shorter-term loan means higher repayments. But when the extra expense is manageable a shorter loan makes good sense. Even better news, and contrary to what you might assume, a 15-year loan is *not* twice as expensive as a 30-year loan. To illustrate this, let's return to the Browns.

Here's a recap of their situation:

The Browns' ability to pay $1,045 monthly will qualify them for a $195,000 loan at 5% over 30 years. For extra clarity, and to show you the precise figures, I'll state that same information slightly differently:

- 30-year loan of $195,000 at 5% will cost the Browns $1,046.80 per month (P+I). After 30 years they'll have paid back a total of $376,850.

Now compare this with a shorter-term loan:
- 15-year loan of $195,000 at 5% will cost the Browns $1,542.05 per month (P+I). After 15 years they'll have paid back a total of $277,568.

You can see that shortening the loan to 15 years added almost $500 to the monthly payment ($1,046.80 increased to $1,542.05). But this 15-year loan builds their equity in the home much more rapidly; it's almost like paying the extra $500 every month directly off the principal.

In these examples, notice another huge advantage of the shorter-term loan. Take a look at the total amounts paid back on the two otherwise identical loans:

- $195,000 at 5% for 30 years. Total payback amount: $376,850
- $195,000 at 5% for 15 years. Total payback amount: $277,568
  Difference: **$ 99,282**

Almost $100,000 saved! This loan, over its 15-year term, will save the borrower $99,282! Serious money! The big point to keep in mind is this: When you go with a shorter-term fixed-rate mortgage (FRM) you'll save money, typically thousands of dollars, often tens of thousands, sometimes more.

Even if you sell after 5, 7, or 10 years, a bigger chunk of the selling price goes into *your* pocket rather than the lender's! So, instead of going automatically for a 30-year loan, have your lender run the monthly repayment figures *and* total payback figures for a 15- or 20- or 25-year FRM, and compare carefully.

One Practical Way to Make a Shorter-Term Loan Work

To illustrate our final point in this section, let's stay with the Browns.

They can afford to pay $1045 P+I per month. And, with that size payment they can borrow $195,000 for 30 years at 5%.

But at the last minute they have a change of mind! A 30-year financial commitment suddenly seems too long. Instead, they decide to go for a 15-year FRM. In what ways will this affect their options? Let's see.

The Browns know their income limits them to a maximum P+I outlay of $1,045 per month. This they cannot change.

They learn that the $195,000 loan over 15 years would require monthly repayments higher than their limit of $1,045 (they wouldn't qualify for the higher repayment). So, they decide to go with the 15-year mortgage, but take a *smaller loan*, and buy a less expensive home.

Now they need a specific answer to this question: *Without exceeding their $1,045 monthly repayment limit, what size loan can they get with a 15-year FRM at 5%?*

Here's what they learn: With a 15-year FRM at 5%, their $1,045 monthly P+I payment will get them a loan of $132,150.

Let's see what has changed (figures are rounded slightly):

Term of loan: 30 years / 15 years
Monthly payment: $1,045 / $1,045

Interest Rate: 5% / 5%
Size of loan obtainable: $195,000 / $132,150

These figures make the advantages of a 15-year loan obvious, when you can handle the bigger monthly outlay. If you cannot afford the higher repayments, consider doing what the Browns did here: buy a less expensive home with the same monthly repayment ($1,045, as illustrated above). You'll own the home sooner and pay back significantly less overall.

But hold on, we're not through. You have yet *another* attractive option, perhaps the best of all, a wealth-building 'trick of the trade'.

You can get all the benefits of a 15-year loan *without* committing yourself to the higher monthly repayments that go with it. Sounds too good to be true, doesn't it?

But it's true! What's more, you can do it on your own, without paying anyone for assistance. It's called *accelerated payments,* or *pre-paying* your loan.

Let's investigate.

Accelerated Payments &
the Miracle of Pre-Paying Your Loan

In recent times the idea of pre-paying your mortgage has gained wider attention. Almost always though, it seems that someone else wants to do it for you, your bank or mortgage company, or an online service — for a fee!

In fact, it's quite simple to arrange. You don't need to qualify with anyone. And you can do it yourself! All you need do is add extra dollars to your monthly payment. Those extra dollars apply against your loan *principal*, thereby reducing your capital debt, which is precisely what you want.

Let's stay with the Browns and see why this is a clever idea. (If you work out the math on this example you'll find slight variations from rounding figures):

We'll assume the Browns are still considering the $195,000 loan and the 30-year FRM at 5%. This loan, as we saw, would cost them $1,045 per month. But recently they heard something about 'accelerated payments' and now they want an answer to this question:

- *How much extra will we need to pay each month to pay off this $195,000 loan in 20 years?*

Here's what they discover:

By paying an extra $241 on top of their $1,045 monthly payment (new payment: $1,286), they'll have the loan paid off in 20 years. But that's not all, not by a long shot! They'll also save $67,990 in interest!

Let's see how:
- $195,000 at 5%. Repayment per month: $1,045
  Loan will be paid off after 30 years: Total payback amount$376,850

- $195,000 at 5%. Repayment per month: $1,286
  Loan will be paid off after 20 years: Total payback amount: $308,860
  Amount saved: $67,990.

But perhaps paying an extra $241 per month is too steep. What if they pay just an extra $95 per month, making their total payment of $1,140 ($1,045 plus $95)? Here's what they find:

- $195,000 at 5%. Repayment per month: $1,045.
  Loan will be paid off after 30 years: Total payback amount: $376,850

- $195,000 at 5%. Repayment per month: $1,140
  Loan will be paid off after 25 years: Total payback amount: $341,980
  Amount saved: $34,870

You can see in the first example that the extra payment of $241 per month saved the Browns ten years of payments and $67,990.

In the second example, an extra payment of just $95 per month saved the Browns five years of payments and $34,870.

This is the miracle of pre-payment! Ask a trusted mortgage advisor to run various term options and extra-payment permutations for you.

How You can Benefit by Paying your Mortgage Bi-Weekly

You can also save significantly by making what is known as *bi-weekly payments*. Here's what that means:

We'll use the example we saw earlier: $100,000 30-year FRM at 5% monthly, P+I repayment will be $537.

Now divide $537 by 2 and you get $268.50. If you pay this $268.50 every *two weeks* you'll make twenty-six such payments per year (the same as making *thirteen* standard monthly payments). If you keep this up, you'll save $16,950 in interest charges, and you'll pay off the loan in just over 25 years (five years early). Yet this bi-weekly payment plan will cost you *only $537 extra per year!*

Here's the computation:

- $268.50 x 26 weeks = $6,981 paid per year
- $537 x 12 months = $6,444 paid per year.

You can see that the extra cost to you per year is $537 ($6,981 minus $6,444), which is equal to just *one extra standard monthly payment,* yet it saves you $16,950 over the *new* term of the loan, a little over 25 years.

If your lender does not offer a bi-weekly program (few do), or tells you they cannot accommodate your bi-weekly payments, press them to do so. Failing that, you can go for yet *another* equally attractive alternative.

Let's explore what that is.

Save Thousands by Making One Extra Payment per Year

Here's the idea, and it's simple: Divide your regular payment of $537 by 12 and you get $44.75. Now add this $44.75 to your standard monthly payment of $537 to get $581.75.

Make this your new monthly payment; it's still just twelve payments per year and it will bring you virtually the same saving as the 26 bi-weekly payments method explained above.

Your monthly mortgage payment coupon book should have a space on it to insert the extra payment amount (in the example above: $44.75). If it doesn't, or if you are making your payment online and there is no separate field to note the extra payment, DO NOT make one single payment for the total. Instead, split it into *two payments*.

In fact, even if your coupon book (or online page) does have a space to insert the extra payment amount, it is still better to send *two separate payments* and mark 'Apply against Principal' on the extra amount.

In our example above, make the regular payment of $537, plus a separate payment for $44.75 marked clearly on the check or coupon or online page that it is to be applied to the principal. This is important, because if you make one single payment for the total amount a lender with no clear instructions, or through error, may apply the extra amount to the *escrow account* for taxes and insurance rather than against the principal. If that happens you have accomplished nothing. You must instruct them *clearly* what to do with the extra payment.

Note: Even though lenders' online systems are constantly evolving and upgrading, you may not be able to activate this pre-payment plan online because there's no field to add your instruction 'Extra payment: Apply against principal'. If so, you'll probably have to mail your checks to the lender, at least at the start. In either case, you should confirm, from the beginning, that your extra payments are in fact being applied against the principal.

On top of this, I advise that you pay a visit to your lender, talk with the person who will be accountable to you; tell them what you are doing, and get their assurance that your extra payment will be handled as your instructed. I advise also putting your instruction *in writing* to your lender. This way you have a comeback if they screw up.

Even More Pre-Payment Ideas that will Save You Big Money

The following pre-payment options show what you can achieve with a 5% interest rate loan. We'll stick with our original model: You are borrowing $100,000 on a 30-year FRM. You already know that your monthly P+I repayments will be $537.

But here's what you'd like to know:

1. What can you save by pre-paying an extra $25, $50, $100, and $200 per month?

2. By how much will each extra amount reduce your 30-year term?

To each standard monthly P+I payment of $537, if you add a pre-payment of:
+ $25: you will reduce the loan term by 2.92 years, and save $10,535
+ $50: you will reduce the loan term by 5.17 years, and save $18,459
+ $100: you will reduce the loan term by 8.75 years, and save $30,706
+ $200: you will reduce the loan term by 13.33 years, and save $45,672.

Clearly, these savings make a very good case for pre-paying whatever extra monthly amount you can comfortably afford.

But your pre-payment does *not* need to be a consistent amount each month. You can pre-pay irregularly, whatever amount and whenever your budget allows. There are no fees, costs, or applications involved. And you do *not* need anyone's permission. Your lender will simply credit the extra payment against the outstanding loan principal, provided you instruct them to do so. As I advised earlier, speak directly with someone at your lender's office who can understand what you are doing and provide the assurance you seek.

Even if your mortgage contract contains a 'pre-payment penalty' clause (few do) this is often waived on request. It's typically a small fee anyway and shouldn't cause you any worry. A sharp real estate attorney will ask for this to be dropped, from the beginning.

Caution: It's worth emphasizing here that it makes sense to pay off your highest interest debts first. If, for example, you are carrying credit card debt, pay this off *before* paying extra off your home loan, which is at a much lower interest rate. The same applies to car loans and even college loans.

Reminder: You do not need to pay anyone to set up a pre-payment program for you. If your lender asks for a fee, as some do, request strongly that it be waived, and expect to be accommodated. Generally, you'll need do nothing more than follow the recommendations here. The final assurance you seek from your lender is that each extra payment will be credited against the principal *on the date it is received*, not at the end of the month (this is unlikely but it has happened; so get confirmation).

How to Benefit from Understanding Your Lender's Loan Pricing Adjustment Chart

This is another smart move that could land you a less expensive loan and lower fees.

Most lenders use a Loan Pricing Adjustment Chart. That's a bit of a mouthful, so I refer to it here as 'the grid' (as they do). It's used to determine your loan rate and how many points you'll be asked to pay on a particular loan.

You might be short on cash and want to pay fewer points, even zero points, or you might want to 'buy down' (reduce) your loan interest rate. Whatever the case, the grid indicates the interest rate that will apply and the points payable. To produce answers, the grid crunches just two criteria, your credit score and the Loan to Value Ratio (LTV) of your loan.

This is important because by adding as little as .1% to your down payment (making it 5.1%, for example, instead of 5%), you might push your loan into the next lower interest rate category on the grid, which means cheaper repayments.

Let's take a closer look.

Get a Better Deal: Increase your Down Payment for a Lower Interest Rate

Here's an example of how you might be able to reduce the loan's interest rate:

Say you're buying a $200,000 home; you plan to put down 5% ($10,000) and borrow 95%, which is $190,000 (LTV 95%).

However, if you increase your down payment to 5.1% ($10,200), this marginal increase of $200 could push your loan into the more favorable 'less than 95% LTV' category on the grid (LTV is now 94.9%). This could qualify you for a one-quarter or one-half percent reduction in your loan's interest rate.

To make this clear, let's work out the exact figures on this $200,000 home purchase:

Option 1:
You put 5% down ($10,000): Lender offers you a $190,000 FRM over 30 years at 5%. Your monthly P I I repayment will be $1,020.
(LTV 95%).

Option 2:
You put 5.1% down ($10,200): Lender offers you a $189,800 FRM over 30 years at 4.75%. Your monthly P+I repayment will be $990. (LTV 94.9%).

Outcome: You save $30 per month: $360 per year, and (believe it or not) $10,800 over 30 years. Just by putting down that extra $200 and thereby cutting one-quarter point off your interest rate. A one-half point cut would double these savings.

Here's what you need to remember:

Homebuyers tend to stick to full figures for their down payments: 5%, 10%, 15%, etc. Sometimes, by adding a tiny fraction you can tip into a category that earns you a cheaper loan, as in the example above.

Tip: Ask your lender or mortgage broker how much you'll need to increase your down payment by to qualify for a lower loan rate. And keep in mind that it's almost always a good idea to put down at least 5%.

Get a Better Deal: Increase your Down Payment to Reduce the Lender's Points (fees)

Now let's look at how the grid affects the points you might or might not pay.(Remember, one point equals 1% of your loan, and 'points' are also fees you pay the lender for processing your loan.)

Here's an example of how to reduce the points on your loan by increasing your down payment:

On the above loan of $190,000, a down payment of 5% ($10,000) coupled with your credit score, might require you to pay fees of 1.5 points to get the lowest interest rate (1.5% of $190,000 = $2,850).

However, by increasing your down payment to 6% ($12,000) you might cut the points fee to one point (1% of $188,000 = $1,880). Your 6% down payment pushed the $188,000 loan into the 'LTV less than 95%' category — (now it's 94%) — and saved you $970 off the fees ($2,850 less $1,880).

Plus, with 6% down payment your monthly P+I will be $1,009 instead of $1,020, an additional saving of $11 per month, or $132 per year. In addition, you own more equity in the home (6%) from the start.

As you would expect, a high credit score coupled with a bigger down payment gives you maximum leverage with lenders. In negotiation terms, you have 'power' and choice.

How Credit Scores are Applied on the Grid

Opposite LTV Ratio on the grid are credit scores; both are equally important. Credit scores run in 20-point increments up to about 740. Of the three scores supplied by the three main credit reporting agencies *only the middle score* is used in qualifying you (not the average).

For example, with scores of 730, 720 and 718, the 720 score rules. This can be critical. *Make sure you ask your lender where you fall on the grid.* Because even a marginal five-point increase in your middle credit score could get you a lower loan rate or save you cash outlay on points. Or both!

Now let's take a look at property taxes and see if there is any money to be saved there.

CHAPTER 17

Are You Over-Paying Your Property Tax?

Even when laws have been written down,
they ought not always to remain unaltered.

— Aristotle

In 2011 the US National Taxpayers Union suggested that as many as 60% of properties in the US were tax-assessed at a higher figure than their actual value. This would mean that the owners of those properties were over-paying on taxes. More recently, a Kiplinger's reader poll revealed that over half of respondents said their property taxes had increased in the past year, yet only one in six planned to appeal the higher assessment. Another recent report I've seen says that only one in twenty homeowners (5%) challenge their tax assessment.

If these figures are accurate, and I know of no reason to doubt any of them, a significant percentage of homeowners may unknowingly be throwing away hard-earned money.

Why is it Worth Checking Your Tax Assessment?

Peace of mind, at least. But possibly more, money. I've heard of successful appeals in high property tax areas where homeowners with strong cases saved $3-$5,000 on their annual bill. More commonly, I'd estimate that an appeal with merit, presented effectively, can save the homeowner from a few hundred to a few thousand dollars annually.

With a little assistance you can estimate potential savings before ever requesting a tax review (more on this shortly). If your case looks promising, you fire ahead; if not, you've lost nothing.

One reason over-payment happens is because property assessments for tax purposes are carried out usually only every two or three years, and in some jurisdictions every four or five years. This creates a disparity; home values change while tax bills remain static.

In 2008 the national recession caused significant widespread depreciation in home values, from which many areas never fully recovered. In addition, whether the economy is up or down, a percentage of homes lose value in every calendar year. This is a natural occurrence; home prices decline in different areas for all kinds of local reasons. Frequently, tax assessments fail to update to reflect these declines.

But outdated tax assessments are not the only problem. Incorrect assessments can occur because the employee or contractor doing the assessment relies on criteria that are inaccurate, incomplete, or entirely wrong, due to administrative and clerical errors. Plus, almost all property assessments are made externally, usually by a person who does not enter or inspect properties, thereby increasing the risk of error. In fact, to a greater or lesser degree the process functions on assumptions.

Do you know how values have been going in your neighborhood? Particularly how this applies to the home you own, or the home you might buy? It's probably time to do some checking, because over-assessment of property tax is more common than most homeowners are aware.

Here's what you need to know about how property tax works.

Understanding How Your Home is Assessed for Tax

The method by which homes are assessed for tax varies quite a lot from jurisdiction to jurisdiction, but the following fundamentals are the same almost everywhere. Just a few figures are used to determine your annual tax bill:

1. Your home's 'fair market value'. This is the price for which you could sell your home on the day the assessment is made, which is determined by the tax assessor. Let's assume $200,000.

2. The 'assessment ratio'. This is a factor set by the local tax authority. Here's what it means: Typically, tax is not imposed on the fair market value of your home but on a lower portion of that value, called the 'assessed value'.

Your tax assessor arrives at the 'assessed value' of your home by multiplying the fair market value by a figure they call the 'assessment ratio' (this can be anything up to 100%).

Let's assume the assessment ratio is 60%. So you multiply $200,000 (fair market value) by 60% (assessment ratio) to get $120,000. Your property tax bill is now based on this assessed value of $120,000.

3. The 'tax rate'. This is the final figure used to determine what you pay. Let's say your local property tax rate is 2.3%. You can now figure your annual property tax bill by multiplying the assessed value ($120,000) by the tax rate (2.3%). That's $120,000 x 2.3% = $2,760, your annual property tax bill.

If the value of your property has declined since it was last assessed, you are probably paying too much tax. Even if no decline has occurred, it's possible the previous fair market value of your home was assessed too high. To check for accuracy and errors, you need to begin by learning what your home is worth now. But you might not need a professional appraisal, at least not initially.

Here's what can you do:

To check if you are overpaying, you query your tax assessment by requesting a 'review' through your local tax assessor's office. Then, if you are not satisfied with the result you can move to a process known as an 'appeal' or a 'challenge', to dispute your tax bill.

Procedures for doing this vary by locality and jurisdiction but certain aspects are universal. You'll first need to learn how your local assessor's office deals with reviews and appeals. This information is usually available online. But check first that you don't already have it explained in your assessment notice, which is frequently the case.

How to Appeal a Tax Assessment

All homeowners receive an annual notice of their home's assessed value and tax payable. This notice also contains a filing deadline, the date by which you must lodge an appeal against your tax bill, usually within 30-60 days of the notice date. Note this deadline! If you are thinking of appealing, don't procrastinate.

Start by collecting evidence of at least five comparable homes whose current values are lower than yours (make sure they are as 'comparable' as possible). In particular, note recent sales of similar properties at lower prices. You can also gather supportive data like this through looking up the 'record card' for each property at your local tax assessor's office, and through other online resources.

The information that pertains to each home is referred to by the assessor's office as the 'record card' for that home, or in some places the 'working papers' or 'workbook'. Check that all details are correct, as far as you can judge. Is the square footage under roof accurate? Number of bedrooms? Number of bathrooms? Number of floors? Age of the house? Are anomalies noted that indicate your home is less valuable than a comparable home across the street; for example: blocked view, inclining ground, disrepair, leaky roof, smaller garden area, smaller block size, etc? If you are a senior, veteran, or disabled person, are you being allowed any additional tax exemptions that apply?

When you have this supporting data in hand you can usually request an informal meeting (a review) with the assessor. This might be all you need do to resolve the matter in your favor. If not, you'll probably have to send the evidence, such as your listing of comparable properties, blueprints, and photographs, to the assessor for formal review (ask for a guide to what data is required).

If the outcome still proves unsatisfactory, you may be able to bring the case before an independent local appeals board. The advantage here is that you'll be making your case in person. If that happens, bring along a handout of information supporting your argument for distribution to each board member.

Should You Hire a Tax Reduction Professional?

If you are not a do-it-yourself type in these matters, a worthwhile alternative is to engage a suitably experienced Exclusive Buyer Agent or other tax reduction professional. Find one who knows your community and understands the relevant tax and value differentials among nearby neighborhoods and jurisdictions. Choose someone who challenges real estate taxes regularly, knows the tax assessors, and is experienced with documentation and presenting successful property tax appeals.

Tax reduction professionals charge either a fixed fee regardless of outcome, or a contingency fee based on their success in getting your taxes reduced, or possibly a refund. Ask for a *free* initial consultation to get a better understanding of the strength of your case and your prospects of success.

From what I've observed, the consensus of opinion seems to be that 20-60% of appeals result in some tax reduction or refund. Generally, the tax professionals have better success than individual homeowners.

Whichever option you choose, a well researched and well presented case with merit will increase those odds in your favor, will bring you at least peace of mind — and could put a chunk of spending money in your pocket.

Final Note:
. . . Now What?

Knowledge is fated to start out as heresy.
— Aldous Huxley

As you apply what you have learned here, your skills will be subtle, even *invisible*. You will *not* be acknowledged as a masterful negotiator.

Fortunately!

I say fortunately because then the advantage will be yours to steal. And steal it you will. For in this quiet strength you have power that's hard to defeat.

In the end you'll be remembered only as someone who could not be talked into or pressured into anything.

The impression you'll leave behind, however, is irrelevant. Your reward is bigger and much longer lasting. And it won't come from a feeling that you have defeated anyone.

On the contrary.

When it's all over, when you've negotiated the best deals on home and mortgage, peace of mind will come from knowing that you protected yourself from risk, loss, mistake and regret.

And even more from counting the money you saved — the money you earned the right to keep and spend as you please, because you were prepared, willing and able to negotiate.

These are the rewards *Not One Dollar More!* makes possible.

You now possess the secrets of invisible negotiation. Use them well.

And welcome to the club!

Call yourself a Smart Buyer!

— *Joseph Éamon Cummins*

ToolBox Resources

Here's a mix of groups, organizations and services dedicated to helping home buyers and home owners in many different ways. For more information go online for a full description of any of these services. If something does not appear clear, request further details online, by phone, or ask your EBA or attorney to explain.

Find an Exclusive Buyer Agent

NAEBA: The National Association of Exclusive Buyer Agents. EBAs are real estate agents with a company that represents buyers' best interests only and never practice dual agency or designated agency. Contact: **www.NAEBA.org**. Also see: *Why Should I Use an EBA?*: **www.youtube.com/watch?v=Qnntlzr7UIA.**

Exclusive Buyer Agent in Massachusetts and Florida

Homebuyer Advisers LLC: Broker/Owner Tom Wemett, an Exclusive Buyer Agent for over 25 years, runs exclusive buyer agencies in Massachusetts and Florida. Licensed as a broker in Florida, Massachusetts and New York, he is on the board of directors of Massachusetts Association of Buyer Agents (MABA) and National Association of Exclusive Buyer Agents (NAEBA).

Tom Wemett is author of *Massachusetts Homebuyers Beware! The Cards are Stacked Against You.*

For more details: 978-633-9090 (office); 518-524-8875 (cell).

Or see Tom's informative websites at:
www.expert-homebuying-help.com and **www.starterhomelistings.com.**

Find Homes-For-Sale Information

Realtor.com: Find homes for sale, go to **www.realtor.com** for the best up-to-date comprehensive database of listed properties.

Warning: *If you give your email address and other information to any online real estate service, expect to be contacted by traditional agents and salespeople.*

Credit Reports and Credit Scoring

Obtain free credit reports from all three major credit bureaus. A federal law, the Fair and Accurate Credit Transactions Act of 2003 (the FACT Act), requires credit reporting agencies to provide consumers with one free credit report every twelve months. The official web site is: **www.annualcreditreport.com**.

For more information about credit reporting and credit scores, go to: **www.myfico.com/credit-education/credit-report-credit-score-articles/**.

You can also obtain all three credit reports and FICO scores for a one-time fee of about sixty dollars by going to: **www.myfico.com/products/three-bureau-credit-report/**.

For additional information about credit reports go to the Federal Trade Commission's web site: **www.ftc.gov**. Click on *Get Your Free Credit Report*.

The three major credit bureaus and their contact information are:
Equifax: **www.equifax.com** 800-685-1111
Experian (Formerly TRW): **www.experian.com** 888-397-3742
Transunion: **www.transunion.com** 800-888-4213.

Credit Repair Scams

The Consumer Financial Protection Bureau (CFPB) provides advice on how to tell a reputable credit counselor from a bogus credit repair company. There are counselors who can help you with your credit report, and others who take your money but don't help. Lots of useful information can be found at: **www.consumerfinance.gov**.

Mortgages: Information and Assistance

CFPB: The Consumer Financial Protection Bureau is an excellent source of information about mortgage financing and home buying. Go to their consumer website at: **www.consumerfinance.gov**. check *Consumer Tools* for information about a number of finance related subjects, including *Owning a Home*.

Additional information is available from CFPB in their *Know Before You Owe* section about two new forms, the Loan Estimate and the Closing Disclosure, at: **www.consumerfinance.gov/know-before-you-owe**.

More information about the Loan Estimate is available at: **www.consumerfinance.gov/owning-a-home/loan-estimate/**.

More information about the Closing Disclosure is available at: **www.consumerfinance.gov/owning-a-home/closing-disclosure/**.

Down-Payment and Closing-Cost-Assistance Programs and Grants: This website links to an organization that maintains a database of down payment assistance programs throughout the country. The site allows you to input information to see if you qualify for any of their programs and grants. Homebuyers will find useful information at: **www.your-homebuyer-advisors.com.**

Down Payment Resource: DPR works to get more buyers into homes. DPR tracks nearly 2,400 homeownership programs across the US through partnerships with over 1,200 Housing Finance Agencies (HFAs), real estate agencies and lenders. DPR's research shows that 87% of US homes are eligible for some type of home-ownership program. Be sure to ask your EBA or salesperson about this. More information at: **https://downpaymentresource.com.**

Bankrate: Bankrate helps consumers make better financial decisions at nearly every stage of life. Also helps you find and compare rates on financial products like mortgages, credit cards, car loans, savings accounts, home equity loans, banking fees, etc. Use Bankrate's mortgage rates tool to find lenders offering the best rates in your area, but consult on this also with your EBA: **www.Bankrate.com.**

Lender Options and Other Programs Worth Knowing About

FHA: A program especially suited to first-time homebuyers and those with a problematic credit history. The FHA guarantees a part of a home loans, which allows lenders to be more liberal with their approval standards. With FHA backing, borrowers can qualify for loans with as little as 3.5% down: **www.fha.com.**

USDA: The US Department of Agriculture operates a home loan assistance program. You don't have to be a farmer or live on a farm. The program focuses on rural areas and allows up to 100% financing by giving guarantees to lenders. Some income limitations exist, which vary by region: **www.rd.usda.gov.**

Good Neighbor Next Door: This HUD-sponsored program was originally called the Teacher Next Door Program, later expanded to include emergency medical technicians, law enforcement and firefighters. It allows 50% discounts off the list price of homes located in revitalization areas. You must live in the property for at least three years. See: **www.hudhomestore.com/Home/GNND.aspx.**

Home Upgrade Programs: The government's Energy Efficient Mortgage Program allows you to buy more home for your investment. It extends your borrowing power when you buy a home with energy-saving improvements or when you upgrade a home's green features. If you qualify for a home loan, you can add the EEM benefit to your regular mortgage. The program simply allows your lender the flexibility to extend loan limits for energy efficiency improvements.
Search: **Energy Efficient Mortgage Program.**

There are also HUD 203(k) loans for buyers who want to tackle a fixer-upper. This special FHA-backed loan considers what the value of the property will be after improvements and allows you to borrow the funds to complete the project as part of your main mortgage. Search: **FHA 203(k)**.

VA: The US Department of Veterans Affairs helps veterans and surviving spouses and service members to buy homes with no down payment or mortgage insurance. Contact: **www.nerdwallet.com/blog/mortgages/va-loan/**.

Fannie Mae and **Freddie Mac:** Fannie Mae and Freddie Mac are government-sanctioned companies and the engines behind the home loan machine. These programs work with local lenders to offer appealing mortgage options, such as 3% down payments. Search: **Fannie Mae** and **Freddie Mac**.

American Homeowners Foundation represents the US's 70m homeowners. Provides valuable, unbiased information (much of it free) to help consumers buying, selling, remodeling, building, financing, or investing in residential real estate. Contact: **www.AmericanHomeowners.org**.

Consumer Advocates in American Real Estate exposes conflicts of interest in real estate. Offers solutions and resources to consumers. See: **www.CAARE.org**.

Note: Many state and local governments offer assistance to home buyers. The Department of Housing and Urban Development has links to this information.

Neighborhood Schools and Amenities Information

WalkScore: Check out **www.walkscore.com** to see how an address rates in terms of proximity to shopping and entertainment.

GreatSchools: This is the leading national nonprofit organization empowering parents to unlock educational opportunities for their children. Information and parenting resources available to help families choose the right school, support learning at home, and guide their children to success. See: **www.GreatSchools.org**.

Professional Home Inspection Information and Services

HouseMaster: HouseMaster of America provides comprehensive home inspection services and property condition reports; also offers checklists and advice for home buyers nationally: **www.HouseMaster.com**.

Pillar to Post: Pillar to Post offers a range of comprehensive home inspection services nationally, a full property report, and can provide a number of specialist inspections for certain hazards: **www.PillartoPost.com**.

American Society of Home Inspectors: ASHI sets and promotes professional standards for property inspections. ASHI certified inspectors operate nationally through local service companies: **www.ASHI.com**.

Note: Most professional home inspection services issue reports that meet or exceed ASHI's internationally accepted standards.
See: **www.homeinspector.org/Why-Choose-an-ASHI-Inspector**.

National Association of Certified Home Inspectors: NACHI is the nation's largest organization of home and commercial property inspectors. Certifies inspectors in US, Canada and overseas. See: **www.nachi.org.**

Also see Freddie Mac for their Home Inspection Kit and Slide Show:
http://myhome.freddiemac.com/buy/home-inspection.html.

Information on Home Testing for Specific Hazards

Radon Testing: Contact: **www.epa.gov/radon**.

Lead Paint Testing: Contact: **www.epa.gov/lead**. Request a copy of the EPA booklet *Protect Your Family from Lead in Your Home.* Or download a copy: **www.expert-homebuying-help.com/EPA-lead-booklet**.

Mold Testing: Contact: **www.epa.gov/mold**.

Chimney Cleaning and Inspection: Contact: **www.csia.org**.

Water Testing and Filtration Systems:
Contact: **www.culligan.com/home/solution-center.**

Amazon Reviews and Readers' Letters
in Praise of Not One Dollar More!

From Amazon

Highly Recommended . . .

Excellent, very comprehensive. Rather than just explaining how to negotiate, the author provides many sample dialogues to refer to, which I found extremely useful. All different situations are covered. I definitely recommend this book for anyone planning to negotiate a home purchase.

Fantastic!

As a trainer for new agents . . . I am using the chapters on negotiating to help them learn how to help their clients negotiate the best deal. Negotiating does not come naturally for most people and these chapters will help almost everyone. I am buying it a second time because one of my agents liked it so much they wouldn't give it back to me! All home buyers should also read this book. An educated buyer working with a buyer's agent is the best way to buy real estate in the US today!

Do NOT buy a house without reading this book . . .

All hyperbole aside, this book saved me six figures on my home purchase! I cannot encourage you enough to read this book before beginning your home search.

Very informative!

An easy read. Thought provoking and if you follow it, it works. Saved us a few thousand when shopping for a loan and gave me courage to negotiate, which also saved us some cash.

Excellent for learning negotiation in business & real estate

Excellent book! Bought copies for friends (rare event) because it's so informative about sales psychology overall - not just real estate. You may get this book for buying real estate, but after reading it you'll be quite informed about buying anything else where negotiation is involved. The book has saved me lots of $$$. It's an easy read too.

Reading it again

As a result of what I learned from this book (and also by not using a realtor), I saved $25K on a $185K house. I also used the techniques in negotiations during a car purchase and during salary negotiations for a new job. Best 17 bucks I ever spent.

I bought this book four years ago when I was shopping for my first house. I got fed up with my realtor and decided I didn't need one, as long as I could handle the negotiations myself. So I turned to this book.

The book is geared toward using a realtor or buying agent, but I found everything was just as applicable when 'going it alone'. Especially some of the resources listed in the back. It's a very easy book to read and it doesn't try to make you a slick rapid-fire negotiator.

It teaches you very simple yet effective techniques that may be common sense to some readers but they weren't to me. Admittedly, Cummins is repetitive in his messages, but I think the repetition serves to firmly ingrain the techniques in your mind so when you do actually get in front of the seller or agent, you don't let your emotions get the best of you.

Now I'm starting to look for my second house, so I'm re-reading the book (and going without an agent again). I'm holding onto the first house as a rental, but I hope that if I ever have to sell, it's not to a buyer who's read this book!

Must-have for a homebuyer (especially first time)

This book is a very easy and entertaining read that is extremely useful for understanding how real estate agents work, how to deal with them and how to negotiate. Although specifically aimed at home buying, the principles can be extended to almost anything. The principles are frequently repeated but are usually expanded upon with more detail or anecdotes.

The book is not just general principles. It shows you how to apply the specific principles through talk and action. For example, you might say X if the seller raises objection Y.

The book is educational and the principles learned will inspire confidence -- the confidence that you will not overpay for your home.

This book was eye-opening for a complete amateur like me

There I was ready to bid my hard earned money away like crazy, ignoring the signs being given off by the seller and agent . . . and then I found this book.

It taught me a number of vital lessons in negotiating a good house price: 1. Shut up! the power of silence and perceived disinterest; 2. Patience - all good things come to those who wait; 3. You, a genuine buyer, are absolute gold dust to a seller and their agent - leverage that power; 4. There isn't 'another buyer' - you're it! and no, it won't be 'stolen out from under your nose'. Best $15 I have spent in many a day -- now all I need to do is make sure they agree to my price and close!!

A Must Read For First Time Home Buyers

Thank you, Mr. Cummins! In today's inflated housing market this book is the light at the end of the tunnel. Every home-buyer should educate him/herself by reading this book. It is amazing how many people over pay for their dream home. Remember (traditional) real estate brokers, agents and home sellers are not your friends; their goal is to make you part with as much of your hard-earned cash as you are willing to give them.

Saved me a Bundle
Never would I have even tried bidding on the house I eventually bought, it was so far out of my range. This book made me give it a try, and I negotiated down a whopping $50,000 less than the asking price. I'm not a natural bargainer, but the book showed me *how* to conduct myself from first walk-through to signing.

UNBELIEVABLE!
My first impression in reading this book was one of amazement, that it took me 38 YEARS being in business to learn what's between the covers of this little gem. No telling where I'd be today if I'd bought this book 38 years ago. GET IT, READ IT, AND LIVE IT, you may well find yourself 38 years ahead in life.

A First Time Homebuyer MUST-GET!
As a first time buyer I am very pleased I picked up this book. It really gives you the insight of the whole real estate process. It will also provide some excellent lessons learned from someone who knows the industry!

The Selling Agent's Worst Nightmare
If you're buying a home for the first time, whether it's an investment or primary residence, read this book. Plain and simple.

Great Book!
I never thought the techniques would work. I shaved (some money) off the asking price. It's worth its weight in gold.

Methodical, with easily-understood worked examples
Sellers have a professional acting for them (the estate agent) which gives them the advantage, so here is a book which helps redress the balance by offering valuable advice to the hapless purchaser.

I found the book's US slant did not distract too much from the useful advice. For me the most useful bits are the role-plays — they illustrate how to play the negotiation game in a very simple yet effective way.

The book does seem to advocate a 'go in strong and low' approach to making offers. This requires nerve, but it's a wonderful antidote to ever-increasing optimistic sellers' prices and I reckon even the most seasoned house buyer should be able to learn something from this book.

A Must-have for every House Buyer
Save yourself some money when buying a house and learn all the techniques explained here; it is gonna save you a lot of money. Besides, you are gonna learn a lot of valuable information about buying and selling property.

Not One Dollar More!
This book is like a good teacher!

I'm a teacher. I read material of all types, usually to learn about a new interest or how to do something. First time I read this book (three years ago) I found it hard to stop reading. It contains lots of brief and interesting stories that illustrate the most important points — how to protect your money, how not to be bluffed, how to offer what you decide, how to respond to your offer being rejected, and so on.

But that wasn't the real test; when I went looking for a new house (nervously, I may add) I discovered that what I had read *had stayed with me!* I wasn't struggling to remember what the book said I should do. The stories just popped into view.

Then the reason for this came to me: the author is a natural teacher — a rarity, in my view — in addition he writes well. He employs extremely smart teaching techniques to make sure you don't just 'learn and forget', what most of our schools do with our kids, and just about every how-to author.

It is also a pleasant, easy read. A different kind of book; no jargon or author bragging so common today in our celebrity-focused society. And it's a practical book.

The end result: I negotiated very successful deals on two houses (sold my first, just purchased my second) that I would never have attempted without knowing what I learned from this book. It definitely does 'take you by the hand' through the negotiation skills. My only criticism, I would like to see a DVD accompanying it, particularly one presented by the author personally. That would be the icing on the cake!

Absolutely the best!

Not One Dollar More! provides a unique perspective on home buying, insight into the roles and motivations of the many individuals involved in a real estate transaction. Empowers you, the homebuyer, to select, negotiate and buy (or reject!) a home on YOUR terms.

Don't be another real estate victim!

Feeling like a lamb to the slaughter? This book provides the tools to fight back. Mr Cummins weaves concepts and real-life illustrations together to create an informative, inspiring book.

Letters from Readers (a few out of hundreds)

As a business coach to mortgage brokers and bankers, part of my job is to inspire my clients to provide more value to their customers. If a lender can provide information like that contained in your book to their home buying customers, it can make a significant difference to the homebuyers' financial well-being.

As you say in your book, the homebuyer is the most under-represented party in a real estate transaction. *Not One Dollar More!* goes a long way toward leveling the playing field, and I'm happy to recommend it to my lender clients who want to provide the best possible service to their home buying customers. Best wishes for your continued success.

Bob Williamson, Professional Coach and Trainer to the Mortgage Industry
www.CoachBobWilliamson.com

Thank You! I recently purchased *Not One Dollar More!*. It has been informative and motivating. Thanks for your great book!

Ron A. C., Rochester, PA

Mr Cummins, my husband and I are first-time buyers. We learned a tremendous amount from your book and truly enjoyed reading it. Here's what happened. The sellers wanted $269,000 for a house we loved; we offered $229,000 attaching a list of comparables. They countered at $260,00 with their own list, which weren't really comparables at all.

To be brief, we made increased offers up to $240,000 and they came down to $253,000. We could not afford to go that high. They ended the negotiation. A few weeks went by, then the agent contacted us with their 'final' price of $247,000. We went up to $245,000, which they accepted.

My husband and I discussed what might have happened had we not read your book. If we had been really 'daring' we'd have begun by offering $240,000 (rather than $229,000) and would have ended up paying at least $255,000, even more. We're very grateful to you. You and your book saved us $24,000! Thank you so much, we wish you continued success. *Not One Dollar More!* is a very useful tool.

Peter and Diane F, Pittsburgh, PA

I'm writing to thank you for all the help your book has given me. I'm a teacher. I felt you'd be interested in my story. I found a house listed at $110,000 (a neighbor told me it had originally been listed at $128,000). That same day I heard someone on KDKA Radio talking about your book. I ordered it immediately, then began making a note of recent sales, like you advised. Similar homes were selling from $90,000 up. The seller was a real estate agent. My lawyer approved my offer and helped with your 'stall and crawl' phase.

On September 2nd I made my first offer, $92,000. The seller countered at $103,000. I delayed three days before giving my next offer, $94,000. She countered at $101,500. I said I was interested in seeing another house. A few days later I offered $95,500 and said it was my final offer. The seller asked for the weekend to consider it.

On Tuesday the agent called to tell me it had been accepted. I'd been fully expecting another round of negotiations. By having the confidence your book gave me, I was able to buy the home for $11,500 below list price, all the more incredible since I was dealing with two seasoned real estate agents. Proof positive it can be done. Thank you again.

Kathryn M. K., PA

My husband and I purchased a home on a wintry day late in November in the DC area and went to settlement on a warm spring day in March. Then seven years later we both retired, we scaled down to an apartment in Bowie, once again we put our deposit down in the first week in December and moved in on February 27.

We negotiated good 'winter' deals on each occasion, guided on each step by *Not One Dollar More!*, the book you featured by Joseph Éamon Cummins, which I found a great help and easy reading.

Letter to Baltimore Sun

Acknowledgments

What's in this book comes from decades of work in businesses of different kinds and from teaching. Naturally, it draws on my first-hand experience of buying and selling property, both professionally and privately. And even more on my work in psychology and negotiation.

But no book of this scale is ever a solo achievement. My research into how consumers buy homes started over twenty-five years ago. In that time I have received support and assistance from too many people to name, as I observed over and over how homebuyers everywhere suffer disadvantages they are not made aware of, that they pay for — and which they rarely learn about after the fact.

As long as diehards in the industry resist ethical reform, the average homebuyer will go on being outwitted and out-maneuvered, being led, pressured or blindly walking into traps that take their money and otherwise stop them getting ahead.

Despite my well-known advocacy for homebuyers, to my surprise I received genuine cooperation from more than a few traditional agents, professionals who privately wish for a conflict-of-interest-free system of exclusive and equal representation for both buyer and seller, which, ironically, is a win-win option for the consumer *and* the industry and what consumer advocates have been calling for for decades.

My most valuable insights, however, came from the exclusive buyer broker community, committed individuals who support the principles and ethics espoused in this book. All contributed directly or indirectly to what I am convinced is *still* the only book of its kind, an objective, fair-minded, plain-English guide that is eminently trustworthy, realistic and practical, that safeguards the most vulnerable party in the real estate arena — the homebuyer.

The list here is incomplete, but to the following people I am indebted:

For her perceptive reading of my manuscripts, her always astute (and sometimes insistent) suggestions for improving clarity, and for her love and sense of fun, I am most grateful to my wife, Kathy Argenti-Cummins.

To Desi and Ann, for preserving the bond, their wellspring of mindful care, and for fighting the good fight.

To Paddy, Keith, Steven and Gerard, companions all, always.

To my parents, Joe and Bridget, for teaching and loving so well.

To Isabel and Tom Argenti, for their warm care and generosity of spirit.

To my good friends: Hop (Anthony Cardelli) for his sensitive writing and wonderful conversation; Harvey for his unique can-do collaboration and business acumen; Bobby Tracy for teaching me how to surf and the right way to 'negotiate' spaghetti; Emma for her spirited narratives; Roberto G for his bright mind;

Desmond G for his positivity and indefatigableness, and Roland P for his kindness when I was studying in Arizona.

To Carol, Karen, Eamon & Hallie, Eileen, Claire, Brigid, Bill & Dawn, Christina & Eric, John & MaryJane, and Dick & Kay, for their gifts and goodwill.

To my clients, students and teaching colleagues on both sides of the Atlantic and in Australia, and especially to Aran, for ensuring I never stop learning.

To all the journalists and broadcasters who have supported the moral correctness and fair-play advocated in this book, and especially to Joseph S. Coyle, senior editor at Money Magazine, for his mentorship and genial company in Manhattan.

To Dawn E. Rae, President of NAEBA, for introducing me to Tom Wemett.

To all the people I have not included or cannot mention here who helped in my research and otherwise: exclusive buyer agents, homebuyers, attorneys, brokers, law makers, salespeople, consumer advocates and educators, for their insights, honesty, openness and time.

I would be remiss not to acknowledge some of those who helped to establish *Not One Dollar More!* for what it is today: Paul R. Roark (Federal Trade Commission), Bill Wendel (Real Estate Cafe, Cambridge, MA), Dr Wayne Dyer, Tony Robbins, Stephen Brobeck (Consumer Federation of America), Steven Kropper, Maureen Glasheen, Andrew Tobias, Sloan Bashinsky, Marc Eisenson, James Scott Tiernan, Jr (American Consumers Assn), Nancy Castleman, Randy Johnson, Elizabeth Razzi, Chris Weimar, Jordan Clark (United Homeowners Assn, Wash, DC), Tom Hathaway, Raymond Stoklosa, Bruce Hahn (American Homeowners Foundation), George Rosenberg, Barry Miller, Keith D. Gumbinger, Jerilyn Coates, The US Dept of HUD, The Council of Better Business Bureaus, and The US Office of Consumer Affairs.

And most especially I extend my sincere thanks to Tom Wemett, exclusive buyer agent, founding member and past-president of National Association of Exclusive Buyer Agents and author of *Massachusetts Homebuyers Beware! The Cards are Stacked Against You.* I went frequently to Tom to check the correctness of things or to understand better what was not clear to me, or to learn what I didn't know. For his compelling knowledge of real estate, his generous assistance with my research for this book, and his dedication to the ethical treatment of homebuyers, I am most grateful.

Needless to say, all responsibility for errors, miscalculations or oversights in this work are mine alone; no blame for such attaches to any other individual.

— *Joseph Éamon Cummins*

Dear Reader . . . Two Requests

Your Success Story: We'd like to hear of your home buying success! Please tell us (at NotOneDollarMore@gmail.com) what you achieved using the tips in this book. The author may email you (with your permission) and/or may use your story online or in future editions. Your personal details will always be kept confidential.

Book Review: If *Not One Dollar More!* has helped you, will you please post a comment on Amazon (or Barnes & Noble, GoodReads, etc). Just a sentence or two saying what you found most beneficial, and please give it Five Stars. Just input '*Not One Dollar More*' to find the book's review page.

As a fully independent, unbiased author providing consumer assistance, I rely on readers like you to spread the word about this book (social media, friends, etc).

Sincere thanks for doing this! Your support really does help. And don't forget to visit this book's website for articles, tips, and more.

To your success . . .
Joseph Éamon Cummins www.NotOneDollarMore.com

Also by the Author

On the Edge of the Loch: A Psychological Novel set in Ireland
Amazon #1 Bestseller in 5 Categories and over 60 4-Star and 5-Star Reviews

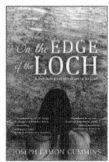

Explores the human passion for freedom, delving inside the lives of characters dealing dangerously with the need to love and belong, and the mountains that must be climbed when life denies these freedoms.

A compelling story of four exceptional people, each obsessed with a dream, each determined to reverse the legacy of the past. But spirit and love and longing can drive people beyond security, even sanity . . .

Executive Workshops, Lectures & Special Events

The author, organizational psychologist and adjunct professor Joseph Éamon Cummins, has provided coaching and training at global organizations such as IBM, Bank of New York Mellon, Pfizer, Dell, GE and others, in areas of resilience, human achievement, performance, leadership, negotiation and emotional intelligence.

To check on his availability for conferences, workshops, coaching, or speaking engagements, or for further details, please email: NotOneDollarMore@gmail.com.

NAEBA to Advocate Even More Strongly for Consumers

As this book goes to press news is emerging that the National Association of Exclusive Buyer Agents (NAEBA) is exploring changing from a trade association to a consumer-focused organization.

'The aim is to provide better information and a higher level of protection to real estate consumers,' a NAEBA spokesperson said.

Since its foundation in 1995, NAEBA has advocated strongly for consumers receiving full and exclusive representation in real estate transactions. Such representation enables consumers to make educated decisions in what is usually one of the largest financial transactions they will make in their lives.

'We believe this shift in focus will better allow us to achieve that mission,' the spokesperson said.

Once the transition is complete, NAEBA expects to have a new name and a new corporate status, but their mission to protect real estate consumers will remain unchanged, as will the web address: www.naeba.org.

NAEBA can be contacted at:
National Association of Exclusive Buyer Agents
1481 N. Eliseo C Felix Jr Way, Suite 100
Avondale, AZ 85323
Tel: 623-932-0098
Toll-Free: 888-NAEBA99 (888-623-2299).